Best of the Web

by the Editors of
Luckman Interactive

BARNES
&NOBLE
BOOKS
NEW YORK

1055 7th Street
Suite 2580
Los Angeles, CA 90017

This edition published by Barnes & Noble, Inc., by arrangement with Luckman Interactive, Inc.

1996 Barnes & Noble

ISBN: 1-56619-903-4

Printed and bound in the United States of America

96 97 98 99 6 5 4 3 2 1

Vice President Directory Services
Jeff Morrow

Acknowledgments
Many thanks are due to the dedicated people who contributed their time and talent to make this book possible. Karen Slovin deserves special recognition for taking the lead and wearing many expert hats, as does Jeri Lloyd for pinch-hitting when it was most needed and for contributing her considerable talents to this project. Thanks to Connie Levinson at Barnes & Noble for her tireless efforts and invaluable editorial expertise. The sage advice and patience given by David Rogelberg at Studio B is gratefully appreciated. Special acknowledgments are due to all the Web site writers and researchers who lent their vast Internet experience to this book.

Managing Editors
Karen Slovin
Jeri Lloyd
Ethridge Smith

Editors
Heidi Bailey
John Farrell
Corinna Moebius
George Muschamp
Thomas Sullivan
Christopher Smith
Spencer Yuen

Proofing
Molly Muschamp
Alan Berman
Amanda Galvin
Andrea Sharp

Database Development
Bob Brooks, RBA Consultants/Los Angeles, CA

Software Development
Publish Right!/Mountain View, CA

Computer Support
New Phase Enterprises, Inc/Westminster, CA

Book Design
Rick Wilson/Intelligent Tool and Eye/San Francisco, CA

Cover Design
Joe Spencer Design/Studio City, CA

Contents

Introduction

Why We Wrote *Best of the Web*

Everybody's talking about the World Wide Web. You see it on the evening news. Your neighbor has a Web page. Elementary schools provide "surftime" to students. If you're curious about the explosion of interest in the Web, you are not alone. Every major player in communications, entertainment, media and computing is formulating a corporate or individual Internet plan. Technological, economic and social landscapes change with every spurt of Internet growth.

With more than 100,000 sites on record to date, exploring the Web may sound intimidating. Each day hundreds of new sites appear on the scene, brimming with colorful images, dynamic navigation, sounds clips, movies and information on practically everything. Although the Web is a pretty straightforward world, there's a lot of it to explore. That's where our job begins.

Our purpose is to introduce you to the true gems of the Web. While surfing the information superhighway has its own rewards, we'll lead you directly to the great resources you want. We'll help you find the best online shopping, business news, and entertainment. Whether you need stock market prices at the closing bell or a recipe for vegetarian chili, the Web is a dynamic global playground with something for everyone.

How Sites Were Chosen for *Best of the Web*

The Luckman editorial team sifts through hundreds of sites each day to round up the best sites on the Web, where quality ranges from brilliant to the mundane. We navigate from the homeless scene to the rave scene, an Irish pub to Seattle public transportation, genetic codes to encryption espionage. Editors with expertise in specific fields like entertainment, computing and business select the outstanding resources that contain comprehensive, timely and pertinent information.

Each Web site is evaluated for its value with regard to elements of content, design and organization. Innovative designs, well-organized presentations and content-rich sites earn the highest ratings.

Introduction

We consider content to be the crucial component of a Web site. Solid content translates into complete and pertinent information on the topic at hand. If a Web site delivers meaningful insight and covers the site in detail, with generous links to related resources, it passes our content evaluation.

Good design is easy to spot. A well-designed site is visually appealing with innovative use of multimedia elements. Intriguing graphics, colorful designs, sound clips, and movies transform a static Web site into an interactive and dynamic spot that everyone wants to visit. We also appreciate clean lines, readability and tasteful use of space.

The third element we examine is the organization, or flow, of a Web document. A clear presentation of text, sound, images and ideas helps users fully realize the content which exists there. Getting lost in a poorly ordered configuration is frustrating and time-consuming. A well-organized Web page is a pleasure to explore.

The combination of the elements of content, design and flow contribute to the overall quality of a Web site. The 500 sites featured in *Best of the Web* lead you through the great resources available today—CNN online news, digital photography from the wilds of Africa, QuickTime™ movies of the latest Paramount release, and sing-along songs from Disney. Research your term paper on Russian literature or order an *X-Files* T-shirt. The online world is as large as your imagination.

Why You Need This Book

I'm new to the Net...

The volume of information on the Web is staggering. If you're new to the Internet, you'll be faced with many decisions about access, software modem speeds, service providers, and more. Once you're connected, you need to know where to look for the great sites. The resources you find in this book will put you in gear.

I know my way around, but I'd like some guidance...

Experienced Web surfers know the depth and scope of the Web. Unearthing a shining jewel which contains just the information you wanted can be an exhilarating experience. Often, though, you come up empty-handed. *Best of the Web* can help you find what you're looking for—whether it's the Louvre or the ESPN SportsZone—we've done the electronic legwork for you.

How to Use This Book

The *Best of the Web* listings are divided by categories of interest like Business & Finance, Children, Entertainment, Online News and others. If you have difficulty locating your interest, check the keyword or title indexes in the back of the book.

Site Descriptions offer an overview of the site's content. Some listings display a screen shot of the opening page.

Site Details define features of the Web site like sound, video, shopping, audio, chat rooms, Shockwave, Java or RealAudio.

Load Time represents the approximate number of seconds it takes for a Web page to appear on your computer screen. Your download time may vary from ours due to several reasons:

- the number of people trying to access the Web site
- the traffic on your Internet Service Provider's system
- the speed of your computer and modem
- the speed of the remote computer serving the information

We measured load times using 28.8 bps modems on Pentium 75-megahertz computers. For an estimate of your download time, extrapolate the speed based on your modem type. For the 14.4 modem user, load times are generally twice as slow as 28.8 modem times. ISDN lines decrease load times by at least half. T-1 lines improve load speed by four times the 28.8 speed or better.

Introduction

What is the World Wide Web?

The Internet is a large, interconnected network of computers. No single entity owns it, nor does one person or organization control it. Created initially as a way for government and academic communities to communicate and share information, the Internet now links nearly 25 million people—students, educators, professionals and children.

The World Wide Web can be considered a multimedia subset of the Internet, transforming text-based documents to pages filled with vivid colors, graphics, sound, video, and dynamic navigation systems. The resulting environments are user-friendly communication forums, global libraries, corporate conference rooms, international shopping malls and entertainment centers. Utilizing a standardized Hypertext Markup Language (HTML), documents and files are linked together in a fashion that allows a user to access the information in a random or circular path.

Web Terms You Need

The culture of the Internet carries with it a host of mysterious terms and jargon. Many of these are not necessary to know in order to use the Web, but you'll enjoy the landscape more if you understand the terminology. Here are some brief definitions of the most frequently used terms. If you're hungry for more information, consult the Glossary of Terms in Appendix A.

Home Page

When you visit a Web site, you arrive at its opening page, called the home page. Usually intended to be an introduction to the assortment of documents linked to it, the home page can be likened to the table of contents within a book.

HTML

Web pages are written in a formatting language called HTML, Hypertext Markup Language. HTML pages contain codes called tags that create the visual appearance and hyperlinks in a Web document.

HTTP

HTTP (Hypertext Transfer Protocol) is a standardized way to exchange HTML documents between different computer types. Along with HTML, it is a distinctive feature of the Web.

Hypertext Links

Also called hyperlinks, or more commonly links, hypertext links are usually underlined and displayed in a different color within a Web document. Click on a hyperlink to connect to other Web documents.

URL

Each Web site has its own unique address, or **U**niversal **R**esource **L**ocator.The following is the standard format for a URL:

http:// sb.stanford.edu/ goodlife/home.html

http Each URL address found in this directory begins with *http* (Hypertext transfer protocol).

//:sb.stanford.edu/ This part of the address displays the computer site where the document is stored. Varying in length, this segment usually ends in **.edu**, **.gov**, **.com**, or **.org** (educational, governmental, commercial, and nonprofit organization, respectively).

goodlife/home.html The final segment indicates the file name of the document, which usually has the extension HTML. Often the HTML gets shortened to HTM when downloaded to computers running DOS. It is not uncommon for the URL to end with the computer site and omit this third section entirely.

Getting Onto the Internet

To access the Web on the Internet, you'll need four things: a computer, a modem, a Web browser, and an Internet connection.

Personal Computer

If you're curious about the Internet, you probably already own a computer. If not, buying one will be your first step. Do some research before you put down your hard-earned money. Pentiums,

386's, 486's, and Macintosh computers will work on the Internet, but do buy as much power, memory, and disk space as you can afford. The hardware you purchase should be as technologically up to date as possible. If you do buy a new computer, make sure it includes a 28.8Kbps (kilobit per second) modem.

Modem

The speed of your modem probably plays the biggest part in how quickly or slowly you can access Web pages. A 28.8 Kbps modem or higher is recommended. A 9,600 Kbps or 14.4 Kbps modem will do the job, but you'll spend a considerable amount of time waiting for Web pages to download. Many of the sites you'll be visiting are filled with graphics and multimedia components. A higher speed modem can handle these files more efficiently than a slow one.

Web Browser

Browsers such as Super Mosaic or Netscape Navigator, are software applications that allow you to navigate and view the Web. Most browsers contain multimedia players like RealAudio, Java, and Shockwave which allow you to enjoy video and audio components of Web documents. Browsers can be purchased through retail and mail-order sources, downloaded from the Web, or may be included in a commercial online service or Internet Service Provider's (ISP) software package.

An Internet Connection

There are many ways to connect to the Internet, from extremely affordable to amazingly expensive. The choice for most individuals is usually between an online service (such as America Online or CompuServe) or an Internet Service Provider. There are advantages and disadvantages to each choice, which we outline below. You'll find listings of commercial online services and national Internet service providers in Appendix B.

Online Services: The Pros & Cons

An Internet connection through an online service has a couple of advantages. Online services like America Online or Prodigy make signup a snap. Pick up a PC magazine containing a registration disk and browser at your local newsstand. A toll-free call will also do the trick. Catering to the newcomer, online services offer Internet tutorials, packaged news and entertainment, as well as guides to the Web.

There are some disadvantages to using an online service for access to the Web. Online services can be expensive if you plan to spend much time on the Internet. Pricing plans vary, but Internet access is almost always extra. The connection to the Internet can be slow, and subscribers are sometimes restricted in where they can go on the Internet.

Internet Service Providers: Pros & Cons

With an ISP, you can select the level of service you need. The connections are faster than those of an online service, and access is usually not restricted. You can pick the browser you prefer, although many ISPs include a browser with their start-up software.

The setup process is not always as easy as with an online service, although some ISPs are approaching the same level of convenience. There are hundreds of ISPs—the quality of service ranges from highly efficient to almost nonexistent. Research an assortment of providers before choosing one. Technical support, connection speed, price, and experience are factors to consider.

How an ISP Works

Basically, your ISP will give you a dial-up number that your modem will use to access to the Internet. It should offer several local numbers in case one is busy. Ask for a free trial account to check availability and technical support response time. If speed is important to you, request information about ISDN and T-1 lines. They are faster than dial-up modem connections, although they are more expensive.

Introduction

A Few Things to Keep in Mind

Times Are Changing

The Web is alive—changing, growing, evolving. Just when you think you understand the landscape, it's likely to change. New sites appear daily on the scene and others disappear quietly in the night. This dynamic exists for a variety of reasons:

- The site has moved to another location on the Web. Sometimes the author will leave a forwarding address, sometimes not.
- The site is closed for maintenance. Try to access the site later; it may reappear.
- The author stops maintaining the site, and the information is outdated.

A Note to Parents

Much controversy exists surrounding the idea of freedom of expression on the Internet. Many individuals feel that guidelines should be enforced that restrict the display of erotic or questionable materials online. Others continue to support open and free expression of the individual. Whatever your opinions in this debate, be aware that materials do exist on the Web that are unsuitable for children.

Art

Artists continually search for new modes of artistic expression. Often, this search results in the expansion of aesthetic boundaries and challenges the status quo. The Web makes it possible to generate and appreciate artistic expression in a new and exciting way. Now, you are not only free to roam the virtual galleries of the Louvre or the Smithsonian Institution, you also are privy to the eclectic and inspiring vision of a collage artist from Nebraska or the raytracings from a digital artist in Japan.

Additionally, the Web is an excellent forum for art criticism and education. Learn more about the compositions and styles of artists like Wassily Kandinsky and Claude Monet at the **Art Exhibits and Reviews** site. The **WEBMuseum** exhibits paintings by famous Old Masters when they were rebellious young turks. The technology of the Web transports artistic expression from the halls of the museum to your home, your conversations, and your communities.

Art Exhibits and Reviews/Millennium Pop

http://watt.emf.net/wm

Art lovers will delight in this exhibit featuring the works of Monet, Kandinsky, Whistler, Kitaj, Durer, L.P. Smith, and Beardsley. Each composition is preceded by a text narrative of the style and an interpretation of the particular piece. Thumbnail images can be enlarged, and reviews are written by award-winning journalists and art editors. Leave the worries of the world behind and revel in the inspiration of artistic creativity. The site is provided by Millennium Pop, an online magazine devoted to covering the "techno-driven transformation" of American society and culture.

Site Details:	Sound, Large Graphics, Good Links
Load Time:	18 seconds

Art on the Net

✯✯✯✯✯

http://www.art.net/Welcome.html

Contemporary visual artists, musicians, poets, and sculptors exhibit their work here. Browse the hallways and foyers of the gallery, where each space highlights a different artist. Read gallery guides and artist biographies, listen to artists' statements on audio, and comment on the shows via an e-mail form. Artists are invited to submit work for exhibition on the site.

Site Details:	Large Graphics, Good Links
Load Time:	27 seconds

Art on the Web

✯✯✯✯✯

http://escher.cs.ucdavis.edu:1024/art.html

Art on the Web explores the art world and provides links, by way of the Web Resource Directory, to innovative art resources. There is a mail-art link where artists can communicate by sending their works to each other, in addition to a list of definitions for the term "true art." Browsers can also view the holdings of various excellent museums, including the Louvre.

Site Details:	Real Audio, Large Graphics, Good Links
Load Time:	32 seconds

Arte & Musei

☆☆☆☆☆

http://www.vol.it/UK/EN/ARTE

This online resource from Italy presents a vast collection of links to the world's finest museums, private collections, and exquisite galleries. Link to Vol.art, Video On Line, or the Leonardo Internet, among others, to explore publications and virtual museums or to plan your next tour of Italian art.

Site Details:	Video, Large Graphics, Good Links
Load Time:	15 seconds

ArtNetWEB

☆☆☆☆☆

http://da.awa.com/artnet/artnetweb

ArtNetWEB presents work fostered by the communal interaction of artists on the ArtNet BBS in New York City. This project aims to establish an art colony in cyberspace. Visitors to this site may browse the online version of *View Magazine*, access gallery information and artist resources, or simply enjoy the variety of artwork featured.

Site Details:	Good Links
Load Time:	24 seconds

Asian Arts

✯✯✯✯✯

http://www.webart.com/asianart

This beautiful Web page features art from Asian cultures. Exhibits, galleries, and articles pertaining to various artistic endeavors are supplied, complete with graphics. The site features a user's guide, calendar of events, and sample letters from Web users and chat line members. Links to a host of other Asian art Web sites are provided.

Site Details: Large Graphics, Good Links
Load Time: 37 seconds

Blue Dot

✯✯✯✯✯

http://www.razorfish.com/bluedot

If you're looking for a gateway to great art resources on the Web, you'll find it at Blue Dot. The graphics are stunning and complement beautiful photo galleries of postage stamps, gargoyles, and the works of James Worrell. Experience the multimedia capabilities of the Web at the exhibition of a smoking cigarette. The art is "moving, converging, vibrating, breathing"—take a look!

Site Details: Animation, Video, Large Graphics, Good Links

Load Time: 157 seconds

Center for Electronic Art

✯✯✯✯✯

http://www.cea.edu

Visitors to the Center for Electronic Art home page will find it easy to access information on the Center and its programs, projects, and people. Stroll through the virtual art gallery or learn about upcoming courses. Snapshots accompany the description of the Center and its mission, vision, and history. You can also discover what former students have said about the Center and its programs.

Site Details: Large Graphics, Good Links

Load Time: 56 seconds

DaliWeb

★★★★★

http://www.highwayone.com/dali/daliweb.html

Visitors to DaliWeb can take a virtual tour of the Salvador Dali Museum and its displays of paintings by the renowned Spanish surrealist. The main exhibit is divided into historical periods, where you may learn about the background of Dali and his work. This Web site also includes a changing feature exhibit. Try out the Dali Quiz for a chance at a free poster or download free Dali Windows Wallpaper. Museum merchandise can be ordered through the online catalog.

Site Details: Large Graphics, Shopping
Load Time: 44 seconds

Electric Art Gallery

★★★★★

http://www.egallery.com/egallery

The Electric Art Gallery presents one of the most comprehensive collections of electronic art on the Web. The exhibition is grouped into different sections: Folk Art, Abstract Realism, Jazz and Blues, Haitian, Southwest, Contemporary, and Journeys. Some of the work on display here is for sale.

Site Details:	Large Graphics, Shopping
Load Time:	90 seconds

Leonardo da Vinci Museum

★★★★★

http://cellini.leonardo.net/museum/main.html

This site provides an excellent overview of the many talents of Leonardo da Vinci. Fascinated by both art and science, Leonardo's insatiable curiosity led him to study human anatomy, of which he made detailed sketches and notes. He conceived and sketched inventions like the helicopter and a device for fastening sequins onto women's gowns. His anatomical studies and inventions are available here, along with a biographical brief of Leonardo.

	Large Graphics
Load Time:	11 seconds

Louvre

✯✯✯✯✯

http://www.paris.org/Musees/Louvre

The Louvre is the most famous and one of the best art museums in the world. Unfortunately, its Web site is not equally grand. The collections are divided into seven categories including paintings, sculpture, prints and drawings, antiquities, and objects d'Art. The web site, part of the Paris Pages, provides practical museum information–its location, hours, and admission costs, along with a brief history, a ground plan, and a few highlights from the collection. There is a link to the Louvre's official Web site, which offers more works of art and information, though the information is all in French at the moment.

Site Details: Good Links
Load Time: 60 seconds

Musei Vaticani

✯✯✯✯✯

http://www.christusrex.org/www1/vaticano/0-Musei.html

Visitors to the official site of the Vatican Museum will find the letters, speeches, and writings of Pope John Paul II, in addition to an enormous gallery of over 1,000 images from Vatican City, the Sistine Chapel, and the Vatican Museums. View a map of Vatican City or read a brief historic background of the area and its rich culture.

Site Details: Large Graphics, Good Links
Load Time: 33 seconds

National Museum of American Art

★★★★★

http://www.nmaa.si.edu

The home page for the National Museum of American Art offers visitors an opportunity to view and read about more than 500 works of art. This page also provides reports of scheduled events and a place to interact with the staff and the artists in the collection. The gallery section showcases online exhibitions, some of which feature RealAudio introductions: The Dark Chamber, The Art of the American Daguerreotype, and the White House Collection of American Crafts.

Site Details: Real Audio, Video, Sound, Large Graphics, Good Links

Load Time: 44 seconds

SITO Home Page

★★★★★

http://www.sito.org

A gathering place for those who create and/or appreciate artistic images, the SITO "artchives" include thousands of pictures sorted by medium and content. Collages, Xerography, Math Art, and Body Art are just some of the media categories listed here. Content categories range from Politics to Comics, Animals to Cover Art. In the Synergy section, view the collaborative, thematic exhibits created via the Internet by artists from around the world. A complete directory of participating artists is also available.

Site Details: Large Graphics

Load Time: 12 seconds

Smithsonian Institution

✯✯✯✯✯

http://www.si.edu

The Smithsonian welcomes visitors to an enormous network of people, activities, museums, research projects, and special performances. Upon entry, enjoy audio and video greetings from the secretary, Michael Heyman. The map of the Washington, D.C., mall area will give visitors a bird's eye view of the location of the nine separate Smithsonian museums and galleries. The many pages of photographs, documents, and research centers may be overwhelming at first glance, so be sure to bookmark this site for return visits.

Site Details: Real Audio, Video, Sound, Large Graphics, Good Links, Shopping

Load Time: 27 seconds

SunSITE's Multimedia Exhibits and Expositions

✯✯✯✯✯

http://sunsite.unc.edu:80/exhibits/exex.html

Visitors can tour the Vatican Library, take a class from the Cordon Bleu cooking school in Paris, and experience a road tour with Elvis Presley at this experiential site. Like an online world's fair, the site presents an enormously eclectic grouping of multimedia sites. Scores of linked topics are arranged under Cultural Studies, Belles Lettres, Visual Arts, Archives, and Miscellaneous.

Site Details: Sound, Large Graphics, Good Links

Load Time: 15 seconds

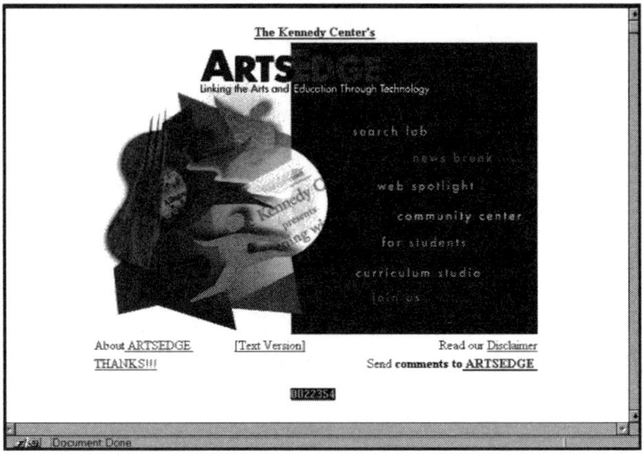

ArtsEdge

http://artsedge.kennedy-center.org

ArtsEdge is a nonprofit organization providing information about artists, organizations, projects, and ideas. It hopes to bring the arts communities together. This dynamic page features several divisions, such as a "for students" section that showcases student artwork. The latest in artistic news is presented here, along with information about the sponsor, the Kennedy Center, as well as links to more arts sites.

Site Details: Large Graphics, Good Links

Load Time: 8 seconds

ArtSource

http://www.uky.edu/Artsource/artsourcehome.html

ArtSource is one of the best starting points for locating Web resources on art and architecture. The site contains links to electronic exhibits, research materials, journals, periodicals, and more. Users can choose from a wide range of topics and graphics at this exemplary art resource center.

Site Details: Good Links
Load Time: 12 seconds

Photo Exhibitions and Archives

http://math.liu.se/~behal/photo/exhibits.html

Here is a rich assortment of photography-related Internet resources. The exhibits and collections are organized by topics such as art, digital, historical, infrared, landscape photographs. Among the exhibits are those showcasing works by Ansel Adams, the *Life* magazine photographer Alfred Eisenstadt, and the American Civil War photographer Matthew Brady.

Site Details: Large Graphics, Good Links
Load Time: 19 seconds

Voice of the Shuttle

http://humanitas.ucsb.edu/humanitas_home.html

The shuttle referred to in the title is not a vehicle for travel in outer space but rather the part of a loom that passes in and out of the thread and weaves it into fabric. The metaphor is apt—the humanities pages found here weave in and out from one another, each subject page connecting to many related links. Subjects range from anthropology to architecture, science to women's studies.

Site Details:	Good Links
Load Time:	40 seconds

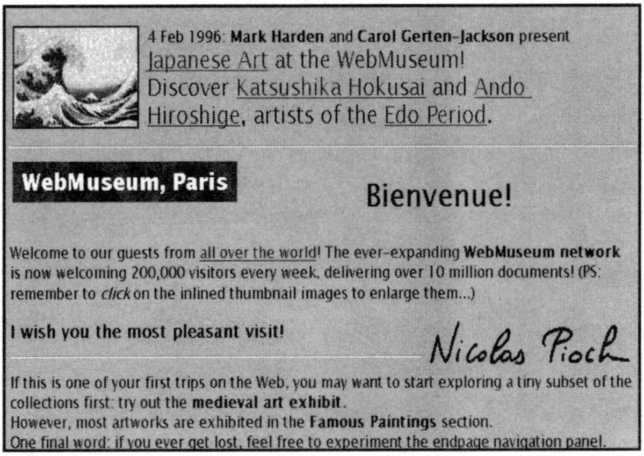

WebMuseum

http://mistral.enst.fr

With its large graphics and succinct curatorial text, this site is sure to appeal to fine art enthusiasts. Scores of paintings by Picasso, Renoir, Cezanne, and others are online here, including a sumptuous rendering of the medieval masterwork *Les tres riches heures du Duc de Berry.* Hypertext links lead to additional resources and commentary. You can also take virtual tours of Paris or 3+ sites in 15 different countries.

Site Details:	Large Graphics, Good Links
Load Time:	26 seconds

World Wide Arts Resources

http://www.concourse.com/wwar

This Web site points to thousands of art resources. Begin with a floor-by-floor virtual tour of the Metropolitan Museum in New York, and embark on an odyssey that includes links to museums, operas, theaters, galleries, schools, and artists around the world. Just how massive is this registry? There are more than 5,000 artists, 120 publications, and well over 100 American museums linked here. Moreover, each museum promises up to a 20-page preview. A search engine rounds out the home page.

Site Details:	Large Graphics, Good Links
Load Time:	37 seconds

Business & Investment

As information becomes a commodity in its own right, thousands of entrepreneurs, professionals, individual investors, and business owners turn to the Internet each day. Whether you're looking for a marketing strategy for your latest business venture or tips on how to be a better manager, the Internet brings a giant collection of business resources to your fingertips.

As global economic indicators rise and fall, the Web keeps pace with up-to-the-minute stock, bond, and mutual fund prices at **NETworth**, **the Stock Room**, and economic forecasts from the **Foundation for Enterprise Development.**

Prepare for the challenges of financing a start-up business with advice from the **CNN Financial Network,** or catch today's headlines with the online version of the **Wall Street Journal.** You'll find other business, technology, and financial periodicals like **Fortune** and **InfoWeek** in the Magazines chapter.

The hands-on investor will profit from information found at the **Dow Jones** page, with leads on hot company profiles and current interest rates. You'll find everything you need on the Web to stay in touch with the pulse of the financial world.

Asia Inc. Online

✯✯✯✯✯

http://www.asia-inc.com

An interactive business magazine, Asia Inc. Online provides valuable business information, daily financial data, and a discussion forum on various topics including China, crime, Hong Kong, current events, and technology. Users can gain access to a wide variety of Internet resources in Asia, too. For the latest Asian stock market closings and financial news, this site proves to be current and informative.

Site Details:	Large Graphics, Good Links, Shopping
Load Time:	38 seconds

Business Researcher's Interests

✯✯✯✯✯

http://www.pitt.edu/~malhotra/interest.html

Researchers will find a rich source of links relating to business technology here. Links are categorized by subjects such as MIS, Human Computer Interaction, Process Reengineering, Organizational Learning, and many other facets of business today. In addition, there are links to pertinent journals and magazines such as *The Economist* and the *Journal of Organizational Computing.* Users will appreciate its search tool, Web site construction help, and careers section.

Site Details: Good Links
Load Time: 22 seconds

Central Source Yellow Pages

✯✯✯✯✯

http://www.telephonebook.com

More than ten million businesses in the United States are accessible through this Web page, which offers links to companies, products, and services worldwide. Search by company name, phone number, or category. An index lists all categories alphabetically, but these are not hyperlinked. Users who wish to search by category must type in the category and state, search criteria can also include the city, zip code, and area code. If the search is successful, users will have access to company addresses. Free one-line listings are available for businesses.

Site Details: Good Links
Load Time: 17 seconds

CNN Financial Network

★★★★★

http://cnnfn.com

This segment of the CNN Interactive News home page is devoted to the world of business. Internal links lead to Wall Street, Market Talk, Your Money, World Markets, and CNN Business Shows. Inside these segments, users will find a short synopsis of the articles but can also choose to view the full article. Corporate agendas, board meetings, women in business, and consumer loans are some of the topics included here.

Site Details:	Large Graphics, Good Links
Load Time:	63 seconds

Dow Jones

★★★★★

http://www.dowjones.com

The electronic publishing division of Dow Jones offers Business Information Services at this site. Research Services, Customized News Services, and Electronic Publications are the three buttons on the home page. Personal investors will find useful tools for researching and investing in the stock market. The newspaper of choice for the business world, the *Wall Street Journal,* contributes to this site.

	Good Links
Load Time:	116 seconds

Foundation for Enterprise Development

http://www.fed.org/fed

For information about business strategies, visit the Foundation for Enterprise Development's (FED) Business Resource Library. Equity compensation, employee involvement, and international employee ownership are a few categories listed. Access FED publications, successful case studies, and the Department of Labor's best practice profiles.

Site Details: Good Links, Shopping
Load Time: 21 seconds

GNN Personal Finance Center

★★★★★

http://www.digital.com/gnn/meta/finance/index.html

The GNN Personal Finance Center is a top-notch resource for users interested in finance and investing. This site is a guide to making investments, and to finding the best Web sites offering financial information. Features of the home page include investment strategies, mortgage advice, and a Q&A section.

Site Details: Good Links
Load Time: 21 seconds

Hoover's Online

★★★★★

http://www.hoovers.com

The creators of the Hoover's Online Web site want to prove that "company information doesn't have to be boring." Users can search a directory of more than 8,500 companies by name, ticker symbol, or location. The week's top business news is rich with hyperlinks to in-depth company profiles and other resources. Also provided here is a hyperlinked list of the top 25 business book bestsellers, hot links to free business information, and feature stories on companies and industries.

Site Details: Large Graphics, Good Links, Shopping
Load Time: 90 seconds

Internet Advertising Resource Guide

http://www.missouri.edu/internet-advertising-guide.html

As businesses flood onto the Internet, advertising inevitably follows. Designed as a tool for businesses new to the Web, this site includes a page describing acceptable advertising practices on the Internet, as well as one devoted to netiquette. In addition to media pricing indexes, the Guide includes resources pertaining to marketing, business, advertising education, and advertising law. Users can also follow links to "exemplary" commercial sites.

Site Details: Good Links , Shopping
Load Time: 21 seconds

Lexis-Nexis

http://www.directory.net/lexis-nexis

Lexis-Nexis is billed as "the world's premier full-text, online legal, news, and business information service." Entrepreneurs and attorneys will want to check out its vast resources, many of which are presented here free of charge. Search the reference library, the small business advisor, companies for sale, and the list of newsgroups Web resources. On the products page, visitors will find a free daily summary of the *New York Times*, as well as software products and services.

Site Details: Good Links, Shopping
Load Time: 37 seconds

Mutual Funds Magazine Online

http://www.mfmag.com

Registered users have unrestricted access to current and back issues of *Mutual Funds Magazine Online*, plus a database of 6,000 funds. Registration is free and includes a weekly personalized e-mail newsletter and a free hardcopy edition of one of the magazine's sister advisory publications: *Mutual Fund Forecaster, Mutual Fund Buyer's Guide, Fund Watch*, or *Income Fund Outlook*.

Load Time: 37 seconds

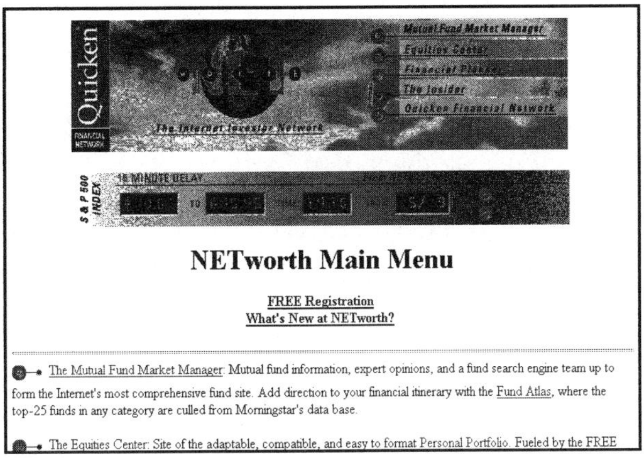

NETworth

★★★★★

http://networth.galt.com/www/home

NETworth offers free, in-depth information on mutual funds to users who fill out its online registration form. Information and stock quotes are available for 5,000 funds. The NETworth Insurance Network provides educational pieces and plenty of facts about traditional insurance products. Users will also find a large sampling of financial newsletters, weekly market outlooks, an updated (every four minutes) S&P 500 Stock Index, and interactive Q&A forums with market experts. The Financial Planning Center provides handy worksheets and tips.

Site Details: Large Graphics, Good Links
Load Time: 35 seconds

Off the Record

http://www.realaudio.com/CGI-bin/nph-redirect.cgi?100168

Off the Record is on the money for information on business and technology management. This Web site provides archives of articles and RealAudio interviews with senior managers who are leading the way down the information superhighway. In the archive of articles, users can follow annotated links to articles from such publications as *Computerland* and *Client/Server Journal.*

Site Details:	Real Audio, Sound , Large Graphics, Good Links
Load Time:	20 seconds

Small & Home-Based Business Links

http://www.ro.com/small_business/homebased.html

Small business owners, and those looking to start businesses, will find information about franchises, distributorships. and marketing opportunties. Although many links are commercial, there are links to newsgroups including news:alt.business.franchise and news:misc.entrepreneurs. The Services section features links to consultants, research services, and Web marketing firms.

	Good Links
Load Time:	63 seconds

Stock Market Charts

★★★★★

http://www.ai.mit.edu/stocks/graphs.html

In development by MIT's Artificial Intelligence Laboratory, this page presents experimental stock market charts. Visitors can click on the name of a company to see charts of its recent price and volume performance, or they can refer to the extensive index of companies. Also available are the NASDAQ Composite Index, S&P 500 Index, and information about artificial intelligence issues.

Site Details: Large Graphics, Good Links
Load Time: 13 seconds

Stock Research Group Inc.

★★★★★

http://www.stockgroup.com

Stock Research Group (SRG) offers the small investor up-to-date stock and investment information about high-growth stocks on the NASDAQ, VSE, and Alberta exchanges. Find out about the hot companies before they take off. Users can read the online version of Tom Kinakin's well respected newsletter, *The Profit Letter*, or learn about the latest developments in the markets. Links to other business and finance resources is also provided.

Site Details: Large Graphics, Good Links
Load Time: 42 seconds

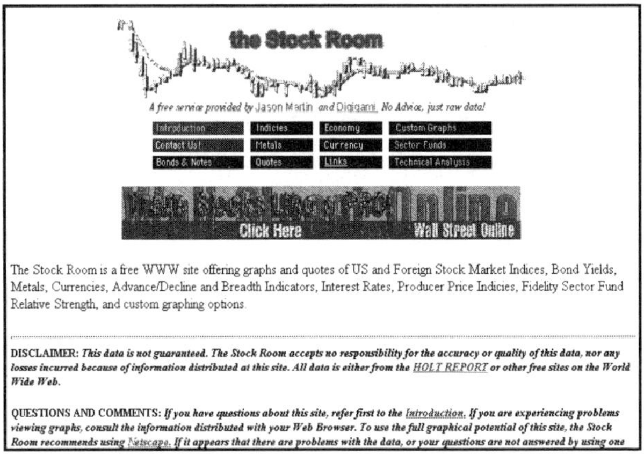

Stock Room

http://loft-gw.zone.org/jason/stock_room.html

Visit the Stock Room for current and past stock quotes, mutual funds prices, and market indexes. A comprehensive and free service, the site covers U.S. and foreign markets, as well as bonds, currency, and interest rates. Follow links to Dow Jones, Standard & Poor, NASDAQ, NYSE, AMEX, and Value Line.

Site Details: Large Graphics, Good Links
Load Time: 16 seconds

U.S. Securities and Exchange Commission

http://www.seconds.gov

The U.S. Securities and Exchange Commission (SEC) is an independent, nonpartisan, quasi-judicial regulatory agency responsible for administering federal securities laws. This well-organized page provides information about SEC, including news digests, public statements, current rules, enforcement actions, and FAQs. Investment guidance and the EDGAR database of corporate information are also provided. Links lead to other U.S. government sites.

Site Details: Large Graphics, Good Links
Load Time: 31 seconds

Wall Street Directory

★★★★★

http://www.cts.com/~wallst/index.html

Wall Street Direct is a comprehensive financial site, with more than 2,500 pages of information. Traders and investors will find useful products, services, and reports. The topics in the main menu include software reviews, analysis tools, market reports, publications, mutual funds, and personal finance.

Site Details: Good Links
Load Time: 3 seconds

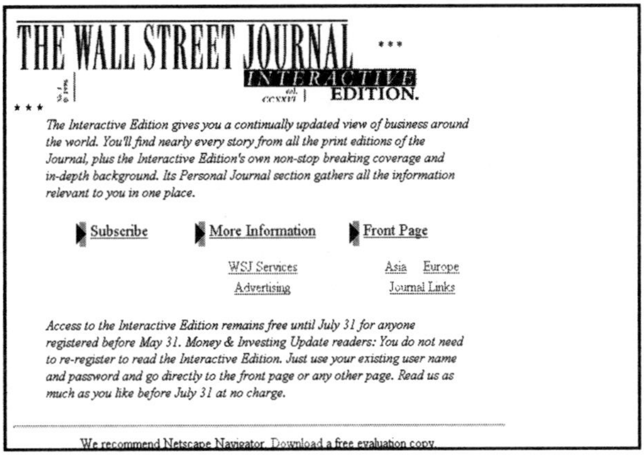

Wall Street Journal

★★★★★

http://www.wsj.com

Don't have time to read the paper thrown on the front lawn? Try the online *Wall Street Journal* offered here. Check in for updates regarding world markets or peruse the headlines from today's paper. Readers will find timely information about economics, business, management, consumer education, and careers. The Journal also offers a special edition prepared for secondary school students. The valuable Money & Investing Update is free to users who register, although a fee is required for ongoing access. Professionals on the go may want to try the customizable Personal Journal, which, for a fee, can be downloaded every day right to your computer.

Site Details:	Sound, Large Graphics, Good Links, Service Fee
Load Time:	43 seconds

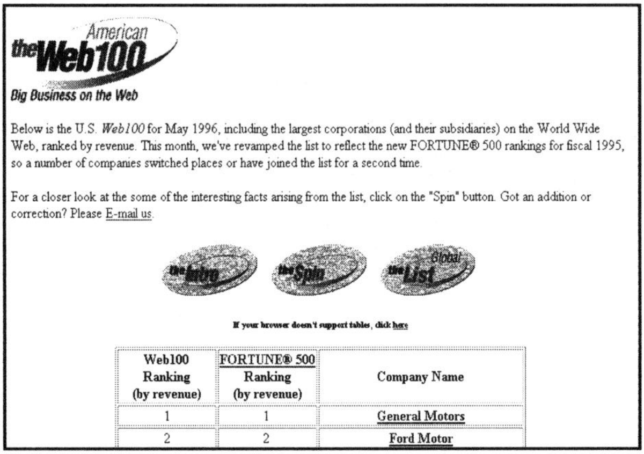

The American Web100

http://fox.nstn.ca/~at_info/w100_table.html

This evolving repository features a list of the largest U.S. corporations on the Web today. The list changes as a company's profit trends are reshaped. Such common household names as Campbell's Soup, Wal-Mart, Ford, and AT&T are among the members of this list, complete with hyperlinks for each.

Site Details: Good Links
Load Time: 42 seconds

Careers

Work is more than how we earn a living—it's a reflection of who we are. The ultimate career is one in which our work is our passion. Experts agree that networking is the key to landing that ultimate job. The Internet elevates the concept of "networking" to a new level.

Today, employers, placement counselors, and job seekers connect over the Internet with up-to-the-minute interaction and international exposure. **Jobtrak** offers career planning tools as well as job listings, while **CareerWeb** provides pointers to polish your interview skills. Employers view resumes from all over the world on **Intellimatch Online**. **America's Job Bank** lists over 100,000 positions. One of them may be the perfect job for you.

America's Job Bank

✯✯✯✯✯

http://www.ajb.dni.us

At least 1,800 state Employment Service offices link to this nationwide listing. For job seekers, it advertises the largest pool of available job opportunities in the U.S. Employers utilize the service for the rapid, national exposure the pool provides. At last review, the pool contained listings for more than 100,000 professional, technical, management, clerical, and blue collar jobs. You can locate job listings and access information about the company.

	Large Graphics , Good Links
Load Time:	34 seconds

Career Magazine

✯✯✯✯✯

http://www.careermag.com

Looking for the perfect job? Users embarking on an Internet job search might want to start the journey here. Career Magazine home page features a huge database of available jobs, which can be searched by job title, region, or specific skills. In addition, the site has employer profiles, news and articles, a career forum, a resume bank, and a huge selection of related links.

Site Details:	Good Links
Load Time:	15 seconds

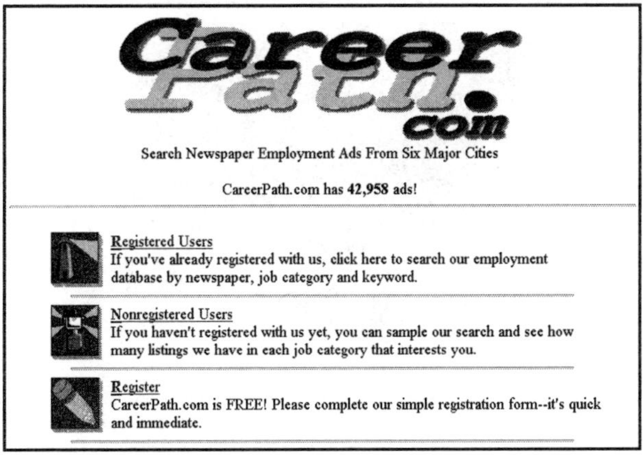

Career Path

http://www.careerpath.com/index.html

A free employment search service, Career Path enables users to peruse six major cities' employment ads for listings in their field. To find out about job openings, select the city that you would like to search and a job category from the listing. This service provides classifieds from the current week and the most recent Sunday papers.

Site Details: Good Links
Load Time: 7 seconds

CareerMosaic

http://www.careermosaic.com/cm

CareerMosaic, hosted by Bernard Hodes Advertising, is an impressive employment resource for recent college grads and career changers. Fill out the online form and search job listings by title, or browse through a long list of companies. The list of job fair locations and dates is updated regularly, and students can follow links to college recruitment information.

Site Details: Large Graphics, Good Links
Load Time: 24 seconds

CareerWEB

★★★★★

http://www.cweb.com

This one-stop location for career- and job-hunters offers a library of resources regarding career choices, self-image, resumes, and interviews. Want to get feedback on your job prospects? Then take the career-fitness test. Users can search for available jobs by location or type.

Site Details: Good Links
Load Time: 16 seconds

College Grad Job Hunter

★★★★★

http://www.collegegrad.com/

Recent graduates who visit this site can browse job listings and find out how to optimize their job searches. Learn interviewing techniques and get tips on writing resumes and cover letters. Job seekers can access many job listing sites. A few of these include E-Span Job Search, Jobnet, JobTrak, and CareerWeb. In addition, users can post their resumes at a wide variety of online resume sites.

Site Details: Sound, Good Links
Load Time: 42 seconds

IntelliMatch On-Line Employment Services

★★★★★

http://www.intellimatch.com/intellimatch

Users who are out of work or in search of better employment can place themselves in the IntelliMatch On-Line Employment Services database. This page presents visitors with a standardized resume form to complete online. Additional features, such as the ability to log back in and alter a previously entered resume, enhance the effectiveness of this forum.

Load Time: 38 seconds

Internet Professional Association

★★★★★

http://www.ipa.com

The Internet Professional Association is one of the world's largest online associations of recruiters, employment agencies, search firms, and employment professionals. Individuals who are seeking employment opportunities will find excellent resources in the Career Center and the employment listings. Firms that desire to post current openings will gain national coverage and online capability to respond to current postings and applications.

Site Details: Good Links
Load Time: 18 seconds

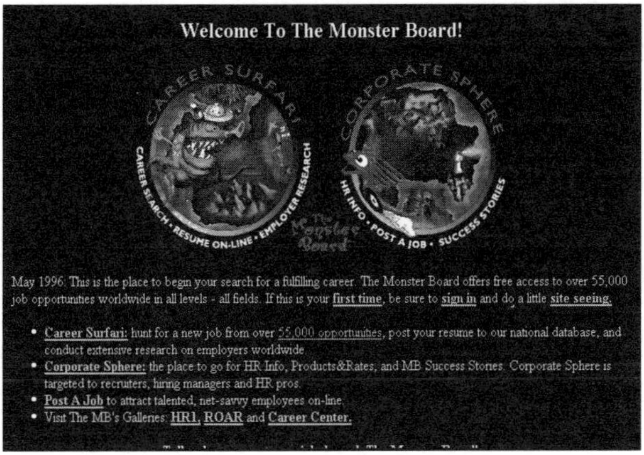

Monster Board

http://www.monster.com/home.html

The Monster Board is an online meeting place for job-seekers and employers. Users can conduct a career search by choosing a field or a specific job. Job openings are posted by many employers, and include company profiles. Resumes may be posted online, too.

Site Details: Good Links
Load Time: 5 seconds

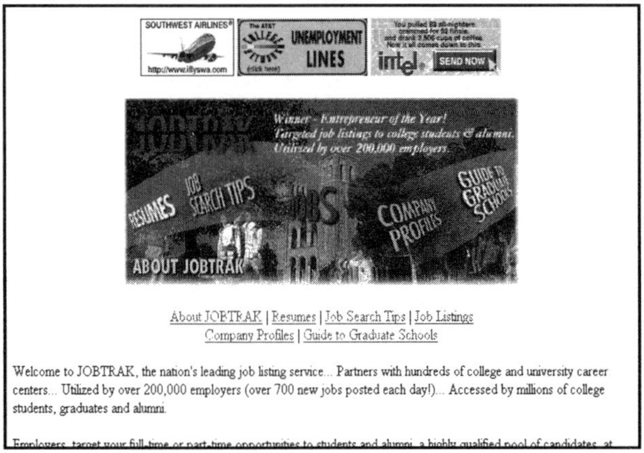

Welcome to Jobtrak

http://www.jobtrak.com

College students and alumni can take advantage of this Web site's job listing service. Review company profiles or access the job listings provided by your school's career center. Also offered here is an online Guide to Graduate School, which includes links to the home pages of graduate schools. The section Job Search Tips provides a number of handy resources, including a Job Search Manual, a Relocation Salary Calculator, and career planning tools.

Site Details: Large Graphics, Good Links
Load Time: 82 seconds

Children

The Web, for all its leading edge technologies, electronic commerce, and super-computing platforms, is still a giant playground for kids of all ages. From puzzles to coloring books, science projects to comics, you and your kids will love exploring the Web.

The younger set can share favorite accomplishments at **Global Show-n-Tell** or hang with the gang at **Maddy Mayhem's Kid's Stuff** page, filled with games, stories, magazines, and software. Tag along with Wile E. Coyote at the **Looney Tunes Page** or join a virtual expedition to the Pyramids of Egypt at the **Great Adventure Home Page**.

Once the kids are tucked in for the night, you'll be tempted to sneak back to the computer for your own romp through the **Electronic Zoo** or a virtual climb to the highest peak in North America with **Outside Kids Online**. Who says grownups shouldn't have fun?

After you've had a little playtime of your own, the Web also offers great parenting resources. Online publications like **Family Planet** and **Family World** deliver helpful hints on issues ranging from toy safety to healthy snacks to creative games for your family. If there's fun involved, you'll find it on the Web!

Global Show-n-Tell

http://emma.manymedia.com/show-n-tell

In the early grades, show-and-tell time is a chance for youngsters to share accomplishments and treasures with their classmates. With the help of the Web, children can share with other children on a global basis. The site follows a museum metaphor, with artwork arranged in different wings by age. The artists include a sentence about themselves, and sometimes include a link to their own home pages.

	Large Graphics, Good Links
Load Time:	42 seconds

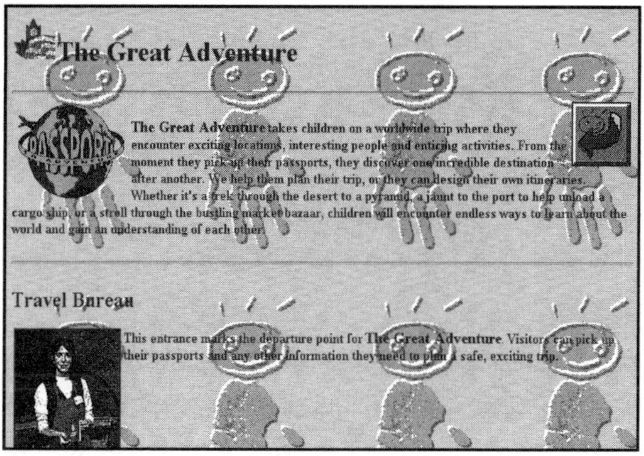

Great Adventure/Canadian Museum of Civilization

http://www.cmcc.muse.digital.ca/cmc/cmceng/childeng.html

The Canadian Museum of Civilization takes children ages 6-13 on virtual adventures around the world. After a stop at the Travel Bureau to pick up passports, children can dive into the past and join an expedition to the Pyramids of Egypt, and visit India or Indonesia. On the tour of Canada's own history, view Coastal Salish Indian houses and totem poles.

Site Details: Good Links, Shopping
Load Time: 33 seconds

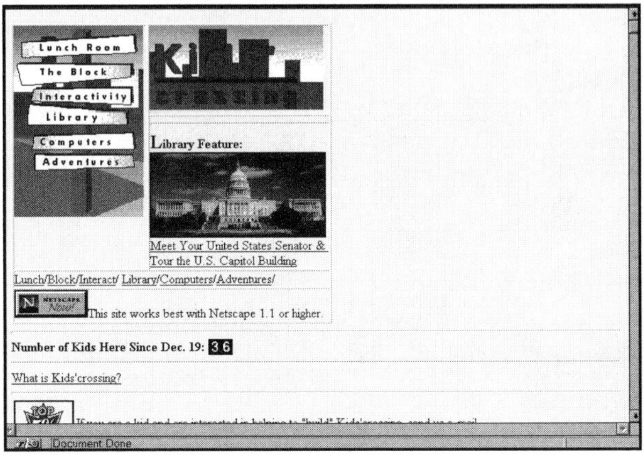

Kids' Crossing

☆☆☆☆☆

http://rmii.com/~pachecod/kidsnet/ckids.html

Join kids under 12 from all over the world on the bulletin board, or follow links to neat places like the Jason Project, where kids can see live video of the moon or tour Hawaii from under the water. Kids can even send mail to space shuttle astronauts. If young users want to become computer savvy, they can check out the tutorials on hypertext markup language and Web page publishing.

Site Details: Video, Good Links
Load Time: 22 seconds

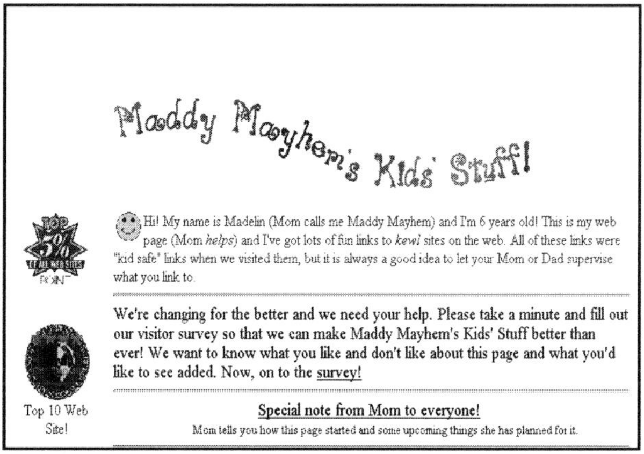

Maddy Mayhem's Kids' Stuff

★★★★★

http://wchat.on.ca/merlene/kid.htm

Here's initiative at a very young age! Sure to be a hit with children ages 3 through 8, Maddy Mayhem (that's what her mother calls her), age 6, has assembled kids-only links on the Internet. Links lead to everything from Disney to Dr. Seuss, Muppets to Animaniacs.

Site Details:	Large Graphics, Good Links
Load Time:	98 seconds

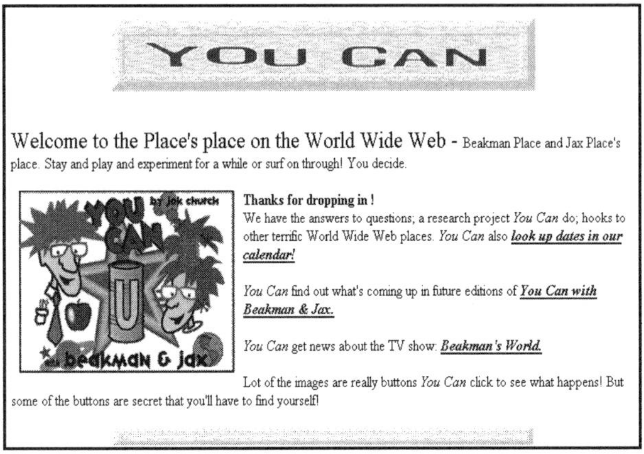

You Can

http://www.nbn.com:80/youcan/index.html

A wonderfully educational site for younger children, the You Can with Beakman and Jax page presents a variety of basic scientific concepts in an amusing and absorbing format. Features include Planet Pictures from the Hubble Space Telescope and real-world scientific applications such as explanations of why feet smell, how mucus protects us, and how glasses correct poor eyesight.

Site Details: Large Graphics
Load Time: 59 seconds

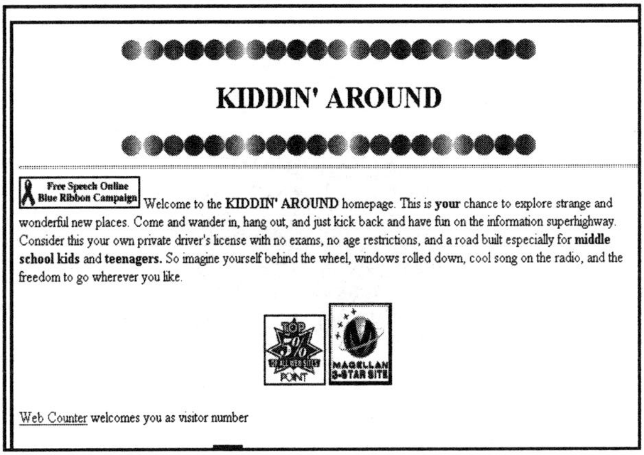

Kiddin' Around

With sections called by intriguing names such as Fantastic Lands, Spooky Spots, Time Machine, and Puzzling Places, the Kiddin' Around page is geared toward middle school kids and teens. Fantastic Lands keys into the interest that older kids have in knights, castles, and fantasy. They can even join the fantasy at the Avalon Roleplaying Page. Not all sections are as comprehensive as Fantastic Lands, but something worthwhile can be found in all of them.

Good Links

Load Time: 56 seconds

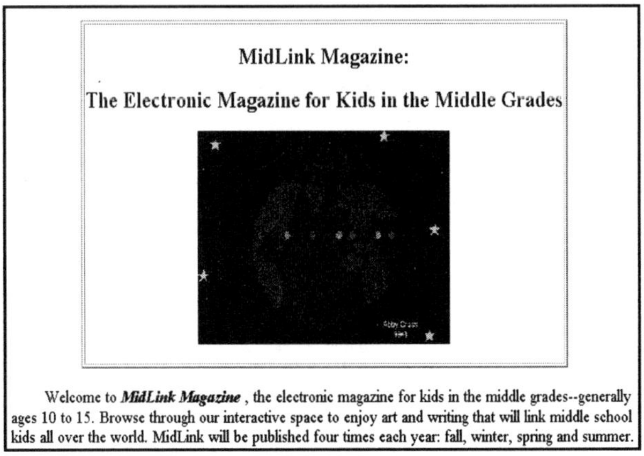

MidLink Magazine for Kids in the Middle Grades

★★★★★

http://longwood.cs.ucf.edu:80/~MidLink

Kids from all over the world can collaborate on fun projects via MidLink Magazine. Instead of doing currency conversion math problems the old way, learn what a hamburger and fries cost across the globe, and post what it costs in your town. Follow the adventures of a real research vessel on its journey around the world in search of new fish species and evidence of the greenhouse effect. Kids can visit the International Book Fair section to find out what other children are reading.

Site Details: Large Graphics, Good Links
Load Time: 29 seconds

Outside Kids Online

✯✯✯✯✯

http://web2.starwave.com/outside/online/kids

Outside Kids Online features articles about kids doing extraordinary things. Learn about a youth who climbed the highest peak in North America, a girl who rescues sea animals in trouble, and a 12-year-old who swam 12 miles from San Francisco to Oakland. Users can also access back issues.

Site Details:	Large Graphics
Load Time:	17 seconds

React

✯✯✯✯✯

http://www.react.com

Designed for teenagers, the weekly online newsmagazine React entertains and amuses with youth-related articles and lively graphics. Young people can voice their opinions by voting in polls about topics ranging from friendship to fashion. Read the joke or insult of the day, too.

Site Details:	Sound, Large Graphics, Shopping
Load Time:	45 seconds

Tum*Yeto Digiverse

✯✯✯✯✯

http://www.tumyeto.com/

Skateboarding, surfing, and snowboarding cultures meet at the very entertaining Tum Yeto Digiverse. Access articles about these outdoor activities and the individuals addicted to them, as well as a virtual art gallery, a food department, and Foxy, an e-zine for girls that features articles, columns, photos, and advice. This dynamic multimedia site is filled with sound and video clips, full-color images, interviews, directories, articles, tips, and much more.

Site Details:	Video , Sound, Large Graphics, Good Links
Load Time:	90 seconds

Young Person's Guide to the Internet

http://www.osc.on.ca/kids.html

The Guide offers "way cool pages by kids, for kids, and about kids." This annotated index of great links is sorted into categories such as Fun Stuff, Explorations, and Cool Schools. Young visitors will find links pertaining to music, ecology, and space sciences.

Site Details: Good Links
Load Time: 85 seconds

Berit's Best Sites for Children

http://www.cochran.com/theosite/KSites.html

Children, especially the younger set, are well served at Berit's Sites. Kids can follow her links for hours of fun. The page is well-organized, with such categories as Just For Fun, Kids on the Net, Creatures Great and Small, and Serious Stuff. Subcategories include crafts, games, and sports pages, elementary school and kids' home pages, animals, art galleries, science and math, world travel, and much more. Each of the well-selected page listings includes a two- or three-sentence annotation.

Site Details: Good Links
Load Time: 60 seconds

Calvin and Hobbes Gallery

http://eos.kub.nl:2080/calvin_hobbes

Calvin and his toy tiger Hobbes, who as far as Calvin is concerned, is very much alive and kicking, are two of the most lovable and hilarious characters to be seen in the comics in a long time. This site offers several panels, single and multiple, color and black-and-white, of the hyperactive and mischievous kid from the comics.

Site Details: Large Graphics, Good Links
Load Time: 46 seconds

Children's Literature Web Guide

★★★★★

http://www.ucalgary.ca/~dkbrown/index.html

From storytellers' resources to children's publishers, book award lists to online children's stories, there is an amazing number of links to children's and young adult literature resources here. Find links to pedagogical tools for parents, teachers, and writers, as well as links to indexes, research guides, and sites pertaining to families, kids, and books.

Site Details: Good Links
Load Time: 11 seconds

Cool Places For Kids

★★★★★

http://www.alaska.net/~steel/coolpls.html

Presented by Internet Alaska, Cool Places For Kids offers a ton of links to many interesting, fun, and educational online delights. Naturally, this extensive list begins with Alaska, then proceeds through the alphabet to Weather, offering literally hundreds of pointers to some of the most informative sites on the Web. This page is a must for children of all ages.

Site Details: Large Graphics, Good Links
Load Time: 5 seconds

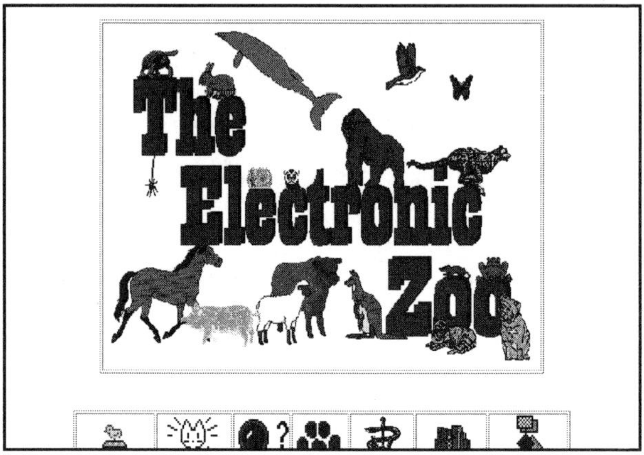

Electronic Zoo

http://netvet.wustl.edu/e-zoo.htm

Although the Electronic Zoo was created initially as a resource for veterinarians and animal-related organizations, kids will love the animal pictures and animal trivia offered. When they click on the pictures of cats, dogs, fish, rabbits, reptiles, marine mammals, pigs, and even fictional animals, kids will bring up links to entertaining and informative sites pertaining to their animal of choice. For instance, they can Talk to a Cat (one of the stranger things on the Web) or view great photos of the African lion.

Site Details: Sound, Good Links
Load Time: 34 seconds

Interesting Places for Kids

★★★★★

http://www.crc.ricoh.com/people/steve/kids.html

Compiled by a parent, Interesting Places for Kids guides children of all ages toward fun and educational sites. Kids can visit the Animaniacs page, the Unofficial Star Trek site, or discover their favorite scientist, Bill Nye, at the Nye Labs Web site. They can also check out other children's home pages. Parents can find out about the latest movies for kids at the Movie Mom's page.

Site Details:	Good Links
Load Time:	16 seconds

Non-Stick Looney Tunes Page

★★★★★

http://www.tncnet.com/~jmccarthy

The unique multiple-window layout and light-hearted content make this Web page a fun place for cartoon enthusiasts. The multimedia pages feature "looney" sounds, great graphics, and a nice collection of links to the home pages of characters such as Wile E. Coyote, Bugs Bunny, and the Animaniacs. There are pointers to related newsgroups, too. "That's all, folks!"

Site Details:	Sound, Large Graphics, Good Links
Load Time:	150 seconds

Uncle Bob's Kids' Page

http://gagme.wwa.com/~boba/kidsi.html

Considered one of the top-notch children's Web sites, Uncle Bob's Kids' Page lists a wide variety of educational and entertaining places for kids. Although the links are annotated with short descriptions, few are sorted by subject. Kids of all ages will find fascinating links including such gems as the Whale Watching Web, the Global Cycling Network, Dinosaurs in Hawaii!, Stereograms, and hundreds more.

Site Details: Good Links
Load Time: 14 seconds

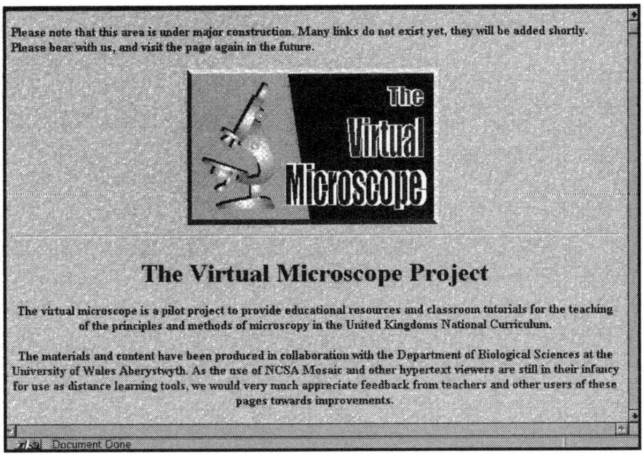

Virtual Microscope Project

http://www.dcs.aber.ac.uk/~mjw/michp.html

The Virtual Microscope Project gives kids of all ages an eye-popping view of the teeming life on the head of a pin. View electron microscope images or take an interactive tour of the microscopic world. A hypertext learning aid is provided, and microscopy movies will be added to the site. In addition, there are links to other interesting biological sites.

Site Details:	Video, Good Links
Load Time:	51 seconds

Children's Literature

http://www.parentsplace.com/readroom/childnew/index.html

Editors, librarians, teachers, and parents are among the reviewers for this annual newsletter. Each year they read and evaluate 3,000+ new children's books and list the top 150. In addition, they profile prominent authors and illustrators and review electronic titles and multimedia. Book reviews are categorized by age group (Children 3 and Under through Young Adult). In the archive section, past reviews are sorted by subject.

Site Details: Good Links, Shopping
Load Time: 10 seconds

Family Planet

http://family.starwave.com

Family Planet, an online magazine for parents, is filled with expert advice from such baby gurus as Penelope Leach, T. Berry Brazelton, and Marguerite Kelly. The '90s juggle of family, work, community, and self is made a little easier with columns such as Working Solutions, the Parents Resource Almanac, movie reviews, toy reviews, and a current events listing. The magazine is well-designed and readable.

Site Details: Large Graphics, Good Links
Load Time: 21 seconds

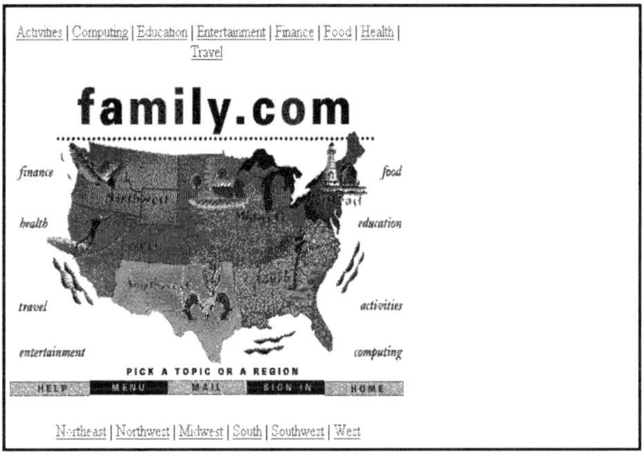

Family.com

http://www.family.com

A collaboration of more than 40 regional, monthly, parenting publications, Family World offers articles on such topics as bonding with dad and healthy snacking. Activities for kids, child development issues, and health and educational resources are included along with book reviews and entertainment ideas. A parents' forum fosters the exchange of stories and ideas. Look at the regional calendar for local activities as well as a listing of the publications contributing to this site.

Site Details:	Large Graphics, Good Links, Shopping
Load Time:	43 seconds

Interesting Places for Parents

✯✯✯✯✯

http://www.crc.ricoh.com/people/steve/parents.html

This helpful and informative page offers Web travel advice and guidance for parents. Once children gain access to the Internet, they may encounter disturbing or offensive material. Here are useful tips and warnings on how to handle or prevent potential difficulties. Along with educational resources, other topics offered include Software for Kids, Resources and Articles, Stuff To Buy, Net Safety, and more.

Site Details:	Good Links, Shopping
Load Time:	12 seconds

Kid-Safety Tips

✯✯✯✯✯

http://www.uoknor.edu/oupd/kidsafe/start.htm

Kids can cruise this easy-to-navigate site and gather lots of safety tips, ranging from Internet safety issues, bike riding safety, dealing with bullies, and home phone safety. Designed like a game, with arrows and entertaining graphics, the site will keep kids here long enough to experience some of the joys of learning.

Site Details:	Good Links
Load Time:	69 seconds

Our Kids

✯✯✯✯✯

http://wonder.mit.edu/our-kids.html

This parenting resource is geared toward parents of kids with disabilities or special needs. Parents will find information about disorder-specific newsgroups, parenting resources, adaptive technology, and publications. The site also features a rare disease database for disability resources on the Net.

Site Details: Good Links
Load Time: 9 seconds

ParentsPlace

✯✯✯✯✯

http://www.parentsplace.com

This resource for parents features articles about children's literature and photography, catalogs and stores geared toward parents, live chat rooms, book reviews, and bulletin boards. Access resources pertaining to baby foods, clothing, diapers, and strollers, or read articles on topics such as fathering, single parenting, twins, and step-parenting.

Site Details: Large Graphics, Good Links, Shopping
Load Time: 20 seconds

SafeSurf

http://www.safesurf.com/index.html

Dedicated to providing children with a pleasant experience on the Internet, SafeSurf points to approved sites as "Child Safe." In the Internet Lifeguard section, parents can review the Online Basics and learn about filtering software. The Parent & Child Agreement is a good starting point for initiating an online safety discussion. SafeSurf can also e-mail parents regularly as new sites appear on the Web. It's not foolproof, but it's a start.

Site Details: Good Links
Load Time: 4 seconds

Computing & The Internet

The age of typewriters, telephones, and adding machines has given way to an era of word processing, e-mail, and electronic spreadsheets. The appeal of the Internet lies in its capacity to exponentially increase work productivity with high-speed global connectivity and information access.

Tasks that once took hours of work time can now be completed in minutes. The graphic artist can download a multimedia viewer from the **Shareware Trade Association** and e-mail finished artwork to an editor with a few clicks of the mouse. The controller of a small business can try a new accounting application found on the Web without a time-consuming visit to a local software retailer. Individuals can locate almost any computer technology company from the **Computer Sites Index**.

As the Web evolves and grows, reference materials and tutorials draw the computer enthusiast into this exciting phenomenon. **Welcome to the World Wide Web** and **Newbie No More** help familiarize the Internet newcomer with jargon, functions, and netiquette. Learn the fundamentals of Web page design from sites like **Global Awards for Excellence in Web Design** or the **Homepage Creator System**. With all this knowledge at your disposal, the limits of time and curiosity are your only constraints.

Computer Sites Index

http://www.ludd.luth.se/~max/computers.html

Users can access the home pages of computer and technology companies through this alphabetical index. The big companies—IBM, Hewlett Packard, Sony, SUN Microsystems, Apple—are here, as well as peripheral manufacturers, such as U.S. Robotics, Creative Labs, and Diamond. Links to many smaller hardware and software companies are listed here as well.

	Good Links
Load Time:	21 seconds

Cult of Macintosh

http://www.utu.fi/~jsirkia/mac/index.html

Cult of Macintosh is an excellent virtual onramp to the fast lanes of Macintosh computing. It contains a comprehensive set of links and descriptions of multiple Macintosh resources on the Internet. Users can select from categories like software, games, Web indexes, newsgroups, magazines, people, questions, and vendors for Macintosh. One section lists the Top 20 Sites on the Internet that cater to Macintosh owners. Nicely designed, this page is a great starting point for Mac lovers everywhere.

Site Details:	Large Graphics, Good Links
Load Time:	73 seconds

Free OnLine Dictionary of Computing

http://wombat.doc.ic.ac.uk:80

Stumped by the latest computer jargon and acronyms? Wouldn't know what a WABI was if it shook your hand? Punch "WABI" into the search form and find out that it is "a software package to emulate Microsoft Windows under the X Window System." Aren't you glad you asked? The Dictionary also categorizes terms by subject, such as Protocols, Programming, Database, and more.

Load Time: 18 seconds

Kim Komando's Komputer Klinic

http://www.komando.com

TV commentator, syndicated talk radio host, and author Kim Komando provides an easy-to-understand site for users who want to improve their computer skills.This home page features categories such as tips and tricks, instant answers to computer questions, and top Internet sites. Users will also find reviews of the latest software, hardware, and Internet resources.

Site Details: Good Links
Load Time: 9 seconds

Shareware Trade Association

http://delta.com/star.org/starhome.htm

Shareware Trade Association and Resources (STAR) provides access to the latest products and companies in the shareware industry. From the home page, users can find shareware available for both Windows and DOS, the Who's Who in Shareware, and the Shareware Bulletin Board. Each month, the authors provide free software to STAR visitors. The site is easy on the eyes and gets the job done.

Site Details: Shopping, Service Fee
Load Time: 16 seconds

Shareware.com

http://www.shareware.com

A service from C|net, Shareware.com is a huge archive of free programs and utilities. Its searchable collection is enormous, with over 210,000 software files for nearly every major platform, including Windows, Macintosh, UNIX, Amiga, and Netware. In one section of the site there are daily reviews of PC and Macintosh titles, and the Survival Kit section features downloading tips and tools. A version of the site without Frames is also available.

Site Details: Good Links
Load Time: 36 seconds

Windows 95

http://fub46.zedat.fu-berlin.de:8080/~banshee/win95/soft.html

Devoted to the Windows 95 operating system, this site contains a vast assortment of Internet resources, tips, guides, software archives, programming applications, and troubleshooting information. Find links to home pages and other Windows '95 pages here. This beautifully designed Web site features information about improving one's system, including directions for setting up virtual memory and checking start-up files.

Site Details: Large Graphics, Good Links
Load Time: 49 seconds

All-In-One Cool Sites Page

http://www.webcom.com/~tbrown/coolsite.html

Yes, the sites listed here are cool, and there are lots of 'em. Browse through the list just for fun, or if in a hurry, take the Autopilot Tour of the Directory. Links are listed by subjects, such as Cars, Electronics, and Shopping.

Site Details: Good Links, Shopping
Load Time: 15 seconds

DejaNews

http://www.dejanews.com

DejaNews is a Web site that contains a search engine for Usenet bulletin boards. Just type in a keyword, and then select one or more of the clickable options: Age of Articles, Method Sorted, and Number of Hits. Here, visitors have direct access to Usenet articles.

Site Details: Good Links
Load Time: 8 seconds

Global Awards for Excellence in Web Design

http://www.river.org/~isaac/global.html

Welcome to the Oscars for the Web. Arranged in such categories as Most Innovative Site, Best Overall Site, and Best Non Profit Site, winners are selected by number of nominations received rather than a judging process. Perhaps recognition of useful, good-looking, high-content pages will spur overall better design on the Web.

Site Details: Good Links
Load Time: 6 seconds

GNN Select Top 50

http://gnn.com/wic/wics/top.new.html

The links listed here lead to popular and comprehensive Web resources. From this list, which is updated weekly, users can go to the 50 most frequently accessed sites from GNN Select—a subject index of links to sites that are useful, up-to-date, effectively designed, and "in touch with Web culture." Many of the GNN Select sites are themselves subject indexes. For more recommended sites, GNN's Best of the Net section is only a click away.

Site Details: Large Graphics, Good Links
Load Time: 13 seconds

NETLinks Newbie Help

http://www.interlog.com/~csteele/newbie.html

The Newbie Help page offers exactly what the title promises: assistance for users new to the Internet. Features of this site include the official NETLINKS! Netiquette guide, recommended newsgroups, an extensive list of search engines, and an HTML guide.

Site Details: Real Audio, Large Graphics, Good Links
Load Time: 25 seconds

Searchers

✯✯✯✯✯

http://gagme.wwa.com/~boba/search.html

Searchers is a tool that consolidates many major Web search engines. Users can submit searches with any keyword to databases such as Yahoo, Lycos, WebCrawler, and Galaxy. Search forms are provided for searches targeting people, documents, and databases. Users can also follow links to numerous retrieval engines and Web indexes.

Site Details: Good Links
Load Time: 10 seconds

The List: Mecklermedia's List of ISP's

✯✯✯✯✯

http://thelist.com

Without question, The List is the most comprehensive collection of information on Internet service providers (ISPs) on the Web. Visitors can browse by country, state, area code, country code, or keyword. Over 1,800 providers are listed, with information on each provider's Web page and/or e-mail address. Examine (and add to) the interactive rating scale of ISPs, and find out the reasons behind the ratings.

Site Details: Large Graphics, Good Links
Load Time: 14 seconds

Tools for Aspiring Web Weavers

http://www.nas.nasa.gov/NAS/WebWeavers/weavers.html

Want to spin your own tale on the Web? This home page contains a starter kit for home page design, complete with HTML and style guides, basic Web-related software tools, VRML and 3D Web tools, and general Web information. Follow the pointers to icons, graphics resources, Internet and HTML standards and specifications—even fast-breaking Web news. An essay included here suggests ways that organizations can make the most of the Web.

Site Details: Good Links
Load Time: 4 seconds

User's Guide to the Internet

http://ug.cs.dal.ca:3400/newbie.html

Frank's Internet resources are comprehensive and helpful. Information and links are provided for Internet documents, services, software archives, UNIX guides, and much more. Users can take an Internet tour, ask for advice from online experts, or retrieve C/C++ programming guides, too.

Site Details: Good Links
Load Time: 4 seconds

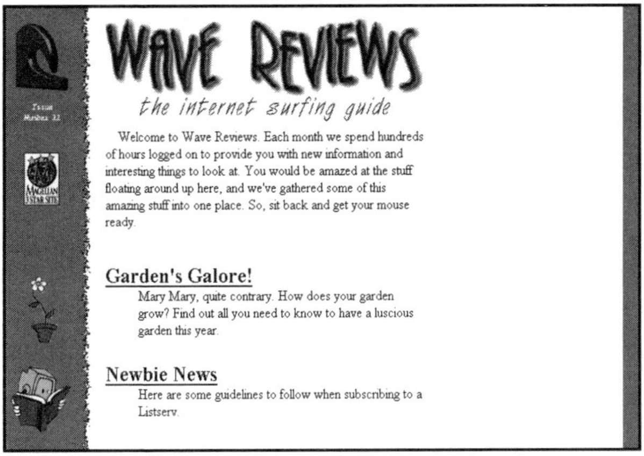

Wave Reviews

http://www.netwave.net/wave_reviews

Wave Reviews, a monthly "Internet surfing guide," offers a succinct yet thorough look at what's new on the Internet. Each issue features annotated links categorized by a certain topic, such as Stupid Web Tricks or Laugh Out Loud. For the busy Web user who wants a high-quality, streamlined e-zine, Wave Reviews makes a great bookmark. Back issues are also accessible.

Site Details: Good Links
Load Time: 22 seconds

Web Masters

★★★★★

http://gagme.wwa.com/~boba/masters1.html

If you're ready to be seen on the Web, the tips Bob Allison offers here can help. Here he addresses the issues of style, content, images, maps, background colors, links, and publicizing your new Web page. He walks visitors through a collection of Web starting points, search tools, and What's New pages that spotlight new appearances on the Web. If you're into graphics and icons, he offers a great list of downloadable icons and tips on how to present them. There's nothing stopping you now!

Site Details: Good Links, Service Fee

Load Time: 22 seconds

WWW Meta-Indexes and Search Tools

★★★★★

http://lcweb.loc.gov/global/metaindex.html

Web sleuths should start their hunt for information here. Sponsored by the Library of Congress, this site lists links to Web indexes and to nearly two dozen search engines. Links to comparison studies of search engines and to lists of Web servers are also provided.

Site Details: Good Links

Load Time: 9 seconds

A Primer for Web Resources

http://www-slis.lib.indiana.edu/Internet/programmer-page.html

Although this page is aimed at beginners, it also makes an excellent resource for the more experienced. The Primer provides information on how to create Web resources. Beginning with how to create and design a HTML document, the material here covers topics such as HTML style guides, reference guides, server management, PERL language, and GUI scripts.

Site Details: Large Graphics, Good Links
Load Time: 23 seconds

Ask Dr. Internet

http://promo.net/gut

With its Q&A format, this e-zine is something of a computing "*Popular Mechanics*" of the Web. Even when questions meander, the good doctor steers the discussion back to the practical mainstream. Dr. Internet answers very specific technical queries in a way that sheds light on much larger practical and theoretical areas. At this site, it's open season and no-holds-barred on all the puzzling aspects of computing, cyberspace, and the Information Age.

Site Details: Good Links
Load Time: 5 seconds

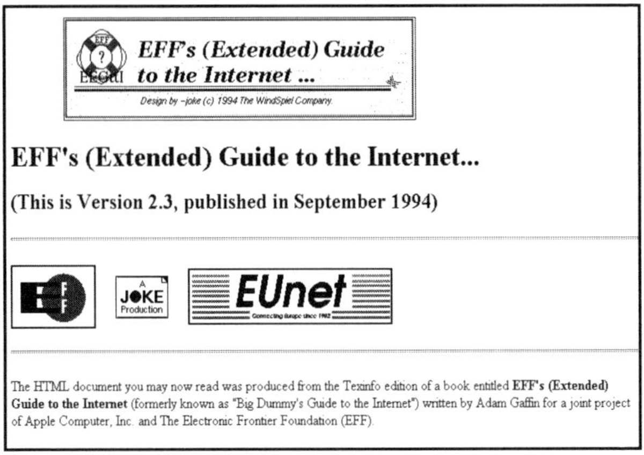

Extended Guide to the Internet

http://www.eff.org/papers/eegtti/eegtti.html

Formerly known as the Big Dummies Guide to the Internet, this site is a must-see for Web newbies—people who have little or no experience with network communications. Follow links to helpful sites such as Setting Up and Jacking In, Public Access Internet Providers from Alabama to Australia, Education on the 'Net, Business on the 'Net, and much more. Links also lead to a host of e-mail, Usenet, Telnet, FTP and gopher sites. This informative gem is not to be missed.

Site Details: Good Links
Load Time: 43 seconds

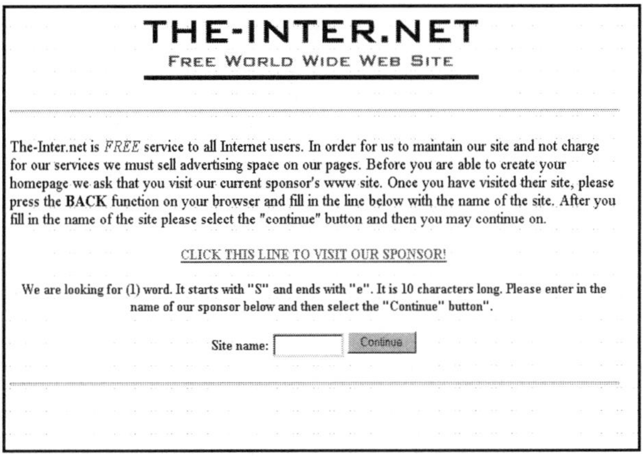

Homepage Creator System

http://the-inter.net/www/future21/create1.html

Here, Web-writing novices can create a home page in minutes by filling in the blanks of a form. Users select background, text, hypertext colors, and line styles, and then write the titles, headings, and the main paragraph. Even the mandatory links are provided, as well as instructions for including the various search engines in your page. For the final touch, users add e-mail information and a closing paragraph. Voila! The novice is now an established Web author. The resulting site may not be fancy, but it's definitely publishable.

Site Details: Good Links

Load Time: 12 seconds

Internet Encyclopedia

http://www.cs.uh.edu/~clifton/encyclopedia.html

If you need to look something up and don't want to leave your computer, make sure you bookmark the Internet Encylopedia. This interactive reference guide will lead you to information available on the Internet. Links are organized in alphabetical order within the MicroReference and MacroReference sections. The MacroReference section contains pointers to large areas of knowledge and FAQs, and is cross-referenced with the more detailed, subject-specific MicroReference section. There are excellent, large graphics throughout this useful site.

Site Details: Large Graphics, Good Links
Load Time: 60 seconds

Internet Roadmap

http://www.ll.mit.edu/Roadmap

Designed to help prevent Internet travelers from getting lost, this Web site offers users an Internet training workshop series. Based on lectures by Internet experts, the series of lessons touches upon such subjects as e-mail, netiquette, LISTSERV user commands, Usenet, Telnet, Gopher, the Web, and much more. Try the pop quizzes or browse through the list of interesting sites found here.

Site Details: Good Links
Load Time: 5 seconds

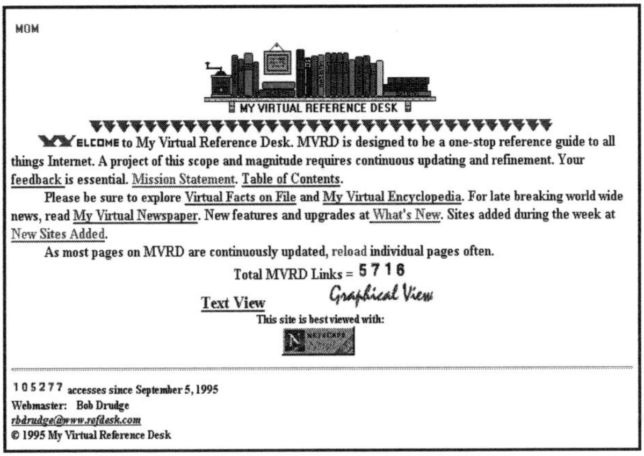

My Virtual Reference Desk

http://www.refdesk.com

My Virtual Reference Desk is an excellent starting point for accessing all that the Web has to offer. Link categories available at this site include Word of the Day, News and Sports, My Virtual Paper, Weather Sites, Hot Web Picks, Best of the Net, Top 25 Sites, and Cool Sites of the Day. Each category is divided into a number of sub-categories, some of which contain links to even more specific subcategories. Users can also refer to the Facts on File and Internet Help sections.

Site Details: Good Links
Load Time: 18 seconds

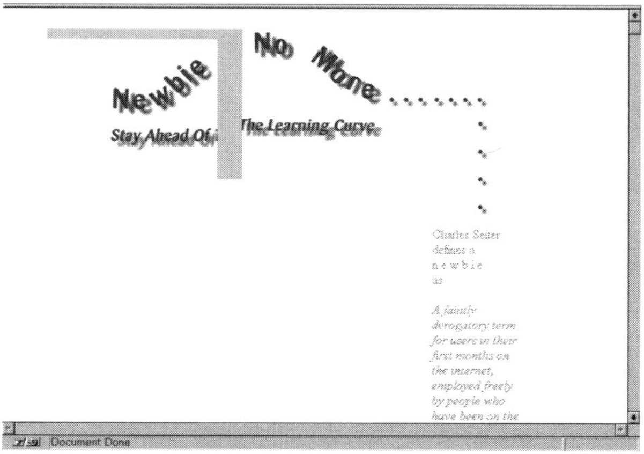

Newbie No More

http://www.netcoach.com

If you've hastily concluded that the Internet can be just as difficult to navigate as a jungle, then this site is for you. The purpose of this page is to "provide information to those seeking to become net-proficient." Visitors will find helpful online tutorials that cover the basics: e-mail, Archie, and UNIX. This page has a nice layout and is effectively organized.

Site Details: Good Links
Load Time: 43 seconds

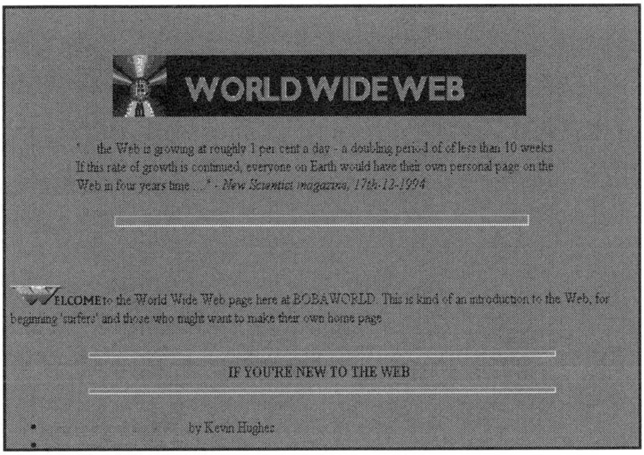

Welcome to the World Wide Web

http://gagme.wwa.com/~boba/web.html

Bobaworld offers this Web page for beginning surfers. The page is an ideal education center to begin exploring the Web. It contains introductory information, Web facts, etiquette guides, and a section on the advantages and disadvantages of the Web. Newbies can also pull up videoteleconferencing information, Yahoo's Web index, and the Hitchhiker's Guide to the Web.

Site Details: Large Graphics, Good Links
Load Time: 9 seconds

Amdahl's Hot Sites

http://www.amdahl.com/internet/general/sites.html

If you're new the the Net, remember this page—its a quick way to find some of the best on the Web. Sorted by subject, most links are annotated. You'll find home pages of museums, TV networks, online sightseeing tours, comics, magazines, and more. Topics are updated regularly.

Site Details:	Large Graphics, Good Links
Load Time:	23 seconds

Big Eye–Selected Web Sites

http://www.bigeye.com

The perfect reference guide for the unconventional thinker, Big Eye's beat is the unusual, weird, and intriguing. The site is a mind-boggling megalink index to hundreds of irresistible sidebars and footnotes to history, science, and life that somehow, taken together, point to greater truths. A lifetime could be spent on everything offered here, from the Anarchy Home Page to the complete writings, letters, and diaries of George Washington.

Site Details:	Good Links
Load Time:	130 seconds

Broach Web List

☆☆☆☆☆

http://www.galstar.com/~heatxfr/craigs.html

The Broach Web List of links is massive, and may require an extra-large cup of coffee and a do-not-disturb sign on the door. Links are sorted by topic. The long, alphabetized list of topics ranges from Art and Art Museums to Human Concern to Volcanos. Several of the headings are subdivided by hemisphere (e.g., Medicine, Eastern Hemisphere; Medicine, Western Hemisphere).

Site Details: Good Links
Load Time: 36 seconds

BUBL Subject Tree: Reference

☆☆☆☆☆

http://www.bubl.bath.ac.uk/BUBL/Reference.html

A large compendium of Web resources, BUBL indexes sites alphabetically or by subject. In the Reference section, users can find dictionaries, Bibles, encyclopedias, the Virtual Reference Desk, and Quotation Sources. The Directories section includes an "800" Number Directory, the Global Online Directory, Business Directories, Internet Access directories, Internet Indexes, and more.

Site Details: Good Links
Load Time: 88 seconds

GNN

http://gnn.com/gnn/index.html

Global Network Navigator (GNN) is a subscription-based, Internet navigational guide and online publisher. Find your way on the Infobahn by starting at the Whole Internet Catalog, NCSA Mosaic's What's New, GNN Best of the Net, or Netizens, a directory of home pages written by users. Shoppers can make purchases online by using GNN Direct or the Business Pages. GNN publications are available in sections, such as The Personal Finance Center, Education Center, Book Story, Sports, and the Web Review. You can spend hours, even days, exploring GNN's many informative pages.

Site Details:	Large Graphics, Good Links, Shopping, Service Fee
Load Time:	70 seconds

NETLiNkS!

http://www.interlog.com/~csteele/hotpage.html

If you want a new page to load up when you start your Web expedition, consider the NETLiNkS! home page. Its very comprehensive categories include everything from Women's Issues and Resources to Games (Classic, MUDs, RPG, Video Games). Each category is divided into easy-to-browse, comprehensive subcategories.

Site Details:	Good Links
Load Time:	43 seconds

Scott's Internet Hotlist

http://sprawl.sensemedia.net:8080/people/scott/scotlist.html

Scott's database of Internet links contains a huge number of connections listed under categories ranging from agriculture and art to weather and Web chat. At last review, it contained 8,120 sites across 69 categories. This on-ramp to the Infobahn is an excellent starting point for searches on a variety of topics.

Site Details:	Good Links
Load Time:	45 seconds

Spider's Web

http://gagme.wwa.com/~boba/spider.html

A good jumping-off place, The Spider offers hundreds of links, both sorted and unsorted. Besides this extensive list, there are Picks of the Day, The Spider's Bookmark, Weekly and Monthly Goodies, and Random Goodies.

Site Details: Good Links
Load Time: 15 seconds

Subject List (Info Bank)

http://www.clark.net/pub/global/subjectlist.html

Here, users can view the very comprehensive Subject List of links alphabetically or as a subject tree. To pull up the tree diagram, click on Return to Subject Page. Under the Ideas topic, there are links to the Freethought Web, Skeptics Society, Philosophy, Feminism, Objectivism, and many more. The Interactive Applications page links to sites such as the Sociable Web, Chats, and WaxWeb.

Site Details: Good Links
Load Time: 23 sec

Discovering Our World

Curiosity leads to discovery. As we gaze at insects beneath a blade of grass or the planet Venus in the evening sky, we marvel at the social order of ants and speculate on the origins of the universe. This sense of wonder brings us to ask questions of science, philosophy and technology.

The graphic and video capabilities of the Web provide a perfect showcase for re-discovering the scientific and natural wonders of our environment. Scientists, who share research findings daily with colleagues, revel in the opportunity to share their explorations and discoveries with the rest of us.

View a real-time image of the sun's corolla or photographs of our galaxy from the Hubble telescope at the **NASA** home page. The **SEDS Galaxy** page features tours of the solar system, astronomy and astrophysics.

Back on Earth, track hurricanes with the help of **Intellicast's** satellite and radar images, or perhaps check on ski conditions in your area. If the possibilities begin to overwhelm you, relax to the haunting sounds of the whale song at the **Whale-Watching Web;** the wonders never cease.

Astronomy and Space

http://www.nuance.com/~cwbol/astro.html

Stargazers should make the time to visit this fantastic and vast space resource page. Links and information on all kinds of astronomical topics are featured. The list includes clubs and associations, newsgroups, beautiful space images, resource listings, comet data, Mars and Saturn information, and eclipse predictions. Links to additional resource pages and astronomy sites are supplied.

Site Details: Large Graphics, Good Links
Load Time: 18 seconds

Astronomy Cafe

http://www2.ari.net/home/odenwald/cafe.html

Students of all ages, as well as the merely curious, will find a universe of information about astronomy here. Written by an astrophysicist, it offers an extensive hotlist of astronomy-related sites. His current favorite is listed in the Catch of the Week. The Guide Book offers students contemplating a astronomy career biographies of prominent astronomers. Students faced with a research paper can find help in the Anatomy of a Research Paper and the Ask an Astronomer sections. A downloadable software library is also included.

Site Details: Good Links
Load Time: 17 seconds

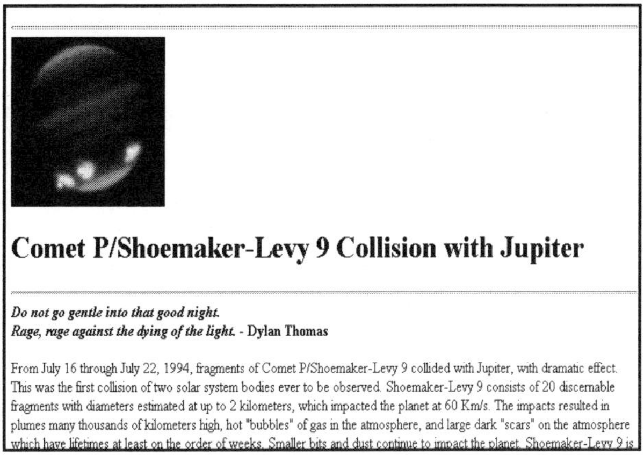

Comet P/Shoemaker-Levy 9 Collision with Jupiter

Do not go gentle into that good night.
Rage, rage against the dying of the light. - Dylan Thomas

From July 16 through July 22, 1994, fragments of Comet P/Shoemaker-Levy 9 collided with Jupiter, with dramatic effect. This was the first collision of two solar system bodies ever to be observed. Shoemaker-Levy 9 consists of 20 discernable fragments with diameters estimated at up to 2 kilometers, which impacted the planet at 60 Km/s. The impacts resulted in plumes many thousands of kilometers high, hot "bubbles" of gas in the atmosphere, and large dark "scars" on the atmosphere which have lifetimes at least on the order of weeks. Smaller bits and dust continue to impact the planet. Shoemaker-Levy 9 is

Comet P/Shoemaker-Levy 9 Collision with Jupiter

http://nssdc.gsfc.nasa.gov/planetary/comet.html

Compiled and presented by the National Space Science Data Center, these extensive scientific images of the collision of the Shoemaker-Levy 9 Comet with Jupiter are indexed by the observatory producing them and by individual comet fragments. Most interesting are discussions of the distinct methodologies used by the different telescopes. The Hubble Space Telescope images are especially beautiful, as are the infrared images from the University of Hawaii. Observatories from around the globe are included along with brief summaries of how the images were made, what they represent, and how they may be interpreted.

Site Details: Large Graphics, Good Links
Load Time: 19 seconds

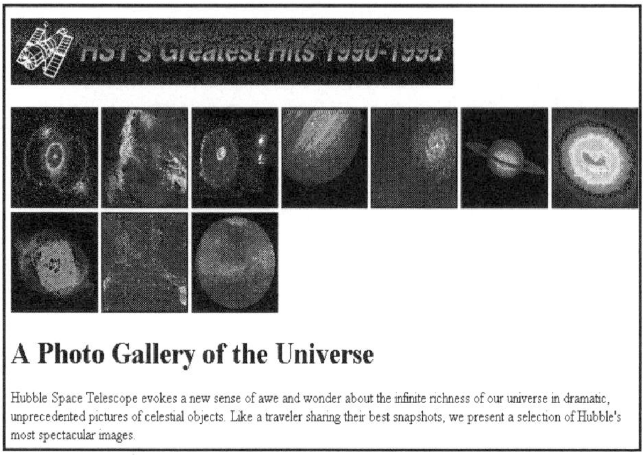

Hubble Space Telescope's Greatest Hits

http://www.stsci.edu/pubinfo/BestOfHST95.html

View some mind-boggling pictures of mysterious and beautiful space phenomena via the Hubble Space Telescope. Some of the color images include a ring around a suspected black hole, a huge storm on Saturn, pictures of Mars, dying stars, and more. Text from press releases and interviews with Hubble astronomers are included. These photographs make us thankful the telescope was repaired.

Site Details: Large Graphics, Good Links
Load Time: 104 seconds

NASA

✯✯✯✯✯

http://www.nasa.gov

Visiting this stellar site may require only one small click, but it's one giant leap for Web travelers. Those who touch down on the NASA home page will find lots of fascinating information to explore. Enter the searchable audio, visual, and video galleries, or find out about events and mission activities at NASA. If the FAQs don't answer your questions, join one of the Usenet newsgroups or search for information by subject. There are also links to specific NASA centers and programs, as well as other space agencies.

Site Details:	Video , Sound, Large Graphics, Good Links
Load Time:	40 seconds

Nine Planets

★★★★★

http://www.seds.org/nineplanets/nineplanets

For lovers of astronomy, this is a must-see site. Visitors will find beautiful color photos of the nine planets, 30 or 40 moons, comets, asteroids, and the sun. Each sub-page is introduced with music, and there are many facts and figures about all the natural features of our solar system, as well as the spacecraft which was launched to explore it.

Site Details:	Real Audio, Sound, Large Graphics, Good Links
Load Time:	38 seconds

SEDS' Galaxy Page

★★★★★

http://www.seds.org/galaxy

Connect to the Galaxy Page to see how astronomy can be brought down to Mother Earth in a very colorful way. Linked to the Students for the Exploration and Development of Space home page, this site features large, beautiful graphics of planets, stars, and galaxies, plus links to: Planets & the Solar System, Astronomy and Astrophysics, Aerospace & Space Sciences, and Visions of the Future—all in a unique split-screen format.

Site Details:	Large Graphics, Good Links
Load Time:	14 seconds

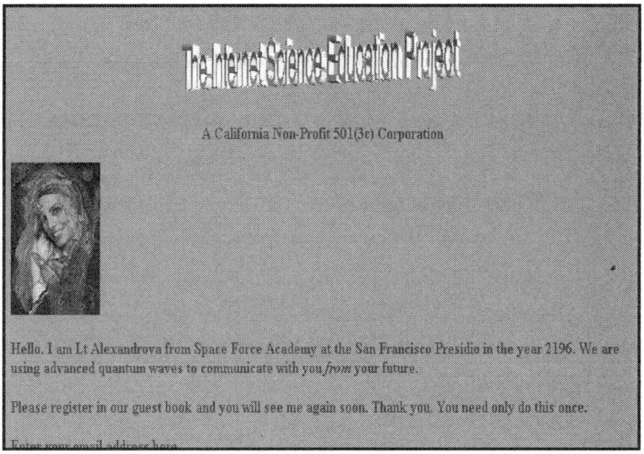

WARP

http://www.hia.com/hia/pcr/home.html

Visitors to this Web site should be prepared for a trip into the black hole of alternative science. Users can explore The Quantum and Beyond, a multimedia, interactive lecture by Jack Sarfatti, Ph.D., or wander to the many other graphics-filled levels at this postmodern site. Users fall in and out of "Web holes" and bump into multimedia documents on quantum physics, wormholes in space, warp technology, time travel, and many more mind-bending topics. Lots of links are available here, but users must explore this site to find them.

Site Details:	Real Audio, Video, Sound, Large Graphics, Good Links
Load Time:	31 seconds

Armchair Scientist

http://www.areacom.it/html/ita/loris/armchair.html

Presented in a fun and entertaining manner, the Armchair Scientist focuses on discoveries and research. Sections include the Science Show, with amazing news and astonishing curiosities, and Heavy Science, with advanced hypotheses. The Technology section takes a look at inventions. Unproved beliefs and assertions can be found in the New Theories section.

Site Details: Large Graphics, Good Links
Load Time: 84 seconds

Cool Science Links

http://www.ee.mcgill.ca/~reach/cool.html

And what cool science links they are! Fly a MIG fighter plane or find your house from space. Take a wild trip with the Fractal Explorer. Look into the science of *Star Trek* or watch a virtual dissection of a frog (yecch!). Whether it's engineering, chemistry, life sciences, mathematics, physics, space, or Just Fun Stuff, science has never been this cool before.

Site Details: Large Graphics, Good Links
Load Time: 38 seconds

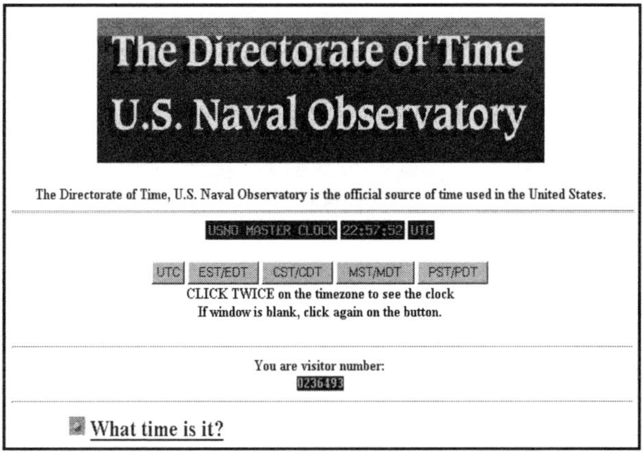

Directorate of Time

http://tycho.usno.navy.mil

The Directorate is the official source of time in the United States. The Navy maintains the Master Clock facility at the U.S. Naval Observatory in Washington, D.C. Children can discover how the time is calculated with atomic clocks, as well as the various definitions of time, and learn that there's an organization to keep an eye on the Earth's wobble—the National Earth Orientation Service.

Site Details: Good Links
Load Time: 14 seconds

Lost Museum of Sciences

http://www.netaxs.com/people/aca3/ATRIUM.HTM

Classical antiquity, the physical sciences, and natural history are the three major departments at the Lost Museum of Sciences. This virtual museum isn't really lost but, rather, it seems to have been designed for those who prefer to get lost in learning. This highly recommended site links to excellent home pages of scores of the world's finest, most respected museums, collections, and research sites in each of the three departments.

Site Details: Large Graphics, Good Links
Load Time: 156 seconds

Whale Watching Web

http://www.physics.helsinki.fi/whale

Part of the Web Virtual Library, the Whale Watching Web is impressively comprehensive. Dedicated to the idea that whale watching can change human perceptions of these huge mammals and thus prolong their survival, the Whale Watching Web allows visitors to hear a haunting whale greeting, view pictures of whales, and link to organizations like Greenpeace and Earthwatch. Access whale watching information by geographic region; find the region's whale watching season, and what kind of whales can be seen there.

Site Details: Video, Sound, Large Graphics, Good Links
Load Time: 9 seconds

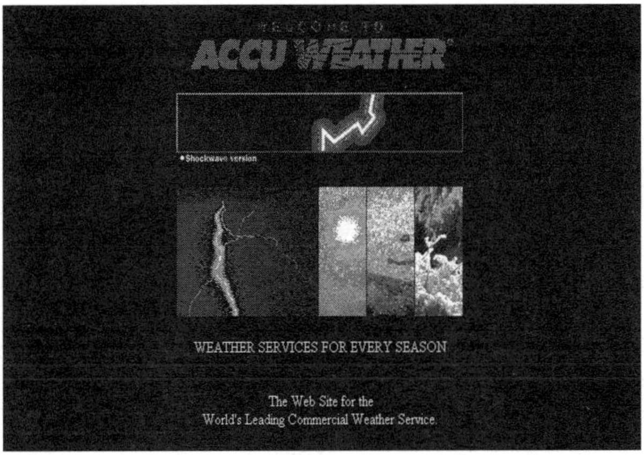

AccuWeather

http://accuwx.com

AccuWeather, Inc., one of the best-known commercial weather services, provides weather forecasts, color graphics, weather systems data, and consulting services to clients throughout the world, in media, business, government, and education. Also on this page is Accu-Weather's News Service, where you'll find news, sports, the lottery, Perfect Date, and more.

Site Details: Large Graphics, Good Links, Shopping

Load Time: 25 seconds

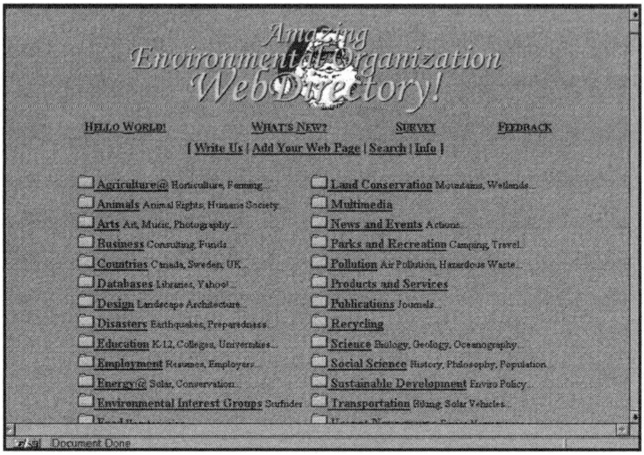

Amazing Environmental Organization WebDirectory

✯✯✯✯✯

http://www.webdirectory.com

The Amazing Environmental Organization Web Directory is a guide to environmental organizations in over 100 countries. This site makes it easy for environmentalists to obtain information on a wide range of subjects, including agriculture, arts, business, education, land conservation, pollution, and recycling. A powerful search engine helps you quickly locate the information you want.

Site Details:	Large Graphics, Good Links
Load Time:	29 seconds

Environmental Information Center

http://www.igc.apc.org/eic

Created to strengthen support for grassroots environmental activism, the EIC works in the political, educational, and religious arenas to improve environmental awareness. The Web site is brimming with information on Congressional activity, environment-related Web links, current news, and hot topics of the week. The EIC offers internship programs and archived materials on issues such as endangered species and global climate changes.

Site Details: Large Graphics, Good Links
Load Time: 52 seconds

IntelliCast

http://www.intellicast.com/icast

NBC brings weather forecasts for the planet to the Internet. This site offers users the opportunity to virtually sample the environment across the globe. For those who ski, here's a convenient, 24-hour hotline for skiing conditions. Visitors can access the NBC page for information about television and entertainment.

Site Details: Large Graphics, Good Links
Load Time: 95 seconds

National Weather Service NetCast

http://www.nnic.noaa.gov/weather.html

The National Weather Service (NWS) provides NetCast, an interactive service where users enter the name of the city and state to receive a particular forecast. Web surfers can also choose to view different types of weather information, including regional weather summaries and zone forecasts.

Site Details: Good Links
Load Time: 15 seconds

Organized Weather Links

http://www.comet.net/weather

Visitors need not be at all interested in meteorology to enjoy this beautiful, well-organized site. In addition to a huge database featuring the latest in weather forecasts, warnings, data sources, and weather servers, Organized Weather Links offers a host of fascinating and colorful satellite, radar, and model images of the Earth's surface and atmosphere. To view the cutting edge of meteorology, along with a refreshing splash of color, access this site.

Site Details: Large Graphics, Good Links
Load Time: 85 seconds

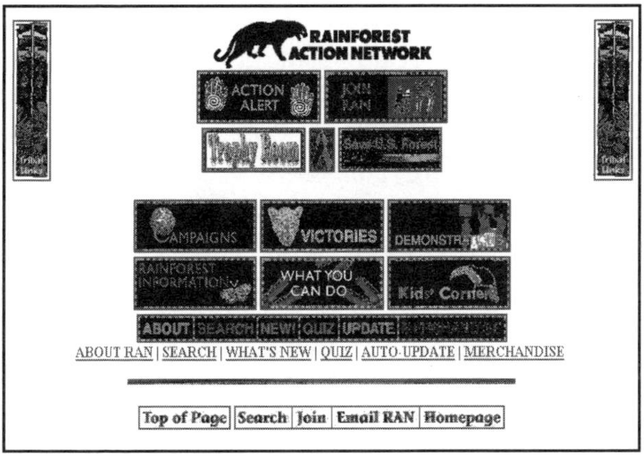

Rainforest Action Network

http://www.ran.org/ran

Those who wonder what they can do about the destruction of the world's rain forests will find ample direction at this well-designed site. Get information on e-mailing government officials, boycotting companies, and demonstrations to attend. Discover which products are sustainable, how to influence corporate decisions, and more. Children can find out how their actions can change the world and learn specific courses of action in the Kids' Corner.

Site Details:	Video, Large Graphics, Good Links, Shopping
Load Time:	40 seconds

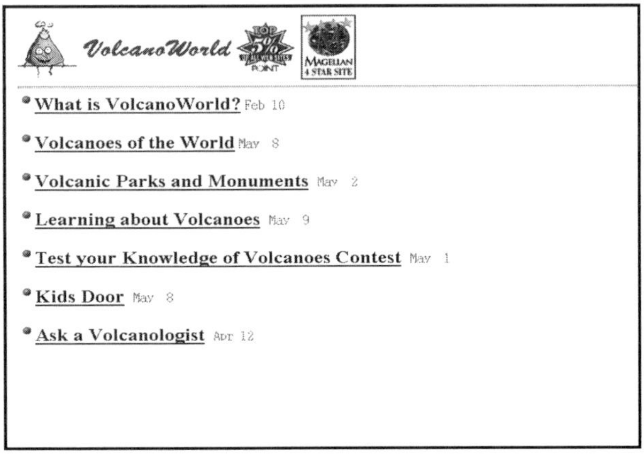

Volcano World

http://volcano.und.nodak.edu/vw.html

Get real time updates on volcanic activity all over the globe at Volcano World. An interactive world map zeros in on active volcanoes. Ask your most burning questions of an expert, and view photographs of cauldrons taken by astronauts in the space shuttle. Volcano Facts lists the largest eruptions and the deadliest. Photographs, maps, videos, and instructional materials are for sale.

Site Details:	Video, Large Graphics, Good Links Shopping
Load Time:	33 seconds

Education

Education is the key to maintaining vitality as individuals, and, ultimately, as world nations. The Internet injects a welcome shot of enthusiasm, expertise, and vision into the educational community. Each day, teachers share lesson plans over the Web, creating synergy and excitement about learning. The once-isolated classroom in Spring, Texas now joins with a literature project being conducted by a group of students in Moscow. The **StarChild Project by NASA** connects astronomy and space science researchers to the K-12 classroom. The Internet brings resources to the student and teacher never before imagined.

Maya Adventure contains activities, photographs and experiments for the young anthropologist. Your budding scientist can learn about electricity, talking lasers or infrared cameras at the **Science/Math Carnival** site. **Doc's Education, Resource Pages** and **Global Online Adverture Learning** deliver comprehensive lists of educational resources on the Web.

The college-bound student will find financial aid eligibility information and application procedures at the **Financial Aid** home page, presented by the U.S. Department of Education. The **Internet College Exchange** page lists over 5,000 universities throughout the United States.

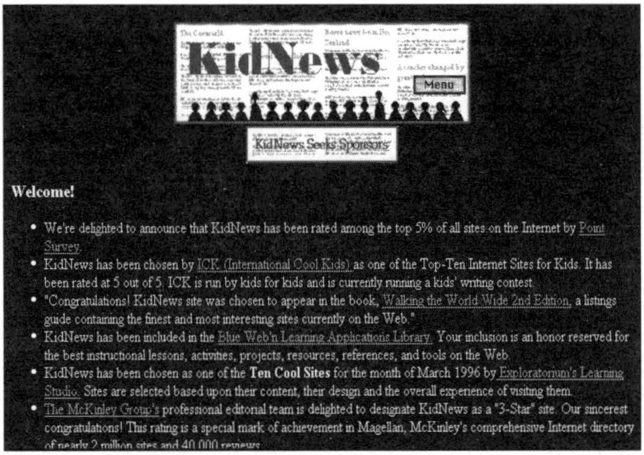

KidNews

http://www.vsa.cape.com/~powens/Kidnews.html

The International Student Newswire (ISN) KidNews site is a news service for kids and teachers around the world. The stories from the service are free to use, and anyone can submit a story. Stories are sorted into the following categories: News, Features, Profile, How-To, Sports, Poetry, and Fiction. Submit a story by filling out the online form provided here. KidNews also offers story reviews, discussion pages for teachers and kids, and a Cool Hangouts section has links to related pages.

Site Details: Large Graphics, Good Links
Load Time: 37 seconds

Maya Adventure

http://www.sci.mus.mn.us/sln/ma/

Visitors to Maya Adventure can trek to the secret-laden jungles of Chiapas, Chichen Itza and Tikal, and explore the ancient civilization of the Maya. A click on the treasure map pulls up photos of fascinating ruins—the remains of temples and cities. During their journey, users can conduct fun scientific experiments. In one experiment, determine the dissolving rate of limestone, the material of the Mayan ruins. Explorers may record their experiences in the Maya Adventure Logbook.

Site Details: Large Graphics, Good Links

Load Time: 24 seconds

MBGnet/Just For Kids

★★★★★

http://www.mobot.org/MBGnet/just_kids.html

Students can discover how to make rain right inside their classrooms by following the instructions at this Web page. Everything from osmosis to ink is explained at the well-designed, educational home page, in terms kids can understand. In addition, young users can participate in educational projects linked to other kids around the world. The many links listed here lead to more fun sites for children.

Site Details:	Large Graphics, Good Links
Load Time:	10 seconds

Mega Mathematics

http://www.c3.lanl.gov/mega-math

Math need not be complicated or dry, as this Web site demonstrates. The fun games and interactive projects at Mega Mathica teach students about map coloring, graphs, knots, algorithms, and much more. Upper level math students can explore the Hotel Infinity or learn about the concept of recursion while making a Sierpinski Gasket.

Site Details: Large Graphics, Good Links
Load Time: 33 seconds

Newton's Apple

http://ericir.syr.edu/Projects/Newton/

Newton's Apple, PBS's highly acclaimed educational TV program, provides an excellent supplement to its broadcasts at this Web site. Users can access 26 lessons on such diverse subjects as movie dinosaurs, hang gliding, earthquakes, garlic, and even the Internet. This highly entertaining and educational site has lots to offer both students and adults.

Site Details: Large Graphics, Good Links
Load Time: 115 seconds

Science/Math Carnival

http://www.ca.sandia.gov/carnival/carnival-cover.html

The Science/Math Carnival provides hands-on activities for K-8 students. A source of fun, encouragement, and learning for both students and teachers, the site features interactive demonstrations and projects on subjects such as air pressure, electricity, infrared cameras, magnetic levitation, and lasers.

Site Details: Animation, Sound, Large Graphics, Good Links
Load Time: 12 seconds

Sea World/Busch Gardens Animal Resources

http://www.bev.net/education/SeaWorld/infobook.html

Are you interested in the animal world and its inhabitants? The Sea World manatee greets you from this home page followed by an encyclopedia of information on animals of all kinds. The educational series offers pictures and sections on animal behavior, diet, conservation, and reproduction. The site also includes pages for Tropical Forests, Nature at Risk, and Animal Training at Sea World.

Site Details: Large Graphics, Good Links
Load Time: 17 seconds

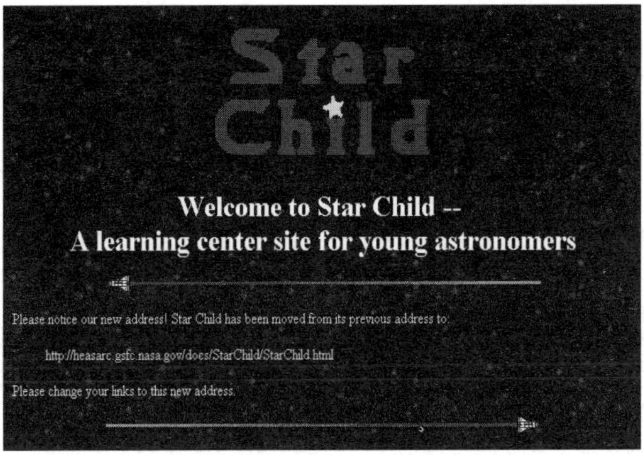

StarChild Project by NASA

★★★★★

http://heasarc.gsfc.nasa.gov/docs/StarChild/StarChild.html

This clear, understandable site is designed for children to learn about space, the Earth, sun, moon, and other astronomy topics. Children choose their area of interest according to the pictures on the home page. Very user-friendly for young people, the site contains hypertext links to definitions for each celestial body. The Earth, for instance, is described as a "large ball of rock spinning through space . . ."

Site Details:	Animation, Large Graphics, Good Links
Load Time:	24 seconds

White House for Kids

★★★★★

http://www2.whitehouse.gov/WH/kids/html/kidshome.html

Kids can get a cat's-eye view of the White House from Socks, the feline resident at the time of this review. Colorful graphics show just where 1600 Pennsylvania Avenue is located on maps, and famous Washington monuments are described in detail. The site includes lighthearted facts about the history of the presidential mansion. In the White House Kids section, kids can read about Lynda Byrd and Lucy Byrd Johnson, John-John and Caroline Kennedy, and other children of presidents.

Site Details: Good Links
Load Time: 20 seconds

Yuckiest Site on the Internet

★★★★★

http://www.nj.com/yucky/index.html

The Yuckiest Site on the Internet is also one of the most educational. The Liberty Science Center and New Jersey Online have put together this site so that children and their families can learn all about cockroaches (and more yucky stuff to follow). Click on the bug bodies to find out lots about the insect world. Lest users forget, these are purportedly the only creatures equipped to survive a nuclear holocaust—so they might have something to teach us. Be that as it may, users are encouraged to raid this site at least once.

Site Details: Video , Sound, Large Graphics, Good Links
Load Time: 37 seconds

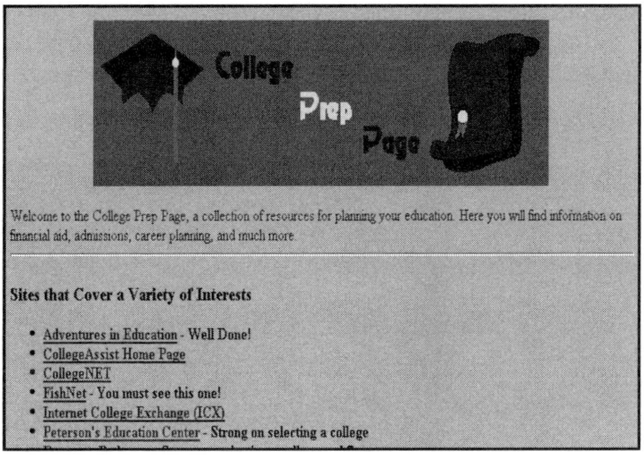

College Prep Page

✯✯✯✯✯

http://www.tpoint.net/~jewels/college.html

High school students plotting their college careers will find many useful planning tools here. Follow links to career information, future occupational trends, and resources for selecting a college. Alternatives such as travel study programs, military academies, and the Peace Corps are explored. Students and their parents can research financial aid, loans, and scholarships online. Additional links lead to the Educational Testing Service and study skills tips.

Site Details: Good Links
Load Time: 11 seconds

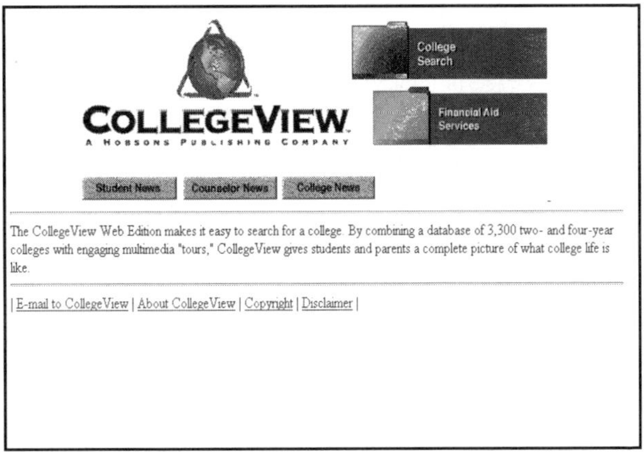

CollegeView

http://www.collegeview.com

Designed for parents and future college students, College View provides the names of colleges which meet certain criteria. The criteria, which is specified by the user, include academic, region, school size, etc. Students can then link to any of the universities and colleges for first-hand information.

	Good Links
Load Time:	21 seconds

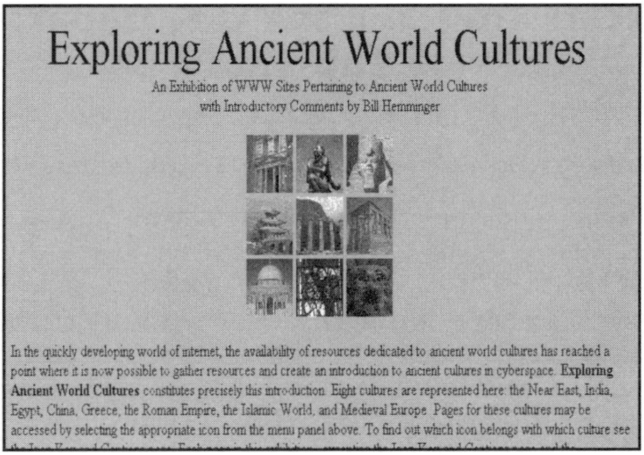

Exploring Ancient World Cultures

http://www.evansville.edu/~wcweb/wc101

This site provides a virtual college course on ancient cultures around the world. Explore the ancient Near East, India, Egypt, China, and Greece, with links to the art, architecture, literature, religious works, and history of each civilization. Other civilizations covered include the Roman Empire, the Islamic World, and Medieval Europe. Each section contains a comprehensive list of links to related sites on the Web. For example, the Greek history section has links to Mythology in Western Art, photographs of the Ancient City of Athens, and the Tech Classics Archive.

Site Details:	Large Graphics, Good Links
Load Time:	30 seconds

Financial Aid from the U.S. Department of Education

★★★★★

http://www.ed.gov/prog_info/SFA/StudentGuide

College-bound students and their parents have a complete Student Guide to DOE Financial Aid at their fingertips. The front page of the site consists of the Guide's hyperlinked table of contents, information on eligibility, financial need, dependency status, and deadlines. The Guide also covers Pell Grants, direct loans, and campus-based aid programs. These include Federal Supplemental Educational Opportunity Grants, Federal Work-Study, and Federal Perkins Loans.

Site Details: Good Links
Load Time: 9 seconds

Global On-line Adventure Learning Site (GOALS)

★★★★★

http://www.goals.com

Hoist the sails and prepare for a sailing trip around the world! Choose from several adventures at sea, from Mick Bird's Trans-Oceanic Rowing Expedition—an attempt to row 24,000 miles around the globe—to sailor Karen Thorndike's solo circumnavigation of the world. The navigator of each real-life expedition provides visitors with updated logbook reports and photos from their journey. View the spectacular photos in the Photo Gallery or offer your suggestions for additional online adventures.

Site Details: Large Graphics, Good Links
Load Time: 10 seconds

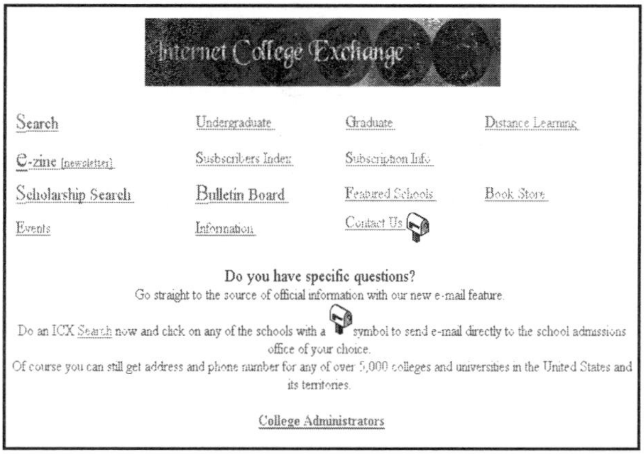

Internet College Exchange

http://www.usmall.com

Searching for the phone number to the admissions office of Stanford University? Here is a valuable resource for the student with plans to attend college. The site links over 5,000 universities in the United States. Locate textbooks through the online bookstore or leave a message on the bulletin board with your questions or ideas about admissions, financial aid, and study plans.

Site Details:	Good Links
Load Time:	34 seconds

Peterson's Education Center

http://www.petersons.com:8080

Peterson's Education Center page provides organized access to information, educational resources, and opportunities at every educational level, including Private Schools, Undergraduate, Graduate, Summer Programs, Vocational, Continuing Education, and Distance Learning. The Center gives users the ability to make inquiries, apply, send transcripts, or interact in other ways with faculty and administrators at educational institutions.

Site Details: Large Graphics, Good Links
Load Time: 43 seconds

Reinventing America

http://www.pathfinder.com/reinventing

Balancing the budget has been the topic of debate for decades in the United States. Reinventing America is an interactive game that runs for 26 weeks, challenging players to review the activities of the federal government, its funding and expenditures, and its programs. Decide on federal salaries, cutbacks, and tax increases in a cyberspace look at this monumental task.

Site Details: Large Graphics, Good Links
Load Time: 6 seconds

Testprep.Com Home Page

http://www.testprep.com

For many students, SAT scores determine their selection by a respected school. The Testprep.Com home page offers free online test preparation, which should help make this ordeal a little easier. The material is clear and easy to navigate, but slow to access, with generally one question per page, so it may take quite a while to get through the practice tests.

Site Details:	Large Graphics, Shopping
Load Time:	1 second

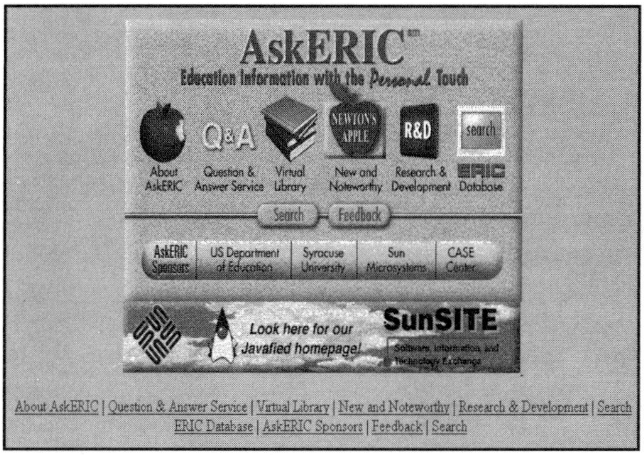

AskERIC

http://ericir.syr.edu

The U.S. Department of Education provides the Educational Resource Information Center (ERIC), a national information system for access to the many education resources on the Internet. Just a few of the resources educators and parents will find here include electronic books through Project Gutenberg, an online dictionary, the CIA World Fact Book, and lesson plans from the TV show *Newton's Apple* and NASA.

Site Details: Good Links
Load Time: 97 seconds

Doc's Education Resource Pages

☆☆☆☆☆

http://www.nmia.com:80/~cram

This site is one of the best compilations of K–12 education links to be found on the Web. Besides the wealth of language arts links, which range from the Emily Dickinson page to the ISN KidNews, there are physical education, science, cultural geography, and current events links. Plus, students will find pointers to news, history, and the arts. For teachers, there is an introduction to the Internet and an Education Resource Page that is filled with lesson plans based on some of the sites. Doc's Pages are a definite "don't miss" for students and educators.

Site Details: Good Links
Load Time: 13 seconds

Math Forum

☆☆☆☆☆

http://forum.swarthmore.edu

This Web site features newsgroups, a problem of the week and project of the month, geometry and math software, and a "math doctor" who answers math-related questions. Try the Internet Geometry Hunt, which has you surfing the Internet for the answers to questions about geometry and mathematics. The site contains plenty of information about current research and links to related sites are included.

Large Graphics, Good Links
Load Time: 13 seconds

Entertainment

It's always Saturday night on the Web. Sound clips, video, animation, and colorful images dance across the screen with sneek peeks at upcoming movies, music, and the latest in games. Nearly every recording artist, television show, film studio, and author is represented on the Web.

Innovation and glamour radiate from cutting-edge television and movie studio Web sites such as **MCA/Universal Cyberwalk, 20th Century Fox Home Entertainment, MGM, the Warner Brothers Network and Paramount Studios.** Television networks feature home pages for popular shows like the "**X-Files**" and "**Star Trek**." Fan clubs, discussion groups, videos, production notes and episode guides are only a mouse click away.

If you're ready for some out-on-the-town entertainment, check out **MovieWeb** and **Hollywood Online** for QuickTime sneak previews of hot movie releases. Pick a film, order your tickets online at **MovieLink**, and pick them up at the boxoffice. Whether your interest is celebrity gossip, prime-time tube talk, or moviemaking—the Web has a part for you.

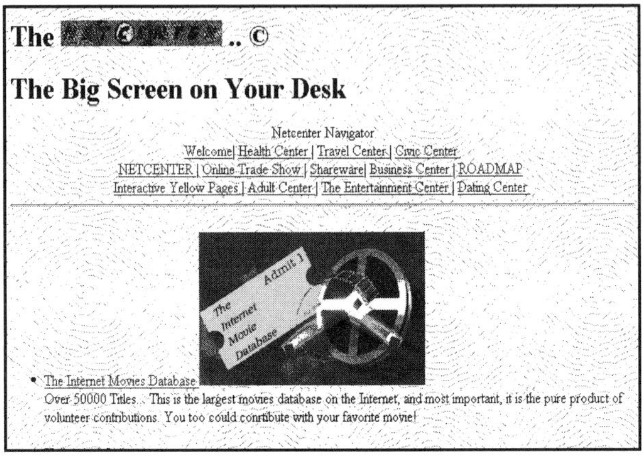

Big Screen on Your Desk

http://www.netcenter.com/netcentr/entertain/cinema.html

This is a must-browse site for film buffs. Link to the Internet Movies Database, with 50,000 films archived and reviewed by other browsers, described as the largest database of films on the Net. Other links include the Academy of Motion Picture Arts and Sciences, theater schedules across the nation for Landmark and Goldwyn theaters, critics' reviews, and home pages for major movie studios.

	Good Links
Load Time:	43 seconds

CNN Showbiz News: Movie News

http://www.cnn.com/SHOWBIZ/Movies

Cable News Network (CNN) provides the latest in entertainment. Showbiz Today, CNN's daily television show about current movies and Hollywood events, is featured here, along with a lengthy list of new movies and reviews. Users can link to CNN's home page or to studios and coming attractions.

Site Details:	Sound, Large Graphics, Good Links
Load Time:	29 seconds

Hitchcock Page

http://www.primenet.com/~mwc

This page takes an impressive look at the life and work of master filmmaker Alfred Hitchcock—seminal influence, mentor, artistic inspiration, and role model to many young "auteur" directors who followed him. Viewers can find a complete filmography, information on stars from his films, and much more. There is an intriguing low-tech presentation of the notorious Janet Leigh shower sequence from *Psycho*.

Site Details:	Animation, Large Graphics, Good Links
Load Time:	60 seconds

Hollywood Online

http://hollywood.com

Visually entertaining, this site is filled with movie promotions. A selection of current movies is highlighted at the top of the home page. From those titles, users can look at clips, hear sound bites and RealAudio segments, and look at notes from the director. Scroll down further on the home page to select from sneak peeks, movie talk, and movie trailers.

Site Details:	Video, Sound, Good Links
Load Time:	56 seconds

Internet Movie Database

http://www.msstate.edu:80/Movies

The Internet Movie Database is a great resource for anyone trying to find specific information ord reviews on a particular movie. It has information on the movie, the cast and crew, the genre, characters' names, the country the movie was filmed in, a brief summary of the plot, accompanying soundtrack information, production notes, movie release dates, and movie quotes. There is a list of the top 100 films, a link to information about the Academy Awards, and a search engine where users can find information by director, actor, editor, or production designer.

Site Details:	Video, Sound, Good Links
Load Time:	22 seconds

Irresistible Force

★★★★★

http://paul.spu.edu/~kevnord/starwars

"May the force be with you" at this Web site for all fans of the *Star Wars* trilogy. It contains information and news about scripts and stories for each of Lucas's masterful movies. Take a look at movie images or listen to sound bites from famous scenes. This site answers some of the questions that die-hard fans may still have about the *Star Wars* movies. It is well-designed and takes full advantage of Netscape 2.0's scrolling capabilities.

Site Details: Video, Sound, Large Graphics, Good Links

Load Time: 39 seconds

Lucy Mohl's film.com

★★★★★

http://www.film.com

A complete and current guide to movies, this site is an excellent resource. The home page lists dozens of options, including spotlight reviews of the popular films currently showing in the theaters. The Coming Soon option displays a grid organized by week, with a release date and plot summary included for each movie. For users who would like an alternative to the current releases, there are video/laser calendars, a film festival guide, a film archive, and hot links to film sites.

Site Details: Sound, Large Graphics, Good Links, Shopping

Load Time: 19 seconds

Movie Sounds Page

✯✯✯✯✯

http://www.moviesounds.com

The Movie Sounds Page is an excellent collection of sound clips from popular movies. Listen to excerpts from favorites such as *Forrest Gump, Pulp Fiction, The Lion King, Wizard of Oz, Casablanca, Midnight Run,* and *The Rocky Horror Picture Show*. The written transcript of each sound clip is also provided.

Site Details: Sound, Large Graphics, Good Links

Load Time: 2 seconds

MovieLink

✯✯✯✯✯

http://www.movielink.com

Never again wait in line at the movies, only to be disappointed by a sold-out show. Moviegoers input their zip code and a list of their neighborhood theaters appears with program information and screen times. Select a time and purchase tickets online for box office pickup at showtime.

Site Details: Large Graphics

Load Time: 15 seconds

MovieWEB

http://movieweb.com/movie/movie.html

Preview the newest movies on MovieWEB with QuickTime videos of trailers. Movie posters, production notes, and synopses are also provided. Connect to motion picture studios and other film-related sites from here. Vote on movies, and view the previous weekend's box office winners.

Site Details:	Video, Large Graphics, Good Links
Load Time:	53 seconds

Paramount Pictures

http://www.paramount.com

Paramount, the major motion picture and television studio, provides this Web site for users interested in its productions. Descriptions of past, current, and upcoming releases are available here, presented in a showy, entertaining format. Movie buffs can read about the Academy Award-winning *Braveheart* and other Paramount films, such as *Clueless* and *Virtuosity*. Previews of television shows, including *Star Trek,* are available, too.

Site Details:	Animation, Sound, Large Graphics, Good Links
Load Time:	104 seconds

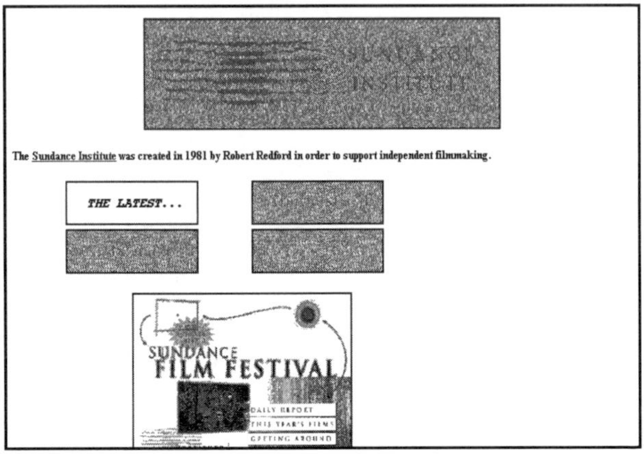

Sundance Institute

http://cybermart.com/sundance/institute/institute.html

Located at the Sundance Resort in the Rocky Mountains of Utah, Sundance Institute is Robert Redford's program for talented young filmmakers, and the Institute's Sundance Film Festival is a highly regarded showcase for new filmmakers. The home page for Sundance features several categories of information: the Calendar, the Resort, the Film Festival, Film on the Web, and the Catalog.

Animation, Good Links

Load Time: 33 seconds

20th Century Fox Home Entertainment

http://www.tcfhe.com

You can relive decades of movie magic at the 20th Century Fox Home Entertainment page. This good-looking site features some of Fox's favorite stars and best-loved films from the '20s to the '90s. Spotlighting titles available on video, you will find family features, studio classics, and contemporary hits. Video and audio clips round out the fare. Fans of the *Star War*s trilogy can download video and read exclusive interviews. Fans of the brilliantly bizarre can follow America's favorite Feds on the Official *X-Files* Page.

Site Details: Video , Sound, Large Graphics, Good Links
Load Time: 40 seconds

ABC Online

http://www.abctelevision.com

ABC's handsome home page posts its weekly schedule, outlines new shows in its lineup, and links to ABC news. The RadioNet section features ABC news reports and programs in RealAudio, including This Week with David Brinkley and Peter Jennings' Journal. Fans of the long-running drama *Murder One* will appreciate the rundown on suspects, breaking news, case history, and Who's Who section, as well as the video clips from the show.

Site Details: Sound, Good Links
Load Time: 42 seconds

Discovery Channel Online

http://www.discovery.com

Here's a real find—the Discovery Channel Online. Providing educational and entertaining programming, the Web site delivers the same high quality material as the TV show. Visitors will find monthly program listings and insightful articles on topics including history, nature, science, people, exploration, and technology. The world is your oyster—explore it with Mr. Curious; find out why the sky is blue, what gene therapy can do, and whether Abraham Lincoln was killed by his physicians. It's an easy site to navigate with search tools and bulletin boards to help you make your discoveries.

Site Details:	Large Graphics, Good Links, Shopping
Load Time:	38 seconds

Eye on the Net with CBS

★★★★★

http://www.cbs.com

Whether your interests swing toward the latest sports scores or the last episode of Late Night with David Letterman, Eye on the Net with CBS has a lot to offer. Get a quick description of the CBS lineup of programs with pictures of the stars, shop for merchandise in the station store, or preview the new schedule. The large and colorful graphics on the home page take a minute to load, but television enthusiasts will find it worth the wait.

Site Details:	Sound, Large Graphics, Good Links, Shopping
Load Time:	36 seconds

NBC

★★★★★

http://www.nbc.com

NBC Hypertext TV provides users with an enormous tour of everything NBC television has to offer. This home page has photos, information on all the network's shows and stars, sports, and news. A clickable map of the United States allows viewers to zoom into their local area and access their local station's Web page.

Site Details:	Sound, Large Graphics, Good Links, Shopping
Load Time:	42 seconds

PBS Online

✯✯✯✯✯

http://www.pbs.org

PBS Online, a beautifully designed site is a thoughtful presentation of the world of PBS. There is, of course, program information and news about the network. You'll find an Online NewsHour presentation of world news, educational pages and links, links to PBS series' home pages, affiliate information, and e-mail feedback options.

Site Details:	Video, Sound, Good Links, Shopping
Load Time:	35 seconds

Sci-Fi Channel: The Dominion

✯✯✯✯✯

http://www.scifi.com

Users interested in traversing the fourth dimension will find The Dominion one of the best science fiction sites around. The Pulp link will transport users to sci-fi comics, an entertainment magazine, and experiments in user-written fiction. The Free Zone offers free downloads of audio, video, and images. Pull up a video clip from *Star Wars* or listen to Rod's introduction to *The Twilight Zone*. If it's just a program schedule for the Sci-Fi Channel you want, you'll find it here, too.

Site Details:	Animation, Video, Sound, Large Graphics, Good Links, Shopping
Load Time:	92 seconds

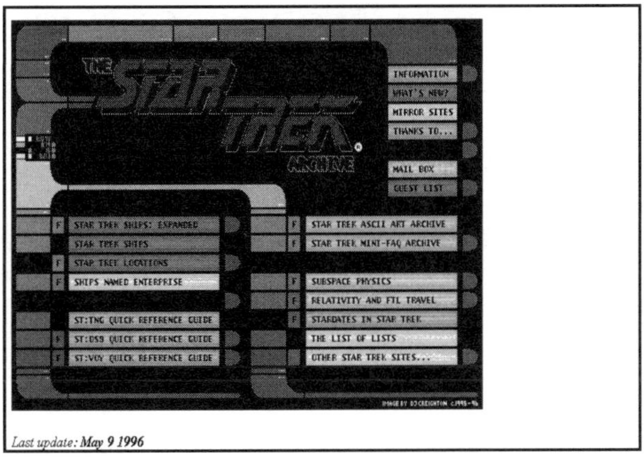

Star Trek Archives

http://www.ee.umanitoba.ca/~djc/startrek

For Trekkers in search of adventure, try the Star Trek Archives. Learn about starships featured in the TV show or review online episode guides. An art archive is also presented as well as a huge list of links to more sites that will help users to "live long and prosper."

Site Details: Large Graphics, Good Links
Load Time: 30 seconds

Star Trek: Deep Space Nine

http://www.cdsnet.net/vidiot/st-ds9

View video clips and listen to audio samples from the *Star Trek: Deep Space Nine* television show at this Web site. Fans of the show have access to air schedules for each season and can review highlights of each show's press release. Photos of the cast are provided, as well as published articles, images of the *U.S.S. Defiant* and links to other *Star Trek*-oriented sites.

Site Details: Video, Sound, Large Graphics, Good Links

Load Time: 44 seconds

Star Trek: The Next Generation

http://www.ugcs.caltech.edu:80/~werdna/sttng

Devoted to *Star Trek: The Next Generation*, this site will delight fans of the popular television show. Users will find information about the cast, the episodes, credits, production notes, a trivia game, a search engine, and a biography of *Star Trek* creator, Gene Roddenberry. In addition, there's a What's New site, the Editor's Pick of the Top 10 episodes, extensive credits, full transcripts of episodes, and promotion information.

Real Audio, Large Graphics, Good Links

Load Time: 37 seconds

TV Net

http://tvnet.com

TV Net is your hot spot for accessing TV-related information on the Web. The site provides everything from the fall preview line-up to job vacancies with national networks. Get the scoop on your city's local network or enter the TV Chat Room to join the buzz. National networks like CBS, ABC, NBC, FOX, PBS, UPN, and WB provide news, entertainment, and sports information. Don't miss The Ultimate TV List, with over 4,000 links to more than 600 shows.

Site Details:	Good Links
Load Time:	17 seconds

Warner Brothers Network

http://www.cs.brandeis.edu/~aaron/wb/wb.html

Here's a Web site for the animated. The Warner Brothers Network's home page includes a list of local affiliates, The WB News, weekly ratings, programming information, and a link to the Official Kids' WB Pages. Take a break from Wall Street news and corporate intrigue with a fun look at Michigan J. Frog, that green, wacky high-stepper, and click on the Dancing Frog link.

Site Details:	Sound, Large Graphics, Good Links
Load Time:	6 seconds

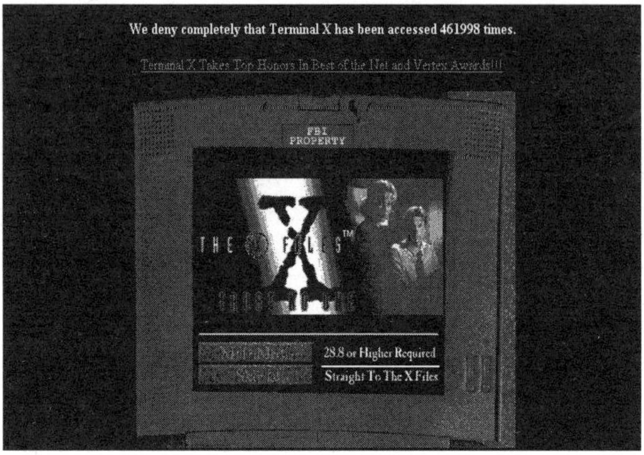

X-Files

http://www.neosoft.com/sbanks/xfiles/xfiles.html

If "the truth is out there somewhere," visitors to this *X-Files* site will find it. Sample video clips, photos, audio clips, bios on the stars, and a guide to the episodes of this popular show. Users will enjoy the QuickTime videos of episode bloopers as well as teasers for upcoming shows.

Site Details:	Video, Sound, Large Graphics, Good Links
Load Time:	9 seconds

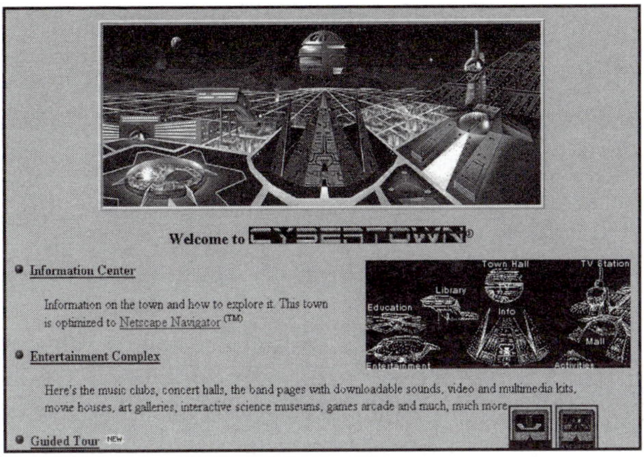

Cybertown

http://www.cybertown.com/cybertown/index.html

The very virtual, but not always virtuous, Cybertown offers so many options that users should plan to take time exploring this site. There are interactive options, movies, large graphics, mazes, music, and much more for Cybertown's visitors. Take a ride on the virtual freeway provided on the home page, but be sure to check out Cyberhood's creative underground, and stop to chat with the locals at Le Cafe.

Site Details:	Animation, Video, Sound, Large Graphics, Good Links
Load Time:	30 seconds

Disney.com

http://www2.disney.com/static/News/docs/HM_T/home.html

Here's "your magical world online." Disney's Web site is a world of its own, one of the great happy places for children in cyberspace. It offers a couple of different tour options to see the site's colorful Disney contents: still photos, movie video clips, movie songs, lyrics, books, a company history, theme park information, television information, interactive news, and shopping. The huge site is attractive and relatively easy to navigate, and even if users get lost in its many pages, they'll probably have fun in the process.

Site Details: Video, Sound, Shopping
Load Time: 20 seconds

Entertain-net

http://userwww.sfsu.edu/~jkafer/welcome.html

Climb aboard a fast moving ride at this Web site for lots of entertainment and interesting links. Updated weekly, this spot provides the Web surfer with hours of exploration into movies, music, graphics, games, improvisational humor, and other interesting links. The author spotlights an entertainment site each week, complete with detailed description and access to the site.

Site Details: Large Graphics, Good Links
Load Time: 59 seconds

Gigabox

http://www.dtd.com/gigabox

There are lots of fun little places to explore at this site. Start with the NFL Two-Minute Trivia Game, the Noise of the Day, and The List of the Day. Browse topics like Top 29 Delusions You Hold Onto and Top 87 Things They Don't Teach You in School. The Evil Little Brother's Excuse Generator is worth a chuckle or two. He'll create a masterful excuse for any dilemma. Her Space features tips on marriage and family, shopping, finance, leadership, artistic expression, and spirituality. The entertainment here changes frequently, so you'll want to visit often.

Site Details: Large Graphics
Load Time: 77 seconds

Gigaplex

http://www.directnet.com/wow

Once you enter the Gigaplex, hold on—a billion pleasures await you. Gigaplex is a whopping 600+ page Web magazine devoted to the arts, entertainment and more. This well-designed site has plenty of great interviews and movie reviews. It covers everything from the Hawaiian Yoga Vacation in paradise to the top 10 hot dogs in America. After an evening in the 'Plex, life will never be the same.

Site Details:	Large Graphics, Good Links, Shopping
Load Time:	50 seconds

Hollywood Network

http://hollywoodnetwork.com

Internet Entertainment Network calls this site an "entertainment cybervillage." It is a site devoted to news and information related to the entertainment industry. The glitz and glamour of Hollywood is showcased at this site, with links to actors' guilds, gossip, chats, and fan clubs. This site will appeal to industry insiders, outsiders, and fans alike.

Site Details:	Sound, Large Graphics, Good Links, Shopping
Load Time:	6 seconds

MCA/Universal Cyberwalk

http://www.mca.com

The home page for this entertainment and media giant provides information and samplings of their latest projects. The Universal Channel is a "behind the scenes" look at TV shows such as *SeaQuest 2032, Law & Order, and Hercules—The Legendary Journeys,* to name a few. Users will also find an interactive game show, exclusive visual/interactive previews of new Universal releases, and access to AMP, the music magazine from MCA Records Online. Visitors can purchase gifts online or visit the interactive Web site of Universal Studios Hollywood.

Site Details: Large Graphics, Good Links
Load Time: 45 seconds

MGM/UA: The Lion's Den

http://www.mgmua.com

Step into the Lion's Den at MGM to prowl the latest MGM film and video releases as well as program schedules. Visit the Executive Suite for studio business news, or the MGM virtual studio store for MGM t-shirts, jackets, and posters. Inside the link labeled Interactive Entertainment, visitors can sample the H.R. Giger screen saver and place an order online if they like what they see.

Site Details: Video, Large Graphics, Shopping
Load Time: 26 seconds

POLLSTAR Concert Hotwire

★★★★★

http://www.pollstar.com

Music industry professionals and fans will find plenty of useful information here. The tour schedule database is searchable by artist, venue, or city. Those in the music industry can subscribe to industry directories, news, and box office results.

Site Details:	Sound, Good Links
Load Time:	54 seconds

Science Fiction Gallery

★★★★★

http://www.scifig.com/scifi/

For fans of science fiction, the Sci-Fi Gallery is the place to visit. Users can explore areas such as Favorites, Classics, Dawn of Film, Monster Movies, Sci-Fi on Television, and Japanese Anime. What's New to the Sci-Fi Gallery provides new categories like notables, sci-fi themes, new this season, and box office heroes. There's also a writer's gallery and links to other science fiction sites.

Site Details:	Large Graphics, Good Links, Shopping
Load Time:	134 seconds

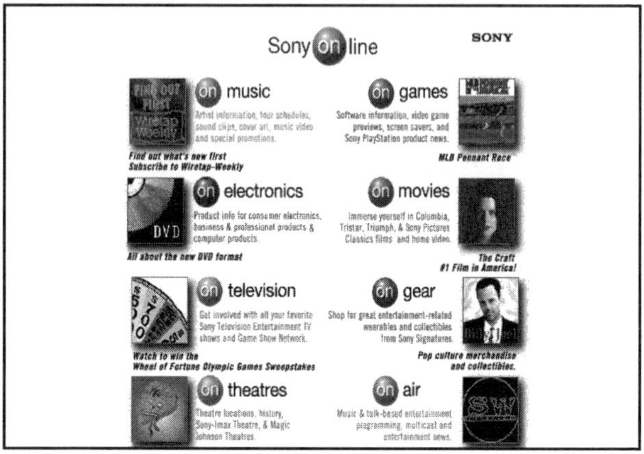

Sony Online

http://www.music.sony.com

Users who want to know what's new in the large world of Sony entertainment should stop by this exciting Web site. Sony covers every aspect of entertainment: artists, music, movies, television, and publishing. There are also audio clips of recent releases.

Site Details:	Video , Sound, Large Graphics, Good Links, Shopping
Load Time:	39 seconds

The Spot

★★★★★

http://www.thespot.com

The virtual world's version of MTV's *Real World* series has the young set buzzing. In a *Peyton Place* sort of way, the cast of characters at *The Spot* bare their real-life dilemmas in an jumble of text, photos, and video clips. Ride along with Lon as he laments the loss of Gina, or listen while Carrie frets over her desire to "move forward" with her boyfriend Stacey. Come to The Spot to find out what everyone's been talking about.

Site Details:	Video, Sound, Large Graphics, Good Links, Shopping
Load Time:	14 seconds

Ticketmaster Online

*****

http://www.ticketmaster.com:80

Ticketmaster's virtual home provides a wealth of information on current concerts, sports events, Broadway shows, and more. A nationwide directory of Ticketmaster outlets is available, supplemented by local charge-by-phone numbers. The databases are searchable, leading to dates for everything from Detroit Red Wings hockey games to a Liza Minnelli or Mr. Bungle concert.

Site Details: Large Graphics, Good Links, Shopping

Load Time: 3 seconds

Games

"A little work, a little play..."
George du Maurier

Games can be as simple as tic-tac-toe or as complicated as chess. They can involve team efforts or require the single-minded strategy of one individual. Whatever the choice, games provide fun, challenge, and companionship. The Internet provides a vast number of games coupled with millions of people to play them with.

Zarf's List of Interactive Games on the Web serves up an enormous list of games including Name That Tune, WebBattleship, Yahtzee and others. Build a virtual business or stage a hostile takeover at the slick, well-designed pages of **Netropolis,** or challenge your digital memory at **Trivia Hot Spots.** The **Internet Chess Club** invites players from beginners to Grandmasters to matches 24 hours a day.

If Chess is a little too solemn for you, sit in for a hand at **NetPoker,** or play the slot machines at the **Internet Online Casino.s** After a long day at the office, a little virtual ferret racing may be just the thing that's needed.

3-D Gaming Scene

http://www.pol.umu.se/html/ac/spel.htm

Action-oriented, 3-D computer games are accessible from this Web site. Each game featured here is tested by the Web author and presented for you to view or play. Read about the latest 3-D games, view screen shots, or download the games. This easy-to-navigate site also offers FAQs and game cheats.

Site Details: Large Graphics, Good Links
Load Time: 7 seconds

Atlantis Cyberspace

http://vr-atlantis.com

The Atlantis Cyberspace home page leads users to an abundance of virtual reality entertainment systems and games. Details on Atlantis itself are included, as well as business opportunities within the organization. Lists of virtual reality entertainment systems, software, and dozens of links to related and interesting sites are provided.

Site Details: Large Graphics, Good Links
Load Time: 27 seconds

BlackJack Server

http://www.datawave.net/blackjack/bj.html

Instead of an expensive trip to Las Vegas or Atlantic City to play Blackjack with real money, play on the Web with pretend money! The game stakes players with $1,000, and players can place bets up to $5,000. It's almost as good as the real thing.

Site Details:	Large Graphics
Load Time:	4 seconds

Centre for the Easily Amused

http://www.islandnet.com/~cwalker/homepage.html

This site is also known as the Ultimate Guide to Wasting Time. It's big, it's varied, and it's funny. Some of the many links include: Mr. Smarty Pants Knows, the Pez Home Page, the Dysfunctional Family Circus, and the Complaint Letter Generator.

Site Details:	Good Links
Load Time:	25 seconds

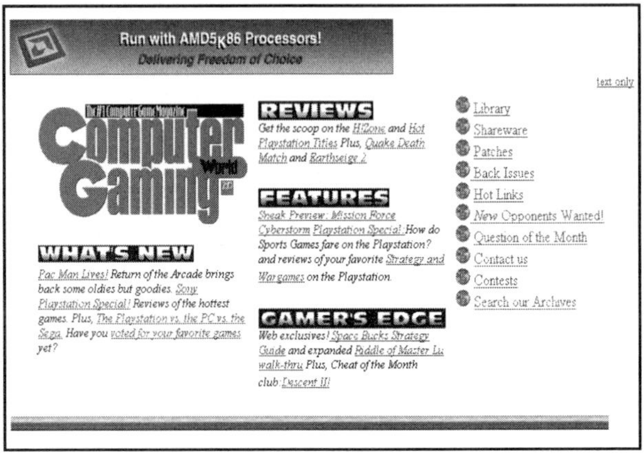

Computer Gaming World

★★★★★

http://www.gamingworld.ziff.com/~gaming

Computer Gaming World is an electronic publication dedicated to news and reviews of current games on the market. You'll get inside information about games, sneak previews, game reviews, and cheat tips. This site is a must-see for all gamers.

Site Details:	Large Graphics, Good Links
Load Time:	36 seconds

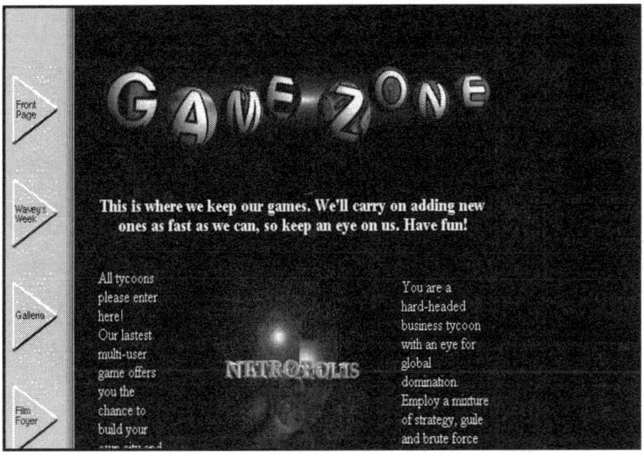

Games Zone

★★★★★

http://www.delphi.co.uk/delphi/interactive/interact.html

The Games Zone has online entertainment for all ages, at no expense to the user. Visitors to this site will enjoy online games such as Netropolis, Ferret Frenzy, Phlong, and the Pigeon Hunt. Tycoons are invited to play Netropolis, a multi-user game of strategy and domination. Want a bit of mystery and intrigue? Put your sleuthing skills to use in the Incan world of Phlong. The diversions are plentiful here.

Site Details:	Animation, Large Graphics, Good Links
Load Time:	10 seconds

Intelligent Gamer Online

★★★★★

http://igonline.escape.com

The Intelligent Gamer Online Web page is intended for home video game players. It's the one-stop location for all that's game-related. Gamers will find news of industry developments and conferences, product reviews, feature stories, and other material. The site includes an interactive component, allowing users to complete surveys or respond to the Intelligent Gamer's contents.

Site Details:	Large Graphics, Good Links
Load Time:	5 seconds

InterLotto

★★★★★

http://www.interlotto.com

Here's the ticket for those who just happen to have stacks of unexamined lotto tickets—an online lottery information service. The page is updated daily and its information covers lotteries throughout the country, with all the various games. It also provides plenty of links to international resources.

Site Details:	Good Links
Load Time:	36 seconds

Internet Chess Club

http://www.hydra.com/icc

All levels of chess players, from beginners to Grandmasters, are welcome at the Internet Chess Club. Registered users can play with rated players from around the world, 24 hours a day. Study games, play in tournaments, and search the database for Grandmaster games. The ICC Chess FTP Library features interfaces for most computers. Fees vary, with discounts for students. Grandmasters play free. Players will also find great links to chess-related sites.

Site Details:	Large Graphics, Good Links, Service Fee
Load Time:	15 seconds

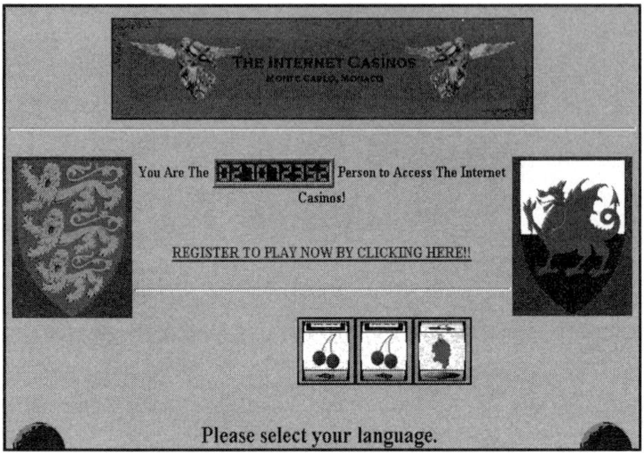

Internet Online Casinos

http://www.casino.org/cc

Try your luck at the Internet Online Casino with slot machines, lotto, sportsbooks, and casino tournaments. Register to play online with major credit cards or digital cash. The site is loaded with graphics, making download time a bit excruciating, but there's lots to explore and your winnings may make the wait worthwhile.

Site Details: Large Graphics, Good Links, Service Fee

Load Time: 44 seconds

Jumble & Crossword Solver

http://odin.chemistry.uakron.edu/cbower/jumble.html

If you need a little help with the Sunday paper crossword puzzles, you'll enjoy the scrambled word solver and the crossword puzzle solver. For crosswords, simply type in the known letters with question marks standing for the unknown letters, and the solver brings up all the possible words. For the scrambled word solver, simply type in the letters, and it will sort them for you. Keep this one a secret!

Load Time: 3 seconds

NetPoker

http://www.libertynet.org/~consult/poker/welcome.html

Can't round up the group for the Saturday night game? Who needs 'em! Play interactive Las Vegas-style NetPoker. The bank stakes players 100 points (you're playing for points, not money, remember) and keeps track of account balances. Aim for the Hall of Fame, where the names of the top 10 players are listed. Free registration is required for play.

Site Details: Large Graphics
Load Time: 2 seconds

Netropolis Game

✯✯✯✯✯

http://www.delphi.co.uk/Netropolis

Visitors can build businesses and alliances or claw their way to the top in the multi-user virtual environment of Netropolis. Users make friends or taunt foes via e-mail but claw their way to the top of the heap any way they can. This game is slick, well-designed, and appeals to the money-hungry back-stabber lurking in so many of us.

Site Details: Large Graphics
Load Time: 119 seconds

NUKES

☆☆☆☆☆

http://www.nuke.com

This site contains a wealth of details about current video games, computer software, movies, television shows, and online malls, with connections to relevant sites and opportunities to purchase merchandise online. Users will also find information on comic books and magazines as well as movie reviews, book archives, and much more.

Site Details:	Animation, Large Graphics, Good Links, Shopping
Load Time:	88 seconds

PC Gamer

☆☆☆☆☆

http://www.futurenet.co.uk/computing/pcgamer.html

After registering at the gateway to Futurenet, British gaming wonks congregate at this major gaming site, a clever e-zine version of *PC Gamer,* the UK magazine. The user is served news, reviews, critiques, features, previews of upcoming games, and hot tips—and those are just the hors d'oeuvres. It's also a neat spot to order cool stuff.

Site Details:	Large Graphics, Good Links
Load Time:	28 seconds

S.P.Q.R.

☆☆☆☆☆

http://www.pathfinder.com/@@EEEOQOAQ5AIAQO0T/twep/rome

This 3-D interactive game takes players to ancient Rome, where the fate of the city is in their hands. In the five notebooks they must find, there is information for rescuing Rome from destruction. To play, users fill out a form to apply for Roman citizenship. Easy-to-understand directions are available, as well as character profiles. The game features beautifully rendered graphics, and may draw users in for hours of play.

Site Details: Large Graphics
Load Time: 4 seconds

Zarf's List of Interactive Games on the Web

☆☆☆☆☆

http://www.leftfoot.com/games.html

This is a wonderful page offering several links to interactive games available throughout the Net. Information about the game is provided along with an overview of how it's played. Games such as Name That Tune, ChessWeb, and Yahtzee are among those provided.

Site Details: Good Links
Load Time: 5 seconds

Government

In its purest form, government fulfills a desire by a people for cohesion, community and leadership. The reality is sometimes far from the ideal. The Web brings government closer and makes it more accessible than ever before. Citizens can untangle in bureaucratic red tape online, and voice opinions to representatives in City Hall, on Capitol Hill, and in the White House.

As April 15th looms on the horizon each year, the **Internal Revenue Service** site can help with online tax forms and answer a complicated questions regarding business travel deductions. Once you've completed your tax return, visit the **Small Business Administration** for information on financing the retail flower shop of your dreams. Save yourself a trip to the **Social Security Administration** by visiting its Web site for online forms to request a Social Security Card application for your teenager; or, plan for your golden years with a Request for Earnings and Benefits Estimate Statement.

E-mail the President or review the Citizen's Interactive Handbook at the online **White House**. Voice your opinion about the endangered white owl to your state senator at the **United States Senate** home page. Whether your concern be beautification of a neighborhood park or global warming, **FedWorld** and the **Federal Web Locator** can help you locate the government agency you need.

Bureau of Labor Statistics

http://stats.bls.gov

Visitors to the Bureau's home page can get a look at the economy and its effect on jobs through the information and statistics provided. This content-rich resource provides regional and national information, including reports, statistics, and news releases. This page allows users a comparative look at labor reports from past years.

Site Details:	Large Graphics, Good Links
Load Time:	57 seconds

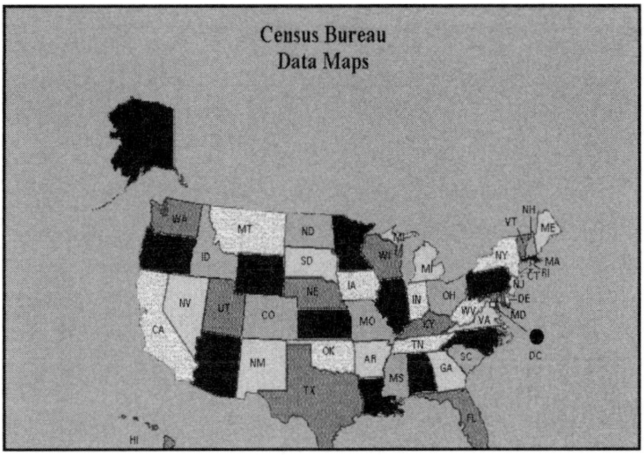

Census Bureau Data Maps

http://www.census.gov/ftp/pub/statab/www/profile.html

This easy-to-navigate site is full of information collected by the U.S. Census Bureau. State profiles, population figures for counties, statistics of U.S. businesses, and state government finances are just a few of the topics covered here.

Load Time: 22 seconds

Federal Reserve Bank

http://www.frbchi.org

Formed in 1913, the Federal Reserve System is the nation's central bank, if you will. Governing 12 regional districts, the Fed's job, under current Chairman Alan Greenspan, is to monitor the nation's money supply, influence interest rates, and stabilize monetary value. These pages provide an overview of the FRB Chicago branch, in addition to a history of the entire system. Visitors will find a glossary of terms, economic indicators, monetary policies, periodicals, and online speeches by Federal Reserve officials.

Site Details: Good Links
Load Time: 20 seconds

Federal Web Locator

http://www.law.vill.edu/fed-agency/fedwebloc.html

Designed as your one-stop shop for all federal information, the Federal Web Locator home page is detailed and comprehensive. It is divided into Legislative, Judicial, Executive branches, Executive Agencies, Federal Independent Establishments (e.g., FDIC, FEMA, EPA, CIA), Quasi-Official Agencies such as the National Academy of Sciences, the Smithsonian, plus the United Nations, the World Bank, and much more.

Site Details: Good Links
Load Time: 30 seconds

FedWorld Information Network

http://www.fedworld.gov

FedWorld offers a central access gateway to government agencies and information. The home page is admirably organized to help the general public find its way through the sometimes intimidating world of the federal government. Users can locate desired data through a subject category listing, browse through recent U.S. government reports, or use the Commerce Information Locator Service.

Site Details: Good Links
Load Time: 53 seconds

Government, Law and Society

☆☆☆☆☆

http://english-www.hss.cmu.edu/Govt

This collection of government, law, and society resources seeks to establish connections in the realm of the global socioeconomic systems in which we live. Substantive research materials, articles, and documents explore topics like economics, gender issues, welfare, political theory, war, and the court systems.

Site Details: Good Links
Load Time: 6 seconds

Internal Revenue Service

☆☆☆☆☆

http://www.irs.ustreas.gov/prod/

The Internal Revenue Service brings users a great-looking page that offers tax forms and instructions, FAQs, filing information, and tax help. There are links to the Department of Treasury home page and the Department of Treasury Bureaus page, as well as a biography of the Commissioner of the IRS, Peggy Richardson.

Site Details: Animation, Large Graphics, Good Links
Load Time: 27 seconds

Lawmarks

★★★★★

http://www.iwc.com/entropy/marks/bkmrkjsm.html

Lawmarks is a fabulous government and legal resource page. Features include courtroom rules and etiquette, a listing of law schools and libraries, the latest legal news, and Web access to law journals. Each division links the user to a wealth of additional law sites, and information on state and federal governments is also available. In addition, a complete listing of human rights and civil liberties organizations is presented.

Site Details: Large Graphics, Good Links
Load Time: 35 seconds

Small Business Administration

★★★★★

http://www.sbaonline.sba.gov/index.html

The U.S. Small Business Administration (SBA) is a government-sponsored organization created to help America's entrepreneurs form successful small enterprises. The SBA home page provides general information, resources for starting, financing, or expanding a business, and a search engine for finding a specific SBA employee. Find out how the government has promoted small business under the Clinton administration. Links lead to many federal and state government servers, as well as SBA's gopher and FTP servers.

Site Details: Large Graphics, Good Links
Load Time: 12 seconds

Social Security Administration

★★★★★

http://www.ssa.gov

Social Security Online offers citizens information about disability, retirement, and other programs managed by the agency. Users can save a trip to the office by downloading a form to request a Social Security Card or to review the 1996 Cost of Living Adjustment brochure online. Compute your retirement benefits using the Social Security Benefit Estimating Program or connect to the Government Printing Office to download thousands of government publications.

Site Details: Large Graphics, Good Links
Load Time: 26 seconds

State and Local Governments

★★★★★

http://lcweb.loc.gov/global/state/stategov.html

Although this site is primarily text-based, this site offers a valuable resource for locating state and local government information. Local councils, state government, and maps of states are provided, along with a link to the National Center for State Courts. Click on a state name and you will be provided with a listing of that state's government pages on the Web. Paths to the popular Web sites of City Link and City Net are provided.

Site Details: Good Links
Load Time: 4 seconds

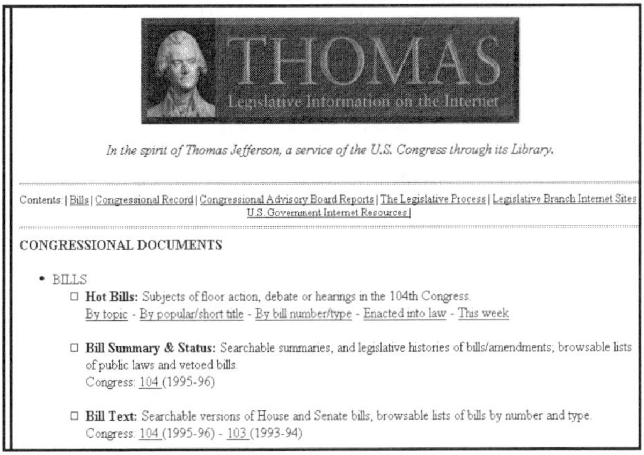

Thomas

http://thomas.loc.gov/home/thomas.html

"Thomas" stands for Thomas Jefferson and for Legislative Information on the Internet. Thomas is a service of the U.S. Congress. It contains the full text of Congressional bills in a database searchable by bill number or keyword. In addition, citizens will find the full text of the Congressional Record, also searchable by keyword. Explore information on the legislative process by reading the article "How Our Laws Are Made" or review the text of the U.S. Constitution.

Site Details: Good Links
Load Time: 21 seconds

U.S. Government Printing Office

★★★★★

http://www.access.gpo.gov

The U.S. Government Printing Office is responsible for printing and distributing the printed and electronically disseminated publications of Congress as well as the executive departments of the federal government. This site provides information on the office, including the personnel, organizational structure, and Congress. Contacts are provided for users who would like more information.

Site Details:	Good Links
Load Time:	34 seconds

U.S. House of Representatives Home Page

★★★★★

http://www.house.gov

This page is the official home page of the House of Representatives. You'll find legislative information as well as data on House Members, Committees, and Organizations of the House. The What's New section updates recent events in the House. Users can also learn about the legislative process, who's who and how to contact them.

	Good Links
Load Time:	3 seconds

United Nations

http://www.un.org

This is the online heartbeat of the United Nations. Learn about the UN Charter, the International Court of Justice, and the history of the UN. Access principal divisions and information centers of the UN, its sister non-governmental organizations, its peacekeeping operations, and more. The presentation is comprehensive and insightful. This global organization offers opportunities to participate in UN events and calendars of upcoming conferences.

Site Details: Good Links, Shopping
Load Time: 12 seconds

United States Community Page Index

http://www.nsbol.com/nsbol/comindex/us_index.htm#main

Find the home pages of communities across the U.S., sorted by state, at this useful and interesting site. Truly an electronic Town Hall, citizens can access their local officials, read about planning issues, and discover recreational opportunities. Since the sites are posted by the individual towns and cities, there is a wide variation of available information.

Site Details: Good Links
Load Time: 28 seconds

United States Senate

http://policy.net/capweb/Senate/Senate.html

The comprehensive directory of names and states at CapWeb's site for the U.S. Senate makes it easy to communicate with your senator. Locate your senator and his or her geographic location, party affiliation, and general personal and professional background. You'll find information on each politician, including date(s) of election, address, phone number, e-mail address, and committees served.

Site Details: Good Links
Load Time: 45 seconds

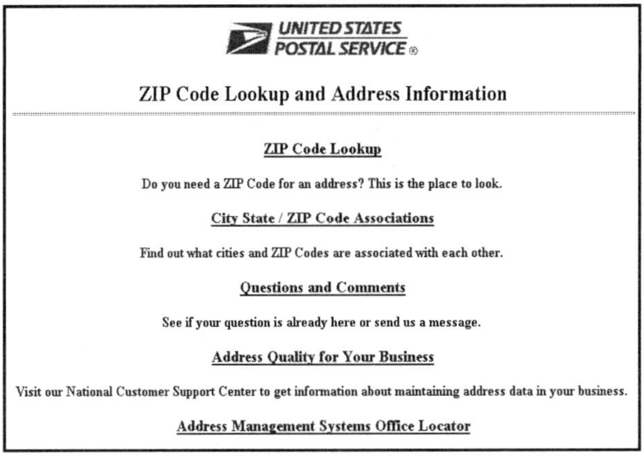

UNITED STATES POSTAL SERVICE®

ZIP Code Lookup and Address Information

ZIP Code Lookup

Do you need a ZIP Code for an address? This is the place to look.

City State / ZIP Code Associations

Find out what cities and ZIP Codes are associated with each other.

Questions and Comments

See if your question is already here or send us a message.

Address Quality for Your Business

Visit our National Customer Support Center to get information about maintaining address data in your business.

Address Management Systems Office Locator

USPS Address Quality & ZIP Code Lookup

http://www.usps.gov/ncsc

Make this site a one-stop spot for all your postal questions—FAQs, Zip+4 dilemmas, and bar coding mysteries. Handy lookup utilities mean that you'll never have to send a letter without a zip code again. Know the zip code but not the town name? No problem. Forgot the official abbreviation for Massachusetts? Or the correct way to abbreviate "Valley"? The thoughtful folks at the Post Office list these and many more abbreviations for you.

Site Details: Good Links
Load Time: 5 seconds

White House

http://www.whitehouse.gov

Visitors to the White House home page have a variety of paths to explore. Listen to a greeting from President Clinton, send him an e-mail, or take a virtual tour of the White House. This page also provides access to Federal agencies such as the EPA, the CIA, the FTC, NASA, FDIC, the FCC, the SBA, and many others. There are also links to the Legislative and Judicial branches. Press releases, archived by date and topic, as well as daily press briefings and weekly summaries, are available. Visitors can browse current and historical documents, such as presidential speeches, the State of the Union address, the 1996 proposed budget, the Declaration of Independence, and the Constitution.

Site Details: Sound, Good Links
Load Time: 15 seconds

Health & Fitness

"If we could give every individual the right amount of nourishment and exercise, not too little and not too much, we would have found the safest way to health."

Hippocrates, c.460–377 BC

Living a vital and healthy life means making informed and intelligent choices about nutrition, exercise, and health care. Whether you need information on mood disorders, pharmaceutical companies, or food labeling, the Internet is a wonderful complement to information and services you normally receive from your fitness trainer, nutritionist, and physician.

Looking for an exercise routine to squeeze between the morning alarm and your 45-minute commute to work? Try the **Balance** home page, offering tips on weight training, running, and aerobics. Once you've finished that final set of sit-ups, you'll want to pack a healthy meal for lunch. The **Body Mechanics** home page can help with low-fat recipes and nutritional guidelines for weight loss.

Research your medical questions at **ChronicIllNet** and learn more about prescription drugs at **PharmInfoNet.** Explore holistic and alternative medical options at the **Alternative and Complementary Medicine Page**.

Acupuncture.com

http://www.acupuncture.com

Health consumers searching for alternative approaches to medical care will find detailed information about acupuncture here. This page also presents detailed coverage on Chinese medicine, massage, nutrition, and much more. Learn how to help hormonal imbalances and substance addiction with the help of acupuncture.

Site Details:	Large Graphics, Good Links, Shopping
Load Time:	82 seconds

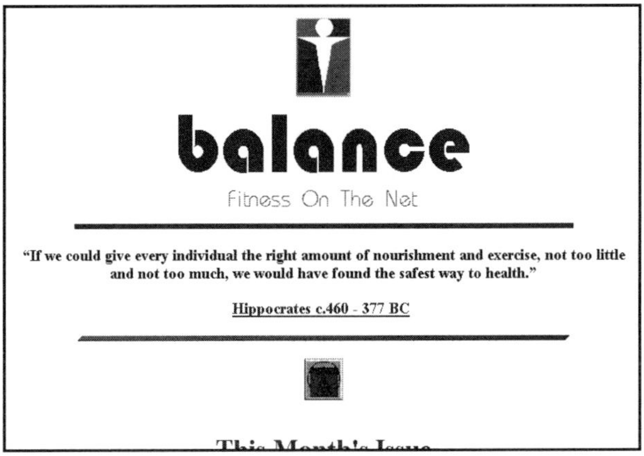

Balance

http://hyperlink.com/balance

Learn about all aspects of fitness and health here. In addition to a rounded offering of topics on weight training, swimming, running, nutrition, and training injuries, the magazine offers a segment, Just for Women that addresses the specific concerns of women's health. Visitors to this Web magazine will enjoy the ease of use of the home page and the great assortment of pertinent and informative articles.

Site Details: Good Links, Shopping
Load Time: 15 seconds

Body Mechanics

http://www.imgsys.com/bodymech/index.html

Fitness enthusiasts are welcomed to a place where the "body and mind are always in a process of change." Visitors to Body Mechanics will find a clean, organized page teeming with training tips, nutrition guidelines, gym ads, and fitness competition information. Fat-free recipes, FAQs, and bodybuilding information are among the many life saving and life lengthening highlights found here.

Site Details: Good Links
Load Time: 23 seconds

Centers for Disease Control and Prevention (CDC)

http://www.cdc.gov

Visitors to the CDC site will find useful information about disease, contagious infections, and mortality reports. Health hazards for children are discussed. Take a look at the Travelers' Health segment for recommendations on vaccinations and nutritional issues before your next international trip. Cruise ship sanitation ratings are also listed.

Site Details: Large Graphics, Good Links
Load Time: 6 seconds

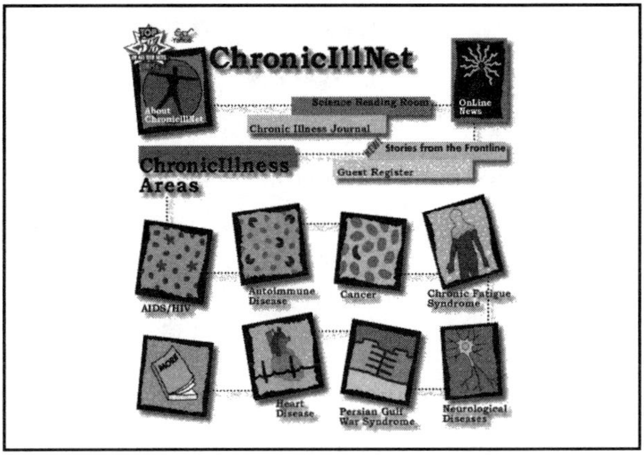

ChronicIllNet

✯✯✯✯✯

http://www.calypte.com

An online library of resources pertaining to chronic illnesses is available here. Subjects covered include HIV/AIDS, autoimmune disease, cancer, chronic fatigue syndrome, heart disease, and Persian Gulf War syndrome. Review the latest news about these chronic illnesses, read key research articles or check out a nationwide calendar of events. Also included at this site or accounts of individuals who have battled chronic illnesses.

Site Details: Large Graphics, Good Links
Load Time: 14 seconds

Diseases, Disorders, and Related Topics

http://www.mic.ki.se/Diseases/index.html

For an extraordinarily comprehensive resource on diseases and disorders of all classifications, as well as symptoms and treatments for many of the ailments, visit this Web site. Explore topics like mood disorders, respiratory tract diseases, geriatrics, and nervous system disorders. Links to additional pages for each topic are listed, and information about surgery, dentistry, anesthesia, and medication is also compiled.

Site Details: Good Links
Load Time: 32 seconds

Emotional Support Guide

http://asa.ugl.lib.umich.edu/chdocs/support/emotion.html

Those who deal with chronic illness, bereavement, or physical problems can find specific support resources here. Support and discussion groups include Usenet newsgroups, gophers, and Web sites. Bereavement groups support parents who have lost children, those dealing with sibling loss, and suicide survivors. Additional features include support for those coping with disabilities, such as amputation, blindness, deafness, traumatic brain injury, and facial disfigurement. There are also resources for those dealing with chronic illnesses, such as multiple sclerosis, AIDS, Parkinson's, and stroke.

Site Details: Good Links
Load Time: 7 seconds

Food and Nutrition Information Center

✯✯✯✯✯

http://www.nalusda.gov/fnic/

The consumer will finds lots of useful nutritional information at this Web site sponsored by the U.S. Department of Agriculture. A few of these resources include publications such as Weight Control, vegetarian recipes, dietary guidelines, information on the new food labeling requirements and more. Users can access the USDA/FDA Foodborne Illness Education Information Center to get educational materials about the Food Guide Pyramid. The list of links—Electronic Sources of Food and Nutrition Information—is especially useful.

Site Details: Good Links
Load Time: 7 seconds

Global Health Network

✯✯✯✯✯

http://info.pitt.edu/HOME/GHNet/GHNet.html

A public health resource with a global outlook, the Global Health Network contains links for public health organizations and agencies, information on worldwide disease and disease-monitoring programs, global healthcare, as well as disaster relief and emergency issues. There are links to other health-related networks on the Internet. Some of these include the World Health Organization, U.N. Information Services, and the AIDS Pathfinder. There are also links for specific diseases and health issues, including CancerNet, Oncolink, tuberculosis, environmental health threats, nutrition, and hunger.

Site Details: Good Links
Load Time: 33 seconds

Health Net

http://www.familyinternet.com/medic.htm

For answers to all your questions related to health, medicine, and fitness, visit this Web page. Make a selection from 22 categories, including baby care, arthritis, blood pressure, nutrition, travel, women's health, or emergency medicine. Learn methods of stress management, how to prevent sports injuries, and which foods help prevent heart disease. A segment on alternative medicine explores herbal, chiropractic, and acupuncture treatments.

Site Details: Large Graphics, Good Links
Load Time: 18 seconds

Martindale's Health Science Guide

http://www-sci.lib.uci.edu/~martindale/HSGuide.html

This online health guide features over 23,000 medical cases, 280 textbooks, and 15,000 teaching files. Visitors will find health resources for the medical, dental, veterinarian, nursing, public health, and nutrition fields. Some of the fields of specialization include pediatrics, radiology, to name a few. This massive site covers some highly practical reference material.

Site Details: Good Links
Load Time: 18 seconds

MedWeb–Alternative Medicine

http://www.cc.emory.edu/WHSCL/medweb.altmed.html

A subsection of the MedWeb archive, the Alternative Medicine MedWeb encompasses the fields of homeopathy, acupuncture, chiropractic, osteopathy, and herbal healing. Users will find online journals including Chiropractic On-Line Today, the Wellness Newsletter, and Conscious Choice. Other resources include The Natural Resource Directory, The Kundalini Resource Directory, and the International College of Traditional Chinese Medicine. For more information, users can access the Holistic Health Directory, and the Homeopathic Resources List.

Site Details:	Good Links
Load Time:	21 seconds

Multimedia Medical Reference Library

http://www.tiac.net/users/jtward/index.html

Consumers, medical students, and physicians will find this page a comprehensive resource for medical and health information. Consumers will find a large medical reference, sorted by disease, with treatment and therapy information. The anatomy section, with its images and movies, will be of interest to the medical student. Cardiology, pathology, and radiology images, along with reference information, make this site a great companion to the medical text. Physicians will find medical software and research journals.

Site Details:	Video, Sound, Large Graphics, Good Links
Load Time:	64 seconds

National Health Information Center

http://nhic-nt.health.org

The National Health Information Center (NHIC) is a health information referral service established in conjunction with the U.S. Department of Health and Human Services. NHIC provides an online database, listing more than 1,000 organizations and government offices, which provide health information upon request. Entries include contact information, short descriptions, and information about publications and services of the constituent organizations.

Site Details: Good Links
Load Time: 15 seconds

Nutrition Pages

http://deja-vu.oldiron.cornell.edu/~jabbo

FAQs about diet and nutrition are the focus of this site. Specific topics include Sports Nutrition and a forum where users submit articles or concerns for discussion. Poisonous Plants, Magnesium in Water, and Saturated Fat are some of the issues covered here.

Site Details: Good Links
Load Time: 24 seconds

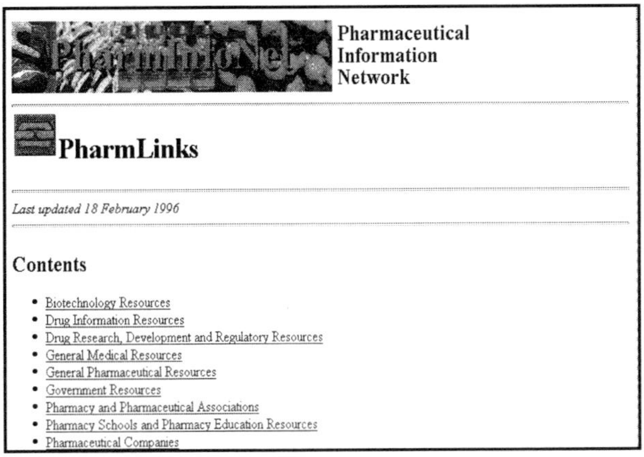

PharmInfoNet

http://pharminfo.com/phrmlink.html

The Pharmaceutical Information Network maintains a large list of links to related data. There are links to pharmaceutical newsgroups, mailing lists, Web servers, and listservs. You will find links to pharmaceutical companies such as Lilly, Searle, Genentech, and Pfizer. Find links to medical information on the Web, such as the Multimedia Medical Reference Library and Medical Matrix, a searchable medical database. To access the drug database, select Drug Information Resources, then click on DrugDB.

Site Details: Good Links
Load Time: 31 seconds

Lifestyles

Your uncle spends his weekends planting tulip bulbs and pruning his rose bushes. Your coworker reads mystery books by the dozen, while your sister spends hours in the kitchen preparing gourmet meals that Wolfgang Puck would envy. Engaging, obsessive, pleasurable—the texture of our lives is patterned by our interests and pastimes. From stamp collecting to wine making, home renovation to wood-working, the Internet not only provides diversions to soothe and satisfy us, but it also connects us with others who share our interests.

The Web can enhance life's pleasures in many ways. Enjoy a special evening among dinner guests with meal suggestions and recipesthat you find within the elegant pages of **Epicurious** or **eGG.** The **American Wine** page helps you select the perfect accompanying beverage. If curling up with a book on a rainy Saturday afternoon sounds inviting, **BookWire Navigator** contains book reviews, bestseller lists, and links to online bookstores.

For the home improvement enthusiast, **Homeplan.com** delivers tips on everything from landscaping to building codes to renovation techniques. Useful consumer booklets and price guides at the **Consumer World** home page help you select a comfortable hammock to hang on the back porch for those long summer evenings. Don't forget the iced tea.

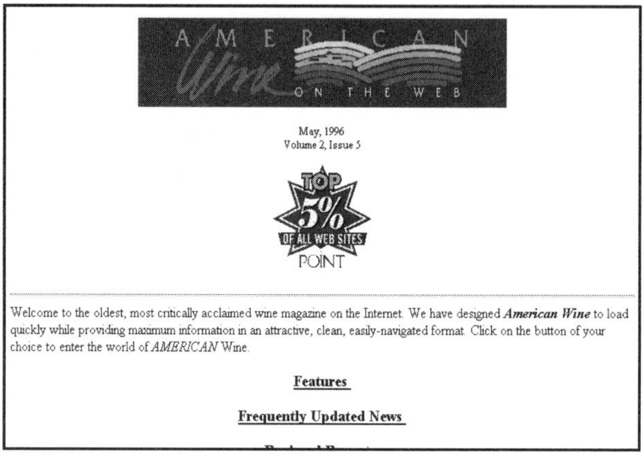

American Wine

http://www.2way.com:80/food/wine

American Wine magazine features American vineyards and winemakers. There are lots of articles, news and regional reports, and links to wine-related sites. Users can find out the ratings of this year's Beaujolais Nouveau and peruse features such as the Winetaster's Events Calendar and book/CD/video reviews. Connoisseurs who enjoy good wines and fine food will find this site just right for their discriminating tastes.

Site Details: Large Graphics, Good Links
Load Time: 11 seconds

Bruce's Wine Page

http://www.pcix.com/wine/index.html

Bruce's Wine Page is a great jumping-in spot for exploring wine-related pages on the Web. Wander down the path to vineyards by the hundreds—from New York State to the West Coast. Shop from a list of retail stores, warehouses, and import/exporters. Search for a particular vineyard or winery by geographic location. The Forum segment offers the opportunity to interact with other wine lovers. Wine reviews, glossaries, and festival information can also be found here.

Site Details:	Large Graphics, Good Links, Shopping
Load Time:	110 seconds

Chocolatier Recipes

http://www.godiva.com/recipes/chocolatier/index.html

If you love the flavor and aroma of chocolate, you will delight in the sweet temptations found at the Chocolatier Recipes home page. A lengthy list of recipes tempts you with creations like chocolate cheesecake, walnut brownie cake, and mango mousse cake. The recipes include pictures and a star rating that measures the level of cooking difficulty. Follow links back to the Godiva home page and the Chocolatier home page.

Site Details: Good Links, Shopping
Load Time: 15 seconds

eGG

http://www.2way.com:80/food/egg/index.html

The electronic Gourmet Guide offers a great cookbook for chefs at every level of ability. Take a look at the fascinating history of food, print a few recipes from the collection, or explore the related-foods links. Also available in this monthly e-zine are a handy Quick Tip link and a feedback form. Need a little splash of something to wash your meal down? Link to American Wine on the Web.

Site Details: Good Links, Shopping
Load Time: 67 seconds

Epicurious

http://www.epicurious.com/epicurious/home.html

Epicurious is an online magazine with recipes, food preparation tips, Gail's Recipe Swap, and a restaurant guide for the United States. An especially useful section details what's in-season at farmer's markets around the country, and then provides recipes using the seasonal ingredients. Users can click on an interactive map to find out what's ripe at their local market, with prices per pound. In addition, cooks can read articles from *Bon Appetit* and *Gourmet Plus*, there are witty features like "Coping with Problem Foods in Public," which give tips on how to eat corn-on-the-cob, lettuce, and cherry tomatoes.

Site Details: Large Graphics, Good Links

Load Time: 12 seconds

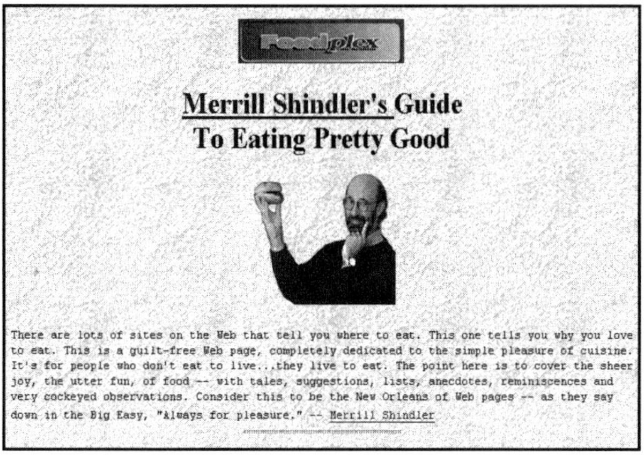

Foodplex

★★★★★

http://www.gigaplex.com/food/index.html

Foodplex showcases the writing of popular Los Angeles print and broadcast restaurant reviewer Merrill Shindler. It's a nice change of pace from the serious tone of most food pages. Shindler's humorous slant on the trendy food world is evident in the article "Food Magazines That I Thought Would Never Last," which meditates on the curious survival of *Chocolatier Magazine* and *The Whole Chile Pepper*, among others. In other articles, Shindler counts the animal distribution in a box of animal crackers, names the best steak restaurants in America and details 10 good places to eat in London. Really.

Site Details: Good Links
Load Time: 52 seconds

Hershey's Recipes

http://www.microserve.net/~hershey/welcome.html

The most notable feature of Hershey's Web site is the online cookbook filled with luscious chocolate recipes. The site also offers guests a virtual tour of the Hershey factory, where you'll find a history of the company, founder Milton S. Hershey, and the Pennsylvania fairyland "that chocolate built." In addition, there are nutrition facts about chocolate from the Hershey kitchens and gift items to purchase.

Large Graphics, Good Links, Shopping
Load Time: 52 seconds

Mama's Cucina

http://www.eat.com:80/index.html

Welcome to Mama's Cucina, where the words proudly state, "no one should go through life without getting a little pasta sauce on the face." This tastefully decorated site will take visitors on a culinary expedition through mama's cookbook with authentic Italian recipes for pastas, pizzas, seafood, desserts, and appetizers. Other great resources include an online Italian speaking tutorial, a virtual tour of little Italy, Italian art and architecture resources, plus general information about Ragu. *Buon appetito!*

Site Details: Good Links, Shopping
Load Time: 82 seconds

Sally's Place

http://www.bpe.com

Sally is a San Francisco-based gourmet cook, writer and editor. She bills her place as a "a worldwide perspective on the finer things of life." The focus is on California wines, international travel, French, Italian (Tuscan), and Cajun cooking, but that's only the tip of the iceberg. There are stand-out, insider-type sections on Californian cities and lots of downloadable audio interviews with noted oenophiles on Wine Valley Radio.

Site Details:	Sound, Good Links
Load Time:	70 seconds

Star Chefs

http://starchefs.com

Chefs and gourmands alike can appreciate this slick Web showcase for top chefs from across the country. Each entry includes a biography, general information on the chef's restaurant, menus, and some of the chef's favorite recipes. There are areas devoted to chefs' secret ingredients and careers in the culinary arts. Nicely done graphics complement the pages.

	Large Graphics, Good Links, Shopping
Load Time:	25 seconds

Virtual Kitchen

✯✯✯✯✯

http://www.pathfinder.com/twep/kitchen

Hungry for a little gourmet cuisine? Visit the Virtual Kitchen, an excellent online resource for recipes, cooking tips, and loads of other food and wine discussions. A huge database of recipes is featured, with desserts, main dishes, beverages, and more. Users can ask a professional chef questions or visit the bulletin boards to leave recipes and advice for other cybercooks.

Site Details:	Large Graphics, Good Links, Shopping
Load Time:	36 seconds

Book Lovers: Fine Books and Literature

✯✯✯✯✯

http://www.xs4all.nl/~pwessel

Pay a visit to this literate site for links to books, rare booksellers, libraries, poetry, and literary journals on the Web. There are links to online research tools, LitWeb, and Andrea's Literary Links.

Site Details:	Good Links
Load Time:	23 seconds

BookWire Navigator

✯✯✯✯✯

http://www.bookwire.com/navigator.html

This incredibly useful home page should appeal to book lovers and writers around the globe. Bookwire provides extensive publishing information, bestseller lists, links to bookstores and libraries, and loads of book reviews. An impressive list of literature and writers' mailing lists is featured, as well as information about the book business and links to several book-related Web sites.

Site Details:	Good Links
Load Time:	111 seconds

Collecting

✯✯✯✯✯

http://www.antika.com//collecting/index.html

Collectors of all kinds will find this section of the Web Virtual Library a great jump site to links throughout the Internet. Whether you collect stamps, candy wrappers, comics, trading cards, antiques, Pez candy, or watches, something useful can be found here. Study groups, newsgroups, shops, and traders' sites are listed.

Site Details: Good Links
Load Time: 15 seconds

Complete Guide to Garden Stuff

✯✯✯✯✯

http://www.btw.com/garden_archive/toc.html

Whether you're all thumbs or have one green thumb, this two thumbs up—way up—site will have you up to your ears in gardening. The 10-chapter book takes a comprehensive look at gardening with information on soil, grass, pest control, tools, weeding, cutting and pruning, equipment maintenance, seed growing, and more. Dig into topics like soil testing, topsoil mixing, watering techniques, and humus products.

Site Details: Good Links
Load Time: 19 seconds

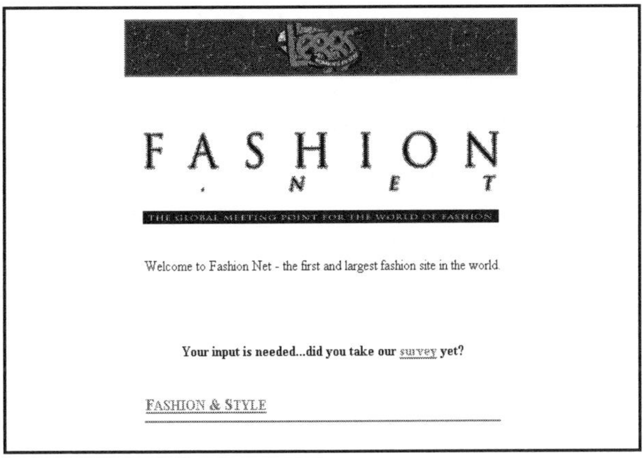

Fashion Net

http://www.fashion.net

Fashion Net creates an electronic meeting ground for the style-conscious consumer and the fashion industry. In the Fashion & Style section, you may shop online for hose, perfume, and jeans. In CNN's Style, get the latest fashion news. An interesting part of Fashion Net is the magazine section featuring *Buzz* Magazine, *ELLE*, *Entertainment Weekly*, and more. This site looks marvelous.

Site Details: Good Links
Load Time: 29 seconds

Gardening Web Directory

http://www.btw.com/urls/toc.html

The Gardening Web Directory is a horticulturist's dream come true. Gardeners will find links to general gardening sites, catalogs, and a FAQ section. In addition, there are links to botany, biology, environmental design, landscape architecture, and entomology.

Site Details: Good Links
Load Time: 5 seconds

Genealogy Toolbox

http://uxl.cso.uiuc.edu/~al-helm/genealogy.html

This master index catalogs about 1,000 genealogical resources on the Web. The tidy site is divided into: Indexes, Family History and Data, Genealogical Resources, Software. Its comprehensive anthology of genealogical resources is an invaluable timesaving tool for anyone conducting ancestral research.

Site Details: Good Links
Load Time: 2 seconds

Joseph Luft's Philatelic Resources on the Web

http://www.execpc.com/~joeluft/resource.html

Stamp collectors will find this a valuable resource. It offers a list of Web pages, including international philatelic sites, stamp shows and societies, postal authorities from around the world, country specific resources, collectors' pages, commercial offerings, and more. The list is extensive and displays this collector's heartfelt passion for his hobby. There is even a list of attractive, downloadable images.

Site Details: Good Links, Shopping
Load Time: 11 seconds

Mysterious Homepage

http://www.db.dk/dbaa/jbs/homepage.htm

This home page has everything for the mystery lover. Sleuths can search out newsgroups, connect to mystery-related home pages, play mystery games, and even read mystery e-texts online. Find mystery e-zines, mystery bibliographies, and Sherlockiana.

Site Details: Good Links
Load Time: 13 seconds

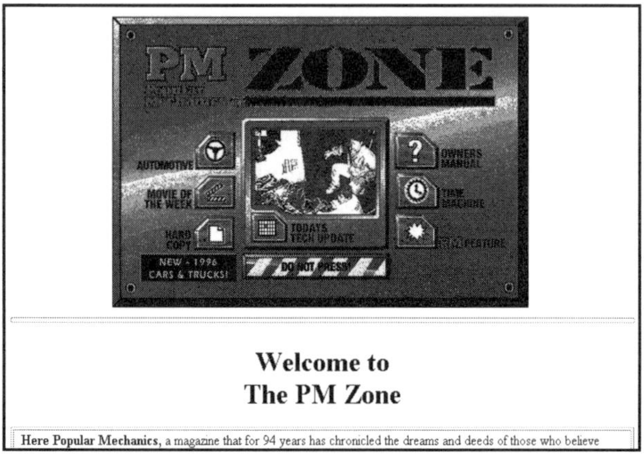

Popular Mechanics PM ZONE

http://popularmechanics.com/homepage.html

Popular Mechanics (PM) launches itself toward the millennium with this Web site. Preview the new car models, find out how to download software from the Internet, and get ideas for do-it-yourself projects. Let the Time Machine take you back through 90 years of technological changes, or read the feature articles from PM's five departments: Outdoors, Boating, Adventure, Aerospace, and Home Improvement. Users can also view QuickTime movie clips, join the Home Computing Forum, or access the Tech Update of the Day. A Web Surfer's Toolkit is also available.

Site Details:	Video, Large Graphics, Good Links
Load Time:	58 seconds

Wonderful Stitches

http://www.needlework.com

Needleworkers searching for inspiration will find plenty of it here. The Decorative Stitch of the Month section features color stitch charts with diagrams and photographs to enlarge and print on a color printer for reference. There are CyberSamplers for counted cross-stitch, needlepoint, and samplers based on quilt patterns. For more inspiration, the Stitches in Action section shows examples of different completed projects. The Textile Resource links are especially notable, with pointers to traditional Andean and Hmong textiles, Bayeaux tapestries, and Medieval/Renaissance embroidery. There are links to the National Museum of Design and the Museum of American History's exhibit.

Site Details: Good Links
Load Time: 10 seconds

Woodworking Catalog

http://www.woodworking.com

The Woodworking Catalog is one of the most comprehensive woodworking sites on the Web. You'll find information on supplies, equipment, schools, lumber, and books on woodworking. From this page, users can access many other resources.

Site Details: Good Links, Shopping
Load Time: 6 seconds

World-Wide Collectors Digest

http://www.wwcd.com/classified/classified.html

For the Web surfer with a garage packed with Hungarian ash-trays, cast-iron Eiffel Towers, Hawaiian refrigerator magnets, and a few dozen bamboo birdcages, this is the perfect site. Collectibles—from hockey pucks to Mr. Spock dolls—are bought and sold at the World-Wide Collectors Digest classifieds section. Voted in the Top 5% of All Web Sites by Point Communications, the Collectors Digest also features a Business Section, Price Guides, Live Auctions, employment information, and a huge list of vendors' e-mail addresses.

Site Details: Good Links, Shopping
Load Time: 36 seconds

Auto Channel

✯✯✯✯✯

http://www.the-autochannel.com

The Auto Channel takes advantage of the Web's multimedia bells and whistles—Java, Shockwave, the latest Netscape extensions, QuickTime, RealAudio, and more. There's a lot of substance behind all the glitz. Car aficionados can view videos of the latest cars. The new car guide, Motorzine, features buying tips, new model reviews, and a chat room. The New Car Database can bring up a list of cars with the most head room or leg room. The Auto Channel even reviews other automotive Web sites for you. Automania has repair tips, accessories and parts, and a shopping mall.

Site Details:	Animation, Real Audio, Video, Large Graphics, Good Links
Load Time:	20 seconds

Better Business Bureau

✯✯✯✯✯

http://www.cbbb.org/cbbb

The Better Business Bureau works to ensure the fair practice of businesses and the fair treatment of consumers. Easy to use, its site features such useful resources as publications, FAQs, and offices of the bureau. The Media Room offers advisories for consumers and several articles about the advertising industry.

Site Details:	Good Links
Load Time:	13 seconds

Comparison

http://www.comparison.com

Trying to figure out which telephone long distance company has the cheapest rates almost makes you miss Ma Bell. Comparison's bar charts make it easier (somewhat) to sort through the different rates. Each provider has different restrictions, though, so it is difficult to determine an absolute cost comparison. Caveats aside, Comparison allows consumers to make more informed telecommunication choices. Day, evening, and night/weekend rates are charted. The rates can also be combined to derive an average overall rate.

Load Time: 10 seconds

Consumer Information Center Catalogue

http://www.pueblo.gsa.gov/

Many consumers know this center as the best source for booklets published by dozens of federal departments and agencies. From their home page, follow the road signs to various categories: Children, Nutrition, Housing, Small Business, Travel & Hobbies, Cars, Employment, Federal Programs, and Money. These avenues lead users to thousands of brochures, some of which are free. You may read many of the brochures online or order a copy of your own.

Site Details: Video, Sound, Large Graphics, Good Links

Load Time: 5 seconds

Consumer World

http://www.consumerworld.org

Consumer World has gathered over 700 of the most useful consumer resources on the Internet. Check an airfare, find an ATM machine anywhere in the world, file a consumer complaint with a state agency, read hundreds of consumer booklets, find a low rate credit card or mortgage, research a law, look up the wholesale price of a car, locate a Better Business Bureau, find a toll-free number, and more, all in one convenient, online spot.

Site Details:	Large Graphics, Good Links, Shopping
Load Time:	16 seconds

Edmund's Automobile Buyer's Guide

http://www.edmund.com

Unless you are Evel Knievel, buying a car is a treacherous and traumatic experience. Edmund's Guide takes clueless car seekers and turns them into confident consumers. Besides new car reviews and specs, the Buyer's Guide includes leasing information and prices for used cars. Don't miss the Buyer's Advice section. Step-by-step instructions, strategies, and revealed insider secrets make the negotiating process almost a pleasure. You'll learn how to determine the true dealer cost and where to find unpublicized factory-to-dealer incentives. All the info is free. Edmund also sells videos, CD-ROMs, and books.

Site Details: Good Links, Shopping
Load Time: 10 seconds

Home Safety Center

http://www.enzoneusa.com

Enzone Incorporated Home Safety Center uses this home page to educate individuals on the dangers of contaminants in the home. Topics include radon gas, carbon monoxide, lead poisoning, microwave radiation, water pollutants, and electromagnetic fields. The company also promotes retail items that help detect these contaminants. An online order form is provided.

Site Details: Large Graphics, Good Links, Shopping
Load Time: 23 seconds

Homeplan.Com

http://www.homeplan.com/homeplan

Homeplan.com, presented by Builders Graphics Custom Home Design & Drafting, is a great resource for home-owners, builders, buyers, realtors and contractors. This page offers an extensive list of tips, resources, suggestions and links, covering everything from custom home planning to landscaping. It makes an excellent starting place for information about homes.

Site Details: Large Graphics, Good Links, Shopping

Load Time: 23 seconds

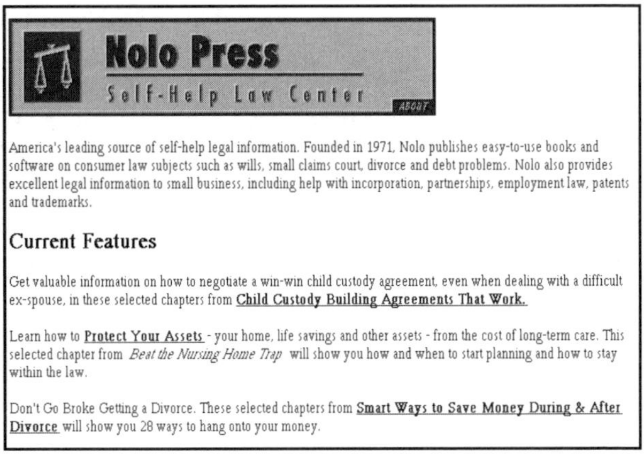

Nolo Press Self-Help Law Center

★★★★★

http://gnn.com/gnn/bus/nolo

Based on the premise that the legal system should be accessible and affordable to all, the Self-Help Law Center offers a variety of publications and books that help consumers take care of their own legal matters. Handle your own claim in court, inform yourself about your rights in the workplace, or file your own divorce papers. A description of each book is offered, as well as pricing and ordering information. Treat yourself to a few lawyer jokes before leaving.

Site Details: Good Links, Shopping
Load Time: 15 seconds

Magazines

Engaging and dynamic—the e-zine, or electronic magazine, is one of the biggest draws on the Web. Online magazines liven feature articles with sound, graphics, and innovative combinations of materials unimaginable before the world of hypertext and multimedia came into focus. You'll find online versions of your long-time favorites like, *Life*, *Fortune*, and *Sports Illustrated* at Time Warner's magazine mega-site, **Pathfinder,** as well as new magazines conceived and developed specifically for the Internet medium.

Looking for a favorite back issue, article or photograph? Forget about searching search through the unmanageable pile of magazines in the garage—online magazines and magazine directories provide huge archives and search features to help you find the back issue you want. The **Electronic Newsstand** houses an enormous collection of magazines, as does the **E-Zines** home page.

Plug into the irreverent take on the technology culture at **HotWired,** or get a glimpse of politics and culture inside the pages of **Utne Lens** or the **Atlantic Monthly**. **Outside Online** connects you to the environment and the great outdoors. Whatever your interest—computer technology, politics, art, pop culture—the magazines of the Internet deliver the goods with style.

HotWired

✯✯✯✯✯

http://www.wired.com/Login

HotWired is an online publication that contains many articles and features about the Internet and cyberspace. To get the full version of *HotWired*, users must sign up for their free services. HotWired is about the Internet as a whole, its culture, its products, online opinions, and much more. Members even have the opportunity to use the search engines and to customize what they read by being told what's new since their last visit.

Site Details:	Sound, Large Graphic, Good Links
Load Time:	25 seconds

MagNet

✯✯✯✯✯

http://www.cris.com/~milewski/magnet.html/

More than 50 of the top computing magazines are gathered on MagNet, from Access to ZD Europe. Readers will find *Home PC, Computer Shopper, Info World, PC Magazine, Windows Magazine,PC Guide,* and many more. Internet-related titles include *NetGuide, .net, HotWired*, and *Interactive Age. Sun World Online, UnixWorld,* and *Mac User* are some of the technically-oriented publications.

Site Details:	Good Links, Shopping
Load Time:	15 seconds

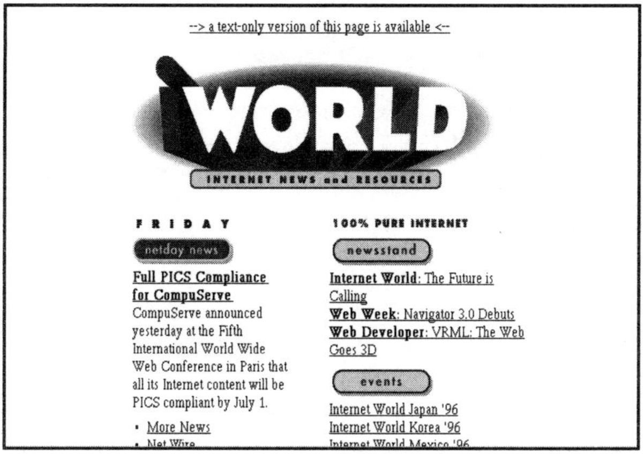

Mecklermedia's iWorld

http://www.iworld.com

Users will appreciate the easy-to-navigate interface of iWorld, a Web site offering a variety of Internet and Web resources. Read sample features from three magazines—*Web Developer, WebWeek,* and *internetWorld*—or access back issues. The Media Suite showcases new multimedia tools, and users can visit the Net House for a live chat. The Bulletin Board hosts discussions of Internet-related topics such as Java and multimedia on the Internet. Internet- and Web-related news can also be found here, in addition to announcements about online events.

Site Details: Large Graphics, Good Links
Load Time: 105 seconds

Magazines

Computer

TechWeb

http://techweb.cmp.com

TechWeb's well-designed and easy-to-navigate page provides links to the home pages for 16 computer and Internet magazines. Visitors to this page can find *Home PC, Net Guide, Windows Magazine, Information Week, Communications Week*, and *Informatiques Magazine*, to name just a few.

Site Details:	Large Graphics, Good Links, Shopping
Load Time:	64 seconds

WWWiz Magazine

http://wwwiz.com

This light and bright magazine is a welcome break from the many other "heavy" sites on the Web. Visitors to these clean pages will find an organized, refreshing mix of news, feature stories, computer tools, contests, shopping resources, editorials, and classifieds. Guests will likely enjoy making good on the invitation found here to read current and past issues.

Site Details:	Large Graphics, Good Links, Shopping
Load Time:	100 seconds

Magazines

Computer

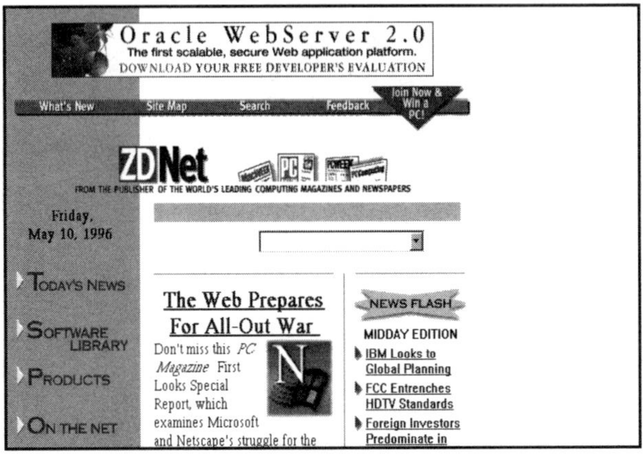

ZDNet

http://www.pcmag.ziff.com

Visitors to the Ziff-Davis Press Computer Magazines home page will find hours of options to explore. Users may register for a free, personalized news service or browse through current and back issues of such popular Ziff-Davis publications as *MacUser, PCWeek, and Computer Gaming World.* Subscription information is also provided for each magazine. Other connections available include the Internet Shopping Network, the Oracle Store.

	Large Graphics, Good Links, Shopping
Load Time:	57 seconds

Buzz Magazine Online

http://www2.earthlink.net:80/~buzzmag/ BuzzHomePage2.1.html

Buzz entertainment magazine has its finger on the pulse of L.A. Sparkling fiction and hard-hitting editorials give the magazine flash and impact. This good-looking site has archives of past issues, and an anthology of *Buzz* fiction. Nominate someone to the Buzz 100, a list of the coolest people in the universe. Take part in interactive happenings, such as the Buzz Salon, or check out some L.A. Hot Links.

Site Details: Video, Large Graphics, Good Links

Load Time: 21 seconds

Cake Times

http://itrc.on.ca/caketimes

Cake Times is a Web e-zine that makes the most of the new Web technology at the same time that it creates the almost-tactile feel of a glossy magazine. Articles are witty, penetrating, and timely, while the graphics entertain and draw readers onward. A recent issue contained articles entitled "The Differences Between Supermodels and Serial Killers," "The New Edwardians," and various poems, book reviews, and drawings.

Site Details: Animation, Large Graphics, Good Links

Load Time: 17 seconds

Condè Nast Traveler

★★★★★

http://www.cntraveler.com

Dreaming of a vacation on a secluded tropical island? A cross-country ski trip? Visit the Conde Nast Traveler before you head out. Headline stories change daily, with news on topics such as boating in Spain or the best time to buy airline tickets. Share a story or ask a question by participating in one of the forums. For a list of recommended travel destinations, fill out the online form with your preferences on everything from the weather to hotel architecture. This online edition features all of the amenities (and more) of its hard-copy sibling.

Site Details:	Large Graphics, Good Links
Load Time:	77 seconds

Discover Magazine

★★★★★

http://www.enews.com/magazines/discover

This page is the online version of *Discover*, the magazine of science and technology, their wonders, their uses, their impact upon our lives. The site offers the current issue, archives, the gallery of covers, the Discover Awards, online subscriptions through the Electronic Newsstand, and Talk to Discover. The Welcome page also has supplemental material for educators and insider interviews. This is a well-crafted yet simple online publication.

Site Details:	Large Graphics, Good Links, Shopping
Load Time:	18 seconds

Fortean Times: The Journal of Strange Phenomena

★★★★★

http://forteana.mic.dundee.ac.uk/ft

Fortean Times is a magazine dedicated to the world's mysteries, everything from alien sightings to dream phenomena. The magazine's Web page contains current and past issues, as well as numerous links, an online chat connection, and short stories from some of the readers. Current mystery and science fiction topics are listed, and interested users can subscribe to *Fortean Times* online.

Site Details:	Large Graphics, Good Links
Load Time:	94 seconds

HomeArts

★★★★★

http://www.homearts.com

Rich in content and beautifully designed, the HomeArts site melds online versions of *Redbook*, *Good Housekeeping, National Gardening, Popular Mechanics, and Country Living* into a unique, seamless whole. Browse the table of contents by topic or magazine.

Site Details:	Large Graphics, Good Links, Shopping
Load Time:	19 seconds

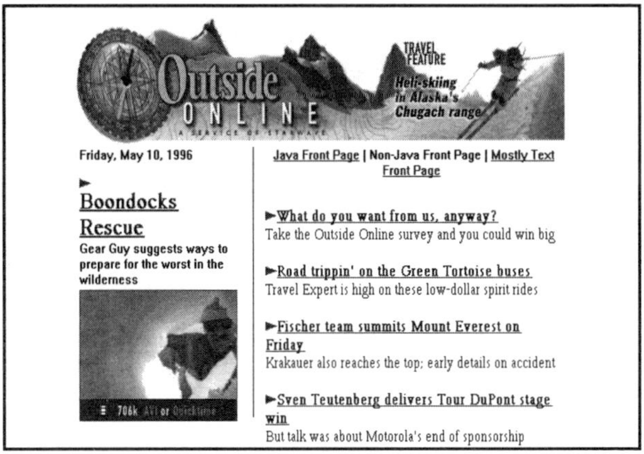

Outside Online

★★★★★

http://web2.starwave.com/outside/online

The online version of *Outside* magazine provides the deskbound with inspiration to get outside. Plan trips, locate outfitters and find travel companions in the Going Places section. Get outdoor and environmental news and read equipment reviews. Find in-depth information on biking, hiking, fitness, mountaineering, water sports, and snow sports. In addition, there are outdoor-related links and a link to *Outside Kids* Online.

Site Details:	Good Links, Shopping
Load Time:	45 seconds

Atlantic Monthly

★★★★★

http://www2.theAtlantic.com/atlantic

Devoted to politics, society, the arts, and culture, the *Atlantic Monthly* magazine offers this online version. Word games and trivia contests, a political forum, and entertainment previews are a few of the options. Take a look at campaign perspectives or review literary tributes to artists like John Steinbeck, Henry Wadsworth Longfellow, or Robert Pinsky.

Site Details: Sound, Good Links, Shopping
Load Time: 56 seconds

Hungry Mind Review

http://www.bookwire.com/hmr

High marks to every aspect of this online version of the delightfully literate and civilized HMR, a production of Dave Unowsky's famous Hungry Mind Bookstore in St. Paul, Minnesota's historic hill district, where F. Scott Fitzgerald, Charles Schultz, Amelia Earhart, August Wilson, Roy Wilkins, Warren Burger, and many other gifted notables grew up. The *Review* itself is amply represented here. Famous and non-famous writers cover all kinds of recently printed literature and topical political, social, and ecological issues. Subscribe using the handy form. You won't regret it.

Site Details: Good Links, Shopping
Load Time: 34 seconds

Mother Jones

http://www.mojones.com/mother_jones/MA95/toc.html

In its online incarnation, *Mother Jones* magazine presents hard-driving coverage of life in the '90s. Recent articles included an exploration of the unadvertised dangers of a new migraine drug, an interview with Studs Turkel, and coverage of the 1996 presidential campaign. Users can access back issues, do a keyword search of the database, or browse through a subject index of articles. MOJO Plugs are links to causes deemed worthy by the editors of Mother Jones, who encourage activism. These links are sorted into categories—Making Our Democracy Work, Keeping Our Media Honest, Promoting a Sustainable Way of Living, and many others.

Site Details: Large Graphics, Good Links, Service Fee
Load Time: 10 seconds

Utne Lens

http://www.utne.com/lens/big.html

The *Utne Reader* is a well-known publication that provides an eclectic mix of articles from alternative media. The same quality and diversity of information is offered at its Web site, the Utne Lens. The online content focuses on the community and issues that have emerged in the electronic-media era. The topics include media and technology, art, travel and culture. Within these categories are book reviews, technology reviews, and editorials. Users are invited to share their opinions at Cafe Utne.

Site Details: Good Links, Shopping
Load Time: 56 seconds

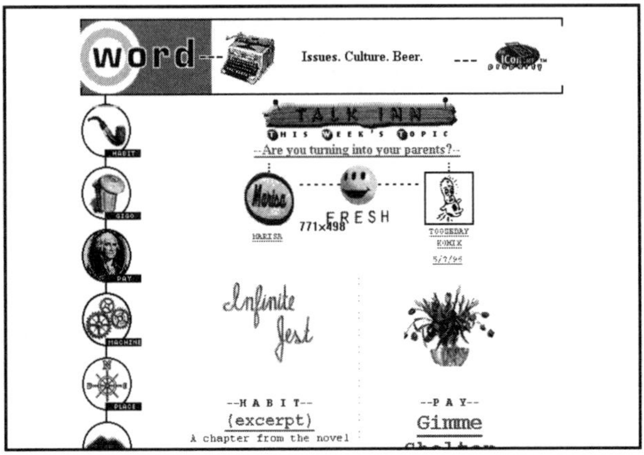

Word Literary Magazine

✯✯✯✯✯

http://www.word.com/

This literary e-zine will keep you spinning, with great graphics, words of inspiration, artwork, and surprises. The contents are categorized under the following headings: Habit, Money, Travel, Machine, Work, Place, Desire, and Gigo. Read poems and thought-provoking commentary or view artwork and photographs. Be sure to visit the online gallery of paintings by Marianna Trofimova.

Site Details:	Video, Sound, Large Graphics, Good Links
Load Time:	10 seconds

E-zines

✯✯✯✯✯

http://www.dominis.com/Zines

This Web page links to some of the most popular online publications currently on the Web. You'll find *Addicted to Noise, Time, Viewfinder, Sports Spectrum, Offbeat* magazine, and many others. Search by alphabetical listing.

Site Details:	Good Links
Load Time:	8 seconds

Electronic Newsstand

✯✯✯✯✯

http://www.enews.com

The folks at the Electronic Newsstand don't mind if customers thumb through the magazines; in fact, browsing is encouraged. Start off with some quick peeks at timely articles in Best of the Newsstand This Week and Editor's Choice. The Monster Magazine List covers over 2,000 'zines categorized by subject area. Although some periodicals offer subscription information only, others also offer impressive content.

Site Details:	Large Graphics, Good Links, Shopping
Load Time:	49 seconds

Magazines

Mega Magazine Resources

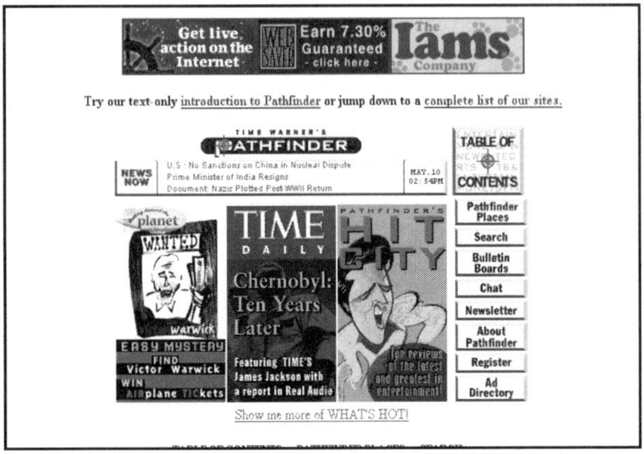

Time Warner's Pathfinder

✯✯✯✯✯

http://pathfinder.com

Time Warner's electronic home page is an extensive news and information resource that links the browser to news, sports, photography, education and shopping sites that are part of the extended Time Warner family. Access is provided to the online versions of *Time, People, Life,* and *National Review.* A Home and Hobbies link takes the user to *Progressive Farmer* Online or The Virtual Garden. With additional categories such as Entertainment, Technology, Kidstuff, Money and Business, and The Digital Pulse, the array of information available is enormous. Subscription information is provided for the more complete home versions.

Site Details:	Large Graphics, Good Links, Shopping
Load Time:	121 seconds

Music

The calming melody of Debussy's *Claire de Lune* spills from the car radio as you commute from home to the office. Scanning the airwaves, you wonder about the new release from Bruce Springsteen—a great gift idea for your daughter's birthday. Back at your computer, the Web offers a convenient and fun way to explore the music of the world with sound clips, RealAudio files, and online shopping. Jazz, blues, rock, classical, and pop artists jam the Web with slick sites brimming with photographs, discographies, music videos, fan clubs, and biographies.

Sites like **SonicNet** and the **Ultimate Band List** bring together compilations of musicians and bands ranging from the obscure to the world renowned. **VIBE** online keeps you plugged into the hip-hop scene, while **Classical World Online** features music categorized by composer, instrument, or title. Venture into the gothic cityscape of **Rocktropolis,** complete with Buzz Café, Church of Rock 'n Roll, Roxy Theatre, and Musicians Exchange. Whether you reside in the **Classics World** or travel the **Blues Highway**, you'll find the beat alive and well—on the Web.

Classical Music Online

http://www.crl.com/~virtualv/cmo

Classical Music Online is a resource dedicated exclusively to classical music. Each month, a "Hot new CD, Artist, Composer or Concert" is highlighted, and a collection of the Top 10 Classical Music Links is updated. Information on artists and composers is available, alongside a Classical CD Titles link, which comprises the latest titles, with indexes by composer, instrument, and title.

Site Details: Sound, Good Links
Load Time: 7 seconds

Classical Net Home Page

http://www.webcom.com/~music/welcome.html

"Classical music" is an umbrella term that includes numerous styles of music spanning 10 centuries. All this music is represented here. A search engine for classical composers can be used to access biographies, photographs, and historical background for each musician. Using the guide provided, site visitors can build a classical music collection by surveying a subjective compilation of the best compact disks of music from each era.

Load Time: 35 seconds

Classics World

✯✯✯✯✯

http://www.classicalmus.com

In addition to selling CDs by mail, Classics World offers much more for the music lover. Read about the life and times of classical composers. Search by name or period. Access audio and video clips in The Concert Hall, and discuss your musical passion on the Bulletin Boards. The Opera section is a delight. Learn the story behind famous operas—there are 40 opera synopses and vocalist biographies to read. In the Artist section, search by name or instrument and peruse your favorite tenor's concert schedule, biography, discography, and more.

Site Details:	Video, Sound, Large Graphics
Load Time:	27 seconds

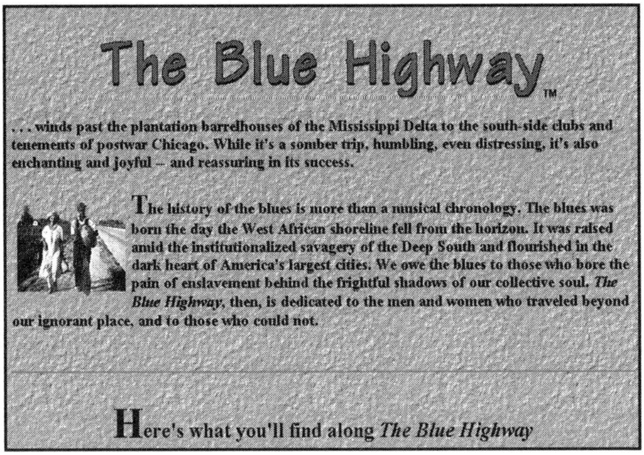

Blue Highway

http://www.vivanet.com/~blues

This is your ticket to the blues. Users will find a wealth of tributes to both living and deceased blues legends, men like Robert Johnson, W.C. Handy, Willie Dixon, and Albert King. Travel down Route 60 to the Mississippi Delta for essays and blues history; listen in on the chats about musicians and their music. Radio listings and links to retail products are also available. What are the current top 15 blues hits? Find this, and more, here.

Site Details:	Large Graphics, Good Links, Shopping
Load Time:	23 seconds

House of Blues

http://underground.net/HOB

Click on the Unity through Diversity link and travel to the world famous House of Blues. With venues in Los Angeles, New Orleans, and Harvard Square, the House of Blues attracts world-class musicians and celebrities. For schedules and information on who is playing where and when, just select a city and an artist. This Web site is phenomenal—enhanced by cutting-edge technology, it contains virtual reality movie clips and real time animation. It is an absolute must for computer users who love blues music and appreciate excellent Internet programming.

Site Details: Video, Sound, Good Links, Shopping

Load Time: 33 seconds

Jazz Improvisation

http://gopher.adp.wisc.edu:80/jazz

Materials from a jazz improvisation class at the University of Wisconsin provide both a wonderful introduction and a thorough examination of many aspects of performance, rhythm, style, harmony, and melody. Jazz/blues resources throughout the Net are listed, as well as pop/commercial, and other educational sites. Photos are included. Some jazz audio clips are available for those with the required download capabilities.

Site Details: Sound, Large Graphics, Good Links

Load Time: 26 seconds

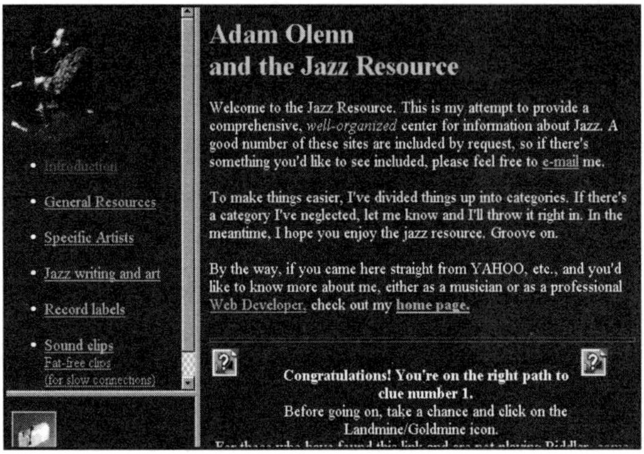

Jazz Resource

http://darwin.clas.virginia.edu/~aro2b/jazz_resource.html

This Jazz resource is packed to the rafters with the sort of goodies Jazz lovers will savor. There are sound clips from Miles Davis's "So What," John Coltrane's "Giant Steps," and Charles Mingus's "Good-bye Porkpie Hat." Also featured are classic album covers, and links to other important Jazz storehouses on the Web. Jazz junkies, stop here, or you'll be "kind of blue."

Site Details:	Sound, Large Graphics, Good Links, Shopping
Load Time:	2 seconds

Country Connection

http://digiserve.com/country

Do you want to know all there is to know about George Strait or the Judds? This Web site is dedicated to a comprehensive coverage of the country music world. From the Country Countdown USA to artist listings, Country Connection will provide hours of entertaining and informative browsing. Check out the online magazine, Cowpie News, or produce your own country song from Dr. Mellow's country song generator. Sound clips, song lyrics, and 80 image links are offered.

Site Details:	Sound, Large Graphics, Good Links, Shopping
Load Time:	20 seconds

Internet Beatles Album

http://www.primenet.com/~dhaber/beatles.html

Beatlemania is rekindled at the Internet Beatles Album. Diehard fans will love its collection of rareties and interesting tidbits. In addition to discographies, song lyrics, and member biographies, this site has a wonderful collection of RealAudio sound files and interview clips. Listen to Yoko Ono comment on art students and John Lennon. Examine the photo gallery of John, Paul, George, and Ringo. Fans will also be able to get background information on manager Brian Epstein, and Pete Best, the drummer who left the band before the Beatles became international superstars.

Site Details: Sound, Large Graphics, Good Links

Load Time: 30 seconds

MTV Online

http://mtv.com

The party continues at MTV Online with music, politics, television, and animation entertainment. The site is filled with great graphics and contains sound clips, bios, and album releases from hot bands. You'll find comic strips from Beavis & Butthead, The Maxx, Aeon Flux, and The Head. The Week in Rock with Kurt Loder takes rockers on an irreverent romp through music stories and celebrity snapshots.

Site Details:	Animation, Real Audio, Video, Sound, Large Graphics, Good Links, Shopping
Load Time:	102 seconds

Rockhall.com

http://www.rockhall.com/index.html

This is the Web site for the Rock and Roll Hall of Fame Museum. Rock aficionados can browse the Top 500 Song list, get rock news, join a rockhall forum, and even win free stuff. Curious kids can get a look at geezer rock.

Site Details:	Video, Sound, Shopping
Load Time:	28 seconds

Rocktropolis

http://underground.net/Rocktropolis

Take a unique journey through the dark and unknown streets of Rocktropolis. This expansive and aesthetically pleasing site illuminates music and concert events with the World Internet Live Music Archive, a comprehensive listing of more than 3,300 clubs in over 800 cities. Leading surfers through the streets of Rocktropolis, the site allows browsers to check out any number of shops, including the Rock Shop, Pentagon CD and Tapes, and the Chat Room. Users will find information on current movies and other links to the entertainment world.

Site Details: Sound, Large Graphics, Good Links, Shopping

Load Time: 45 seconds

RockWeb Interactive

http://www.rock.net/rwi

RockWeb Interactive is a music resource that features rock bands from around the world. You'll want to try out a sound clip or two from the new music section, or enjoy some of your tried-and-true favorites. RealAudio allows users to sample the music, which ranges from soulful to hard rock. Photos, graphics, interviews, and more are available at this cutting-edge site.

Site Details: Animation, Real Audio, Sound, Large Graphics, Good Links

Load Time: 6 seconds

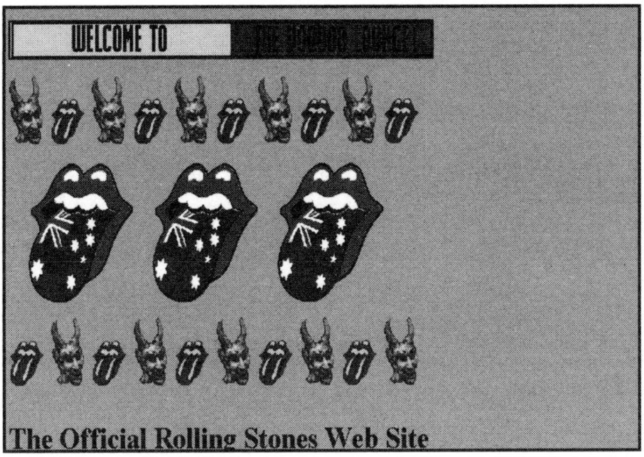

Rolling Stones

http://www.stones.com

Hang out with the Stones at the official Rolling Stones Web site and enjoy photos of the band, RealAudio songs, and a sampling of interviews and reviews. Listen to two-minute excerpts from songs taped in Toronto, Foxboro, or Dallas live concerts. Visitors to the site can participate in a collective effort to write some Rolling Stone-based fiction. Add on to an existing story, or start one of your own. Want to catch the Stones in concert? Check here for a schedule of tour dates and towns.

Site Details:	Video, Sound, Large Graphics, Good Links
Load Time:	45 seconds

BLAM!—The Big List of Artists and Music!

★★★★★

http://www.primenet.com/~virogen/blam!.html

The Big List of Artists and Music page is appropriately named. In addition to general music resources like links to major-label home pages, and information about styles such as "techno" and "progressive rock," the page houses an epic list of popular bands' home page links. Sites representing bands ranging from Alice In Chains to Machines of Loving Grace to ZZ Top can be accessed at BLAM!

Site Details:	Sound, Good Links
Load Time:	39 seconds

Categories of Music Links

★★★★★

http://orpheus.ucsd.edu/harmony/

This site catalogs over 750 music links. Major headings include Artists, Classical, Cultures, Discographies, Events, Instruments, Jazz, Magazines, Radio stations, Studios, and Styles. You'll find links to Atlantic Records, Motown, Polygram, Sony, and other major labels. Wondering what acid jazz is? You'll find the answer here.

Site Details:	Sound, Good Links
Load Time:	5 seconds

Guitar.Net

http://www.netcentral.net/guitar/index.html

Guitar players of every ability level will find useful resources here, including OLGA, the Online Guitar Archive, where users can access words and music in both chord and tablature format. Beginners can sharpen skills with the Chord of the Week feature, with a complete description, diagram with tablature, and audio clip. Abe Wechter, an acoustic guitar maker, answers questions in Ask the Guitar Maker.

Site Details: Sound, Large Graphics

Load Time: 54 seconds

HitsWorld

✯✯✯✯✯

http://www.hitsworld.com/

Find links to *Billboard's* music charts, Nielson's TV ratings, Rick Dees's Weekly Top 10, and Casey Kasem's Top 40, *Cash Box* charts, and more, here on the Hitlist. Rate your favorite album, or tell HOMR Recommendation Service what albums you like, and receive a list of recommendations. Play Music Wars or Name That Tune.

Site Details:	Sound, Good Links
Load Time:	44 seconds

IndieWeb

http://www.forfood.com/~indieweb/index.html

IndieWeb is a page devoted to the coolest independent records labels and fanzines. This work-in-progress site currently offers links to Flipside, Dionysus, Hell Yeah, No-Fi, Last Resort, Bomp, Voxx, Alive Records, and more. Check on new releases, tour schedules, catalogs, and other stuff from your favorite indie label. IndieWeb is also building a D.I.Y. section where people can exchange information on the mechanics of manufacturing and distribution, booking, touring, and other aspects of the indie scene. A good site that's getting better for adventurous music tastes.

Site Details: Sound, Large Graphics, Good Links

Load Time: 15 seconds

IUMA Home Page

http://www.iuma.com/artist_01.html

IUMA (Internet Underground Music Archive) is a compendium of alternative music from around the world. The design here is retro and very clever. Users can take a virtual world tour of the cutting edge of alternative music and order groovy merchandise and the music of those bands in the archive.

Site Details: Sound, Large Graphics, Shopping

Load Time: 101 seconds

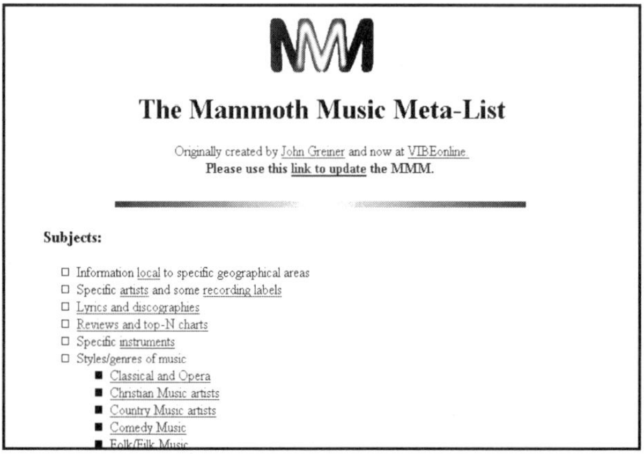

Mammoth Music Meta-List

http://www.pathfinder.com/@@z13BZQAAAAAADjL/vibe/mmm/music.html

For a huge index of links to music resources on the Web, head over to this Web site. Users can look up sites by geographic area (local music), artist, recording label, musical instrument, radio station or show, or festival. This index also includes lyrics and discographies; reviews and charts; music schools, libraries, and research; and music services such as e-zines. Search for music by genre or style—from Classical and Opera to Morris Dancing, from Comedy Music to Native American Music. The Archive section of this index features scores, catalogs, newsgroups, and much more.

Site Details: Good Links
Load Time: 12 seconds

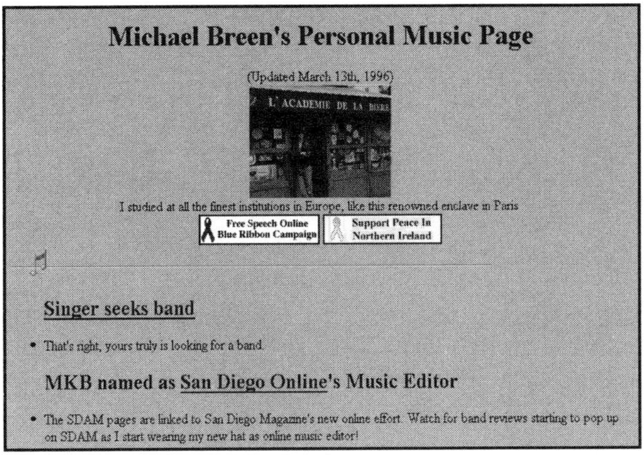

Michael Breen's Music Page

http://orpheus.ucsd.edu/webmaster/music.html

Maintained by a music enthusiast, the Music Harmony List contains over 2,000 listings covering such topics as Artists, Classical, Jazz, Styles, Music Studios, and Magazines. Within each category are more categories. Selecting Solo Industry Artists brought up a large list of such performers as Paula Abdul, Eric Clapton, Jackson Browne, Elvis Costello, and Elvis Presley. The Classical section is divided into Composer, Artist, and General sections. Some of these links include the Opera Schedule Server, classical CD catalogs, Early Music FAQs, and more.

Site Details: Good Links
Load Time: 14 seconds

SonicNet

★★★★★

http://www.realaudio.com/CGI-bin/nph-redirect.cgi?100059

SonicNet captures the attention of the weary Web surfer with a home page that features continually changing images. RealAudio software allows users to hear a soundtrack presented on the home page or full-length songs from a selection of music by alternative bands. SonicNet also provides video from several music festivals, including Lollapalooza and the Warped tour.

Site Details: Real Audio, Video, Sound, Large Graphics, Good Links

Load Time: 61 seconds

Ultimate Band List

★★★★★

http://198.147.111.1/WWWoM/ubl/ubl.shtml

Portions of this site are rich with information on current punk and underground bands and albums, and this page offers a huge number of excellent links to the vast Web Wide World of Music, and many other top-notch resource sites (American Directory, Infinite Zero, Ventrue, Onion, Too Pure). There are contests, online chats, polls, forums, reviews, graphics, and a periodicals section called News-Stand. Parts of the site are quite sketchy, non-existent, or ostensibly anti-social.

Site Details: Sound, Large Graphics, Good Links

Load Time: 13 seconds

VIBE Online

★★★★★

http://www.pathfinder.com/vibe

This is the online version of *VIBE*, the hip-hop- and rap oriented magazine. It offers visitors real audio on VIBEline, QuickTime music video clips on VIBEvideo, feature stories, regular departments, VIBE promos, and Killer Apps. There are new album reviews, style reviews, comments on the American political scene, and more. Users interested in hip-hop culture and related information should check out VIBE online.

Site Details:	Real Audio, Video, Sound, Large Graphics, Good Links
Load Time:	29 seconds

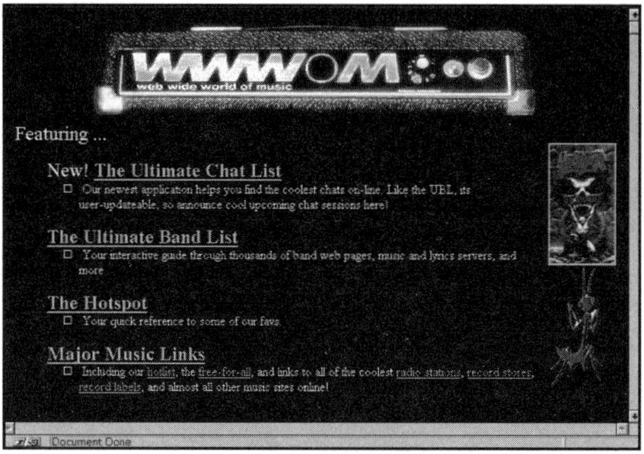

Web Wide World of Music

★★★★★

http://american.recordings.com/wwwofmusic/index.html

The Web Wide World of Music is a cool music resource on the Web. Not only can you keep in touch with the latest in music, but there are plenty of links to other interesting experiences on the vast Web. Provided here are The Ultimate Band List, the Web's largest interactive list of music links; the Hotspot, a quick reference to music and other fun places; and Major Music Links to the coolest radio stations, record stores, record labels, reviews, and almost all other online music sites. This is one for your hotlist.

Site Details:	Real Audio, Large Graphics, Good Links, Shopping
Load Time:	42 seconds

Online News

In the 1700s, sending a letter to America required a messenger to travel by ship for weeks across the Atlantic. Whether the message carried personal news or the announcement of the death of a king, the letter could be delivered no faster. In 1860 America, Pony Express riders carried news from Missouri to Sacramento in a mere 10 days. The invention of the telegraph reduced the wait to the time it took the operator to transcribe the message.

Radio, telephone, television, and satellite technologies changed the way the world communicates. Today news is received practically as soon as it happens.

The Internet adds a new dimension to communication: control. Instead of waiting for the evening news, the 7 a.m. radio broadcast, or the morning paper, you can gather the information you want, when you want it.

Follow the heat of the stock market or the pulse of American politics with **Nando Times.** Transcripts of breaking news, bulletins, commentary, and economic analysis is yours for the asking. Skim the headlines with **Trib.comNews** or **USA Today**. You'll find QuickTime footage and Real Audio broadcasts from **ABC**, **NBC**, **CBS**, **CNN**—you name it, the Web has it.

Sites & Sounds: ABC News Reports

★★★★★

http://www.prognet.com/contentp/abc.html

For world news around the clock broadcast in RealAudio every 15 minutes, tune this sub-page of the American Broadcasting Corporation site. Visitors can hear the Peter Jennings Journal, Johnny Holliday Sports, and read feature articles.

Site Details: Animation, Real Audio, Sound, Good Links

Load Time: 22 seconds

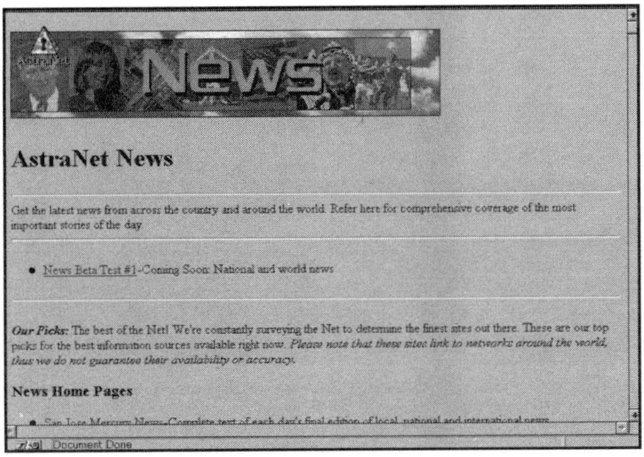

AstraNet News Home Page

http://www.astranet.com/newstp1.html

The AstraNet News page offers a selection of the latest news from some of the best and most comprehensive resources on the Web. This one-stop shop for news has links to national, world, and special interest news services, including White House daily summaries, GNN's I-Media Center, Time-Warner, the *San Jose Mercury News*, *Der Spiegel*, and hundreds more.

Site Details: Good Links
Load Time: 38 seconds

BBC

✯✯✯✯✯

http://www.bbcnc.org.uk/

Visitors are afforded a glimpse into the vast world of the London-based British Broadcasting Corp., a radio/TV giant employing some 30,000 people worldwide. Follow the links to the "BeeB" international radio, education, television, and Internet resources. Radio archives and program schedules are offered, as well as sessions on music, art, technology, science, and women's issues. The television schedules feature programming on the subjects of consumer affairs, drama, and weather. BBC Education Online presents resources for primary, secondary, and adult education.

Site Details:	Large Graphics, Good Links
Load Time:	25 seconds

CBC

✯✯✯✯✯

http://www.cbc.ca

The Canadian Broadcast Corporation's page presents television and radio programming information and news services in French and English. Get the latest on the '96 TV shows and times, or browse the video vault for historic footage. A link is provided that contains information on CBC celebrity biographies and pictures. Newslink offers daily breaking stories and newsreels.

Site Details:	Sound, Large Graphics, Good Links
Load Time:	36 seconds

CBS News: UTTMLink

★★★★★

http://uttm.com

The multimedia nature of the Web is put to good use by UTTMLink, CBS News' "up to the minute" online presence. Download a RealTime Video player for news footage, listen to RealAudio reports of world news, or read the day's headlines. A "Campaign 96" section profiles the candidates and the polls, reports on funding, delegates, and strategies. The site also focuses on the latest Internet and CD-ROM developments, as well as movie reviews, women's health reports, parenting, and news from space. Links bring the visitor to reporters' resources or a complete list of CBS affiliates.

Site Details:	Video, Sound, Large Graphics, Good Links
Load Time:	43 seconds

CNN Interactive

✯✯✯✯✯

http://www.cnn.com

The CNN Interactive home page keeps users in touch with daily news, entertainment, weather, sports, politics, technology, and health. The top sheet gives headline world news and QuickTime footage of the stories on Bosnia or shuttle touchdown. CNN offers a search engine with which users may specialize their search for daily news. Link to CNN On-Air to locate program information, or browse through the CNN Environment page to get an update on topics like tiger poaching or pollution problems in Lake Tahoe. Before leaving, check out stock quotes and prices at the closing bell on Wall Street.

Site Details:	Video, Sound, Large Graphics, Good Links
Load Time:	33 seconds

CReAte Your Own Newspaper

✯✯✯✯✯

http://crayon.net/

Have you ever wanted to publish your own newspaper? Do you find it too time-consuming to wade through the daily paper? If so, explore this creative home page, which manages news sources on the Web. Simply follow the directions and you can create your own periodical from the hundreds of links to news resources provided here. Not only is this page informative, it is a fun alternative for getting the news.

Site Details:	Large Graphics, Good Links
Load Time:	17 seconds

Nando Times

http://www.nando.net/nt/nando.cgi

This online newspaper provides visitors with everything but the Sunday coupons. Sections covering World, Politics, Nation, and Sports news are all readily accessible, and each delves deep to bring the most important issues to the screen. The Top Story is featured on the home page, in addition to access to low-graphics and Java versions of the Times. Additional areas include Weather, Business, Health & Science, and Entertainment.

Site Details:	Large Graphics, Good Links, Shopping
Load Time:	151 seconds

NBC News

✯✯✯✯✯

http://www.nbc.com/news/index.html

The home page for NBC News offers the online version of the news of the day plus business and financial news, weather, sports and feature stories on the Web. Visitors to this page can get the home pages of NBC's *Sunrise*, *Today*, *Nightly News*, *Dateline*, *Nightside*, *Meet the Press*, *Weekend Today*, and *Weekend Nightly*. This page also has special reports, the daily TV schedule, and sneak previews of new programs.

Site Details: Large Graphics, Good Links
Load Time: 42 seconds

Newspaper Services Available on the Internet

✯✯✯✯✯

http://mfginfo.com/htm/newspapers.htm

The easy and instantaneous access to newspapers published in towns across America and the world is one the best uses of the Web. Cultivating a global attitude becomes possible when reading the events and the concerns of our neighbors in South Africa, Australia, or Scotland, or any state in the U.S. Those who have left their home countries can keep in touch in Chinese, Polish, or Italian language newspapers.

Site Details: Good Links
Load Time: 9 seconds

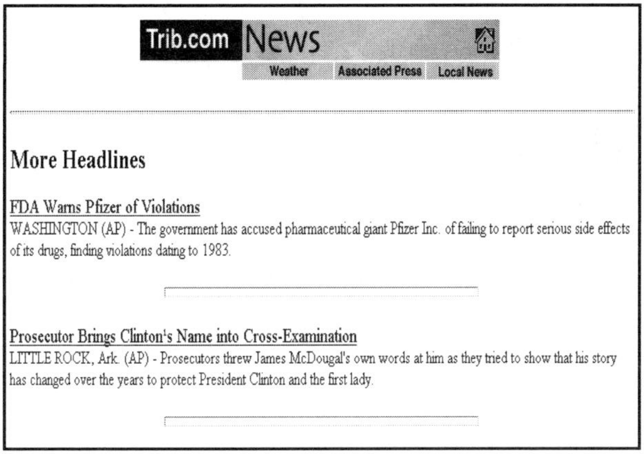

Trib.com News

http://www1.trib.com/NEWS

For the latest news, try Trib.com. Headlines from Associated Press, Reuters, the *New York Times*, and the Electronic Newsstand are available. Hear ABC Radio News, CNN, and NPR News with RealAudio. In addition to national news, read news from sources all over the world, in English. Access the BBC, Tass (the Russian news agency), African, Japanese, Australian, and Canadian news sources.

Site Details:	Real Audio, Sound, Good Links
Load Time:	21 seconds

USA Today

★★★★★

http://www.usatoday.com/

The newspaper that specializes in short news summaries, *USA Today*, is online here. Users will find headline stories in five categories: News, Sports, Weather, Money, and Life. Other features include a daily snapshot, a feedback option, and online surveys. Colorful graphics and easy navigation make this site a winner.

Site Details: Large Graphics, Good Links
Load Time: 30 seconds

Politics

The American political system has served as a model of democracy the world over. Envied for its ideals of individual liberty and communal ethics, a democratic society thrives only with the involvement and participation of its members. With its revolutionary technology, the Internet recaptures the immediacy, personal relevance, and direct communication of the time-honored town meeting essential to the democratic process.

As did the revolutionaries who founded this nation, the voices on the Web speak with passion on a range of political issues: the deficit, health care, crime, welfare, housing, fairness, taxes, immigration, jobs, race, civil rights, and individual liberty. The perspectives range from the liberal—**The Progressive Directory** and **The Mojo Wire**—to the conservative—The Heritage Foundation, the NRA, and the Christian Coalition represented through links at **Campaign Central** and the **Jefferson Project**. Two prominent organizations of the political mainstream, **The Republican National Committee** and **The Democratic National Committee,** have embraced the Web and are online in force, side-by-side with outsiders and even fringe groups. Serious debate, research, and campaigning exist alongside a healthy dose of political humor and satire.

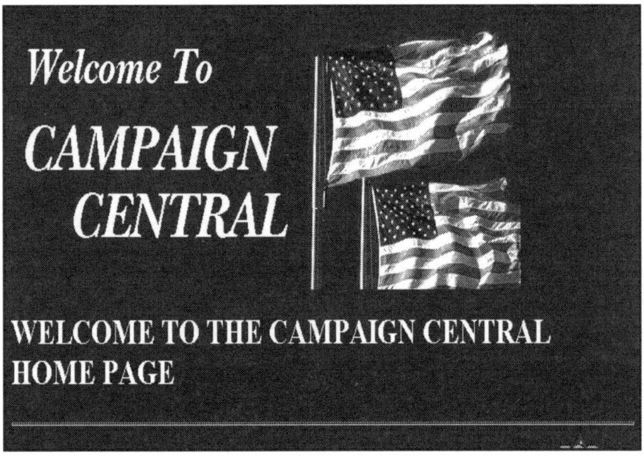

Campaign Central

★★★★★

http://www.clark.net/ccentral

This Web site promises to be one of the most comprehensive political sites on the Web. At last review, the site offered links to 1996 Presidential Campaigns, party organizations and non-profit agencies, government agency links, and top political stories for each calendar day. Follow a specific candidate with updated news briefs, voter education data, and background information.

Site Details: Large Graphics, Good Links
Load Time: 53 seconds

Democratic National Committee

http://www.democrats.org

The Democratic National Committee page offers visitors numerous views, news, and topical events connected with the Democratic Party. Many of the presentations are humorous, while others are made interesting through the use of RealAudio (with President Clinton himself), cartoons, and full color photos. Users can become a member of the Democratic National Committee using an online form, or play a game of Hangman with a New(t) Twist. Links to other politically-oriented sites are provided.

Site Details: Real Audio, Video, Sound, Large Graphics, Good Links

Load Time: 42 seconds

Human Rights Resources

☆☆☆☆☆

http://www.traveller.com/~hrweb/resource.html

This site is a comprehensive assortment of human rights resources and organizations. A subpage of Human Rights Web, it is organized geographically according to international and regional/national resources. Users will find newsgroups, government sites, and a list of organizations, including the Freedom House, Amnesty International, Human Rights Watch, and the PEN International Writer's Union. Other resources include links to PeaceNet and the Dred Scott Society home page. Go to the home page for additional human rights information.

Site Details: Good Links
Load Time: 19 seconds

Jefferson Project

☆☆☆☆☆

http://www.stardot.com/jefferson

The Jefferson Project offers comprehensive information about politics and government. The page is organized according to liberal, conservative, and radical political ideologies. There is information about politicians, political humor, and activism. Learn more about political watchdogs, human rights issues, and environmental politics.

Site Details: Good Links
Load Time: 19 seconds

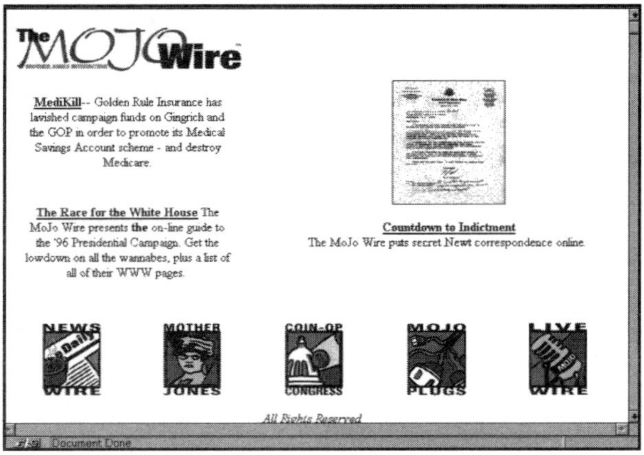

Mother Jones Interactive--The Mojo Wire

http://mojones.com/motherjones.html

The MoJo Wire is the latest offering from "Mother Jones," a magazine for independent thinkers. Explore the archive of past issues which contain thought-provoking and unexpect"ed articles like "The Best Congress Money Can Buy" and Find Out Who Gave What To Whom." Check in for a chat session with Live Wire.

Site Details: Sound, Large Graphics, Good Links

Load Time: 28 seconds

Political Scientist's Guide To the Internet

✯✯✯✯✯

http://www.trincoll.edu/pols/home.html

You don't have to be a political scientist to find this site useful. Students, gadflies, and citizens who want to be well-informed can find research archives, issue-oriented links such as gun control and political party information. Guides to international thinktanks, primary source documents, and governmental agencies provide up-to-date information.

Site Details:	Good Links
Load Time:	101 seconds

Progressive Directory

✯✯✯✯✯

http://www.igc.apc.org

The Institute for Global Communications presents this Web gateway to progressive and environmental resources. Link to PeaceNet, EcoNet, ConflictNet, LaborNet, and WomensNet. Users may network, research, and share information via the Internet. Find out the latest on acid rain, animal rights, toxic waste, endangered species, and other global issues. This site is easy to navigate and contains valuable information.

Site Details:	Good Links
Load Time:	15 seconds

Vote Smart Web

http://www.vote-smart.org

Vote Smart Web offers an excellent online resource for political information. From information about current elections to extensive coverage of voter registration, this page helps the voter make educated decisions. Reference resources like Historical Documents and How the U.S. Government Works are available, along with political humor links and information on how to become a member of this nonprofit organization.

Site Details:	Sound, Large Graphics, Good Links
Load Time:	32 seconds

Republican National Committee

http://www.realaudio.com/CGI-bin/nph-redirect.cgi?100167

The Republican National Committee's home page is designed as a virtual town. Users can click on the Post Office, Newsstand, School, Headquarters, and several other virtual venues to learn about the party and the committee. This is a good political resource, as well as a fun site to visit.

Site Details: Real Audio, Video, Sound, Large Graphics, Good Links, Shopping

Load Time: 46 seconds

Rock The Vote

HTTP://www.rockthevote.org/

Rock the Vote is an organization of young people devoted to the idea of participation in government. The Web site is a nonpartisan presentation of current political issues facing the nation. From health care reform to teen pregnancy to crime, the organization strives to inform. Young people can use the site to learn about the political issues surrounding substance abuse, STDs, violence, and mental health. Get informed and vote!

Site Details: Large Graphics, Good Links, Shopping

Load Time: 95 seconds

Reference

The neighborhood library holds distinct memories for us all—the smooth slide of card catalog drawers, unending aisles of bookshelves and hushed voices from across the room. Today, banks of computer screens replace card catalogs, microfiche files replace magazine bins, and touch-sensitive directory screens replace the information desk. In this progression, an enormous network of online information now reaches beyond the doors of the library into our homes, offices, schools and research labs.

The Internet houses the library of all libraries. Anything you might hope to find in the reference section of a library, you will certainly find on the Internet. World demographics, climates, maps and geographical data are situated within the voluminous pages of the **CIA World Factbook**. Download a hardcopy of your favorite play from the **Complete Works of William Shakespeare** or double-check your composition style at the **Elements of Style** by William Strunk. Online **Dictionaries** will keep your documents well spelled and the **Language Guide** can help with translations, interpretations, and alphabets for over 100 languages. For the insatiably curious, **Planet Earth Home Page** leads visitors through a multimedia tour of science, history, government, and education presentations. For research, discovery and play, the Web is well worth the visit.

Alex: A Catalog of Electronic Texts on the Internet

http://www.lib.ncsu.edu/stacks/alex-index.html

Alex is an enormous collection of books available over the Internet in electronic form. Visitors can read the plays of Aristophanes, the novels of Jane Austen, and the poetry of Denise Levertov. Spanning centuries and continents, the collection includes Moliere in French and "Sir Gawayne and the Grene Knight" in Middle English.

Load Time: 18 seconds

American Bar Association Network

http://www.abanet.org

The ABA's home page provides a wealth of information regarding the legal profession and the organization itself. General information, details on ABA structure, the ABA Journal, and legal news are all here. The home page also features the ABA Store, which offers publications, video tapes, and periodicals. ABA events are listed, along with links to other law-related pages on the Web.

Site Details: Large Graphics, Good Links, Shopping

Load Time: 39 seconds

Bartlett's Familiar Quotations

http://www.columbia.edu/~svl2/bartlett

Great for anyone at a loss for words, Bartlett's provides the visitor with some of the world's most famous quotes from its alphabetical and chronological list of classical writers and authors including Geoffrey Chaucer, Sir Walter Raleigh, and Shakespeare. Users may insert a word in the search engine to find a plethora of quotes.

Site Details: Good Links
Load Time: 12 seconds

Bill's Library

✯✯✯✯✯

http://www.io.org/~jgcom/library.htm

Novelists, poets, essayists, and other literary aficionados will love this site. It's the mother of literary indexes, providing links to both popular and obscure resources on the Web. You'll find magazines, e-zines, novel, poems, and authors, from *The Far Side* to Omar Khayyam, from *The Decameron* to the *New Republic.*

Site Details: Good Links
Load Time: 34 seconds

British Library Portico

✯✯✯✯✯

http://portico.bl.uk

Cheaper than a trip to Britain, the British Library Portico is a superb site for scholars. It provides access to the British Library's resources, as well as European libraries. Visitors will find a link to CERL, the Consortium of European Research Libraries, and Gabriel, the Gateway to Europe's National Libraries. In addition, there are links to the Portico Guide to Resources on the World Wide Web, a guide with a distinctly European slant, as well as the UK Government Information Service, the BBC and The Electronic Telegraph.

Site Details: Good Links
Load Time: 45 seconds

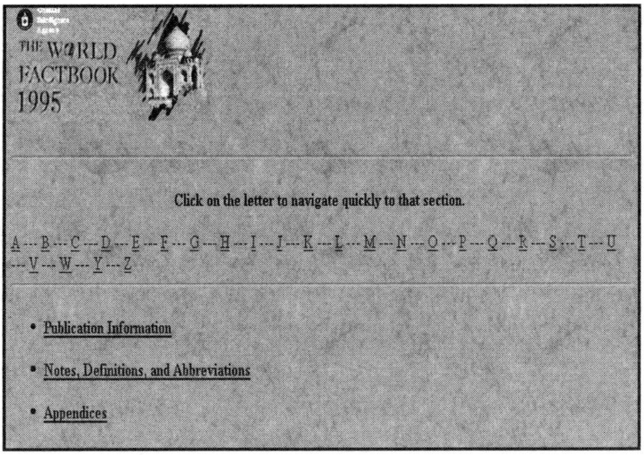

CIA World Factbook

http://www.odci.gov/cia/publications/95fact/index.html

Published annually, the CIA World Factbook is an encyclopedia of facts about the countries of the world. The site provides an invaluable guide for geographic information. Click on a country and you will be offered a map of the area, land boundaries, climate, terrain, natural resources, and demographics. Also offered are details on the agencies that contributed to the resources found here, as well as a key to abbreviations and definitions of terms used within the Web pages.

Site Details: Good Links
Load Time: 163 seconds

Classics Archive

http://the-tech.mit.edu/Classics/index.html

This compilation of Greek and Roman texts is searchable by author, title, date, or translator. New features of the page include a commentary area, suitable for discussion of the various works, and information segments on the author. Many well-known works, including Plato's *Republic*, Virgil's *Aeneid*, and *The Prince* by Machiavelli, are contained here.

Site Details: Good Links
Load Time: 23 seconds

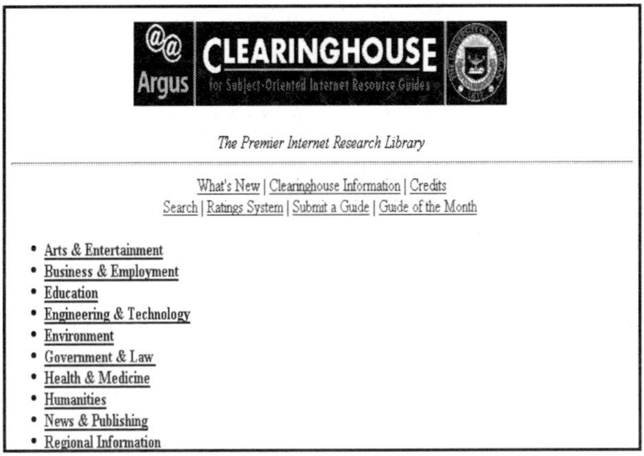

Clearinghouse for Subject-Oriented Internet Resource Guides

http://www.lib.umich.edu/chhome.html

The Clearinghouse is a popular Internet resource. All the Clearinghouse guides are created and maintained by independent Web citizens who have an interest in repackaging the Internet's information in useful ways and in sharing their results with others. This great site presents an alphabetized index to information on virtually every subject including education, humanities, the environment, and science.

Site Details: Good Links
Load Time: 7 seconds

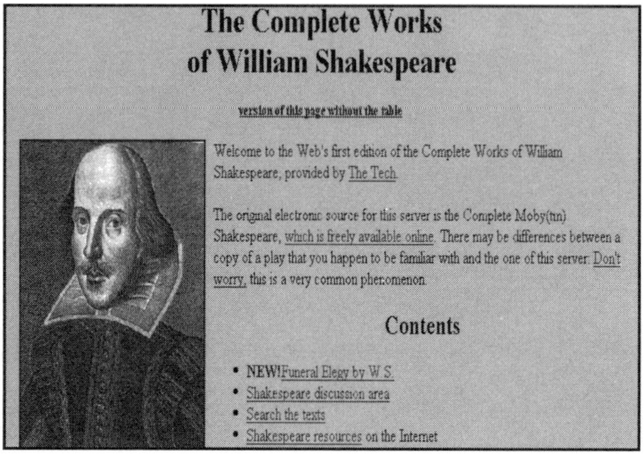

Complete Works of William Shakespeare

http://the-tech.mit.edu:80/Shakespeare/works.html

The title says it all. But there is more—the entire works of the Bard are in hypertext—searchable, annotated, and categorized. There are links to FAQs, a glossary, related resources on the Internet, and Bartlett's Shakespearean quotations, to name a few. Students, teachers, and readers everywhere should bookmark this site for easy access to the greatest works in world literature.

Site Details: Large Graphics, Good Links
Load Time: 21 seconds

Dictionaries

http://math-www.uni-paderborn.de/HTML/Dictionaries.html

This is a wonderful resource for definitions in a number of languages. You'll find translation dictionaries for German, American English, and Technical English. There is a Thesaurus, Foreign Language for Travelers, and even a Hacker's Dictionary. Some references are immediate, others are gopher files. This is a great site to bookmark.

Site Details: Good Links
Load Time: 57 seconds

Elements of Style, Strunk & White

http://www.cc.columbia.edu:80/acis/bartleby/strunk

"Elements of Style" has long been the definitive reference book for writers. Issues of language, punctuation, word usage, and composition are clearly explained by author William Strunk, Jr. The online version of "Elements of Style" is as thorough and user-friendly as the hard copy. Even in cyberspace, style is important.

Load Time: 4 seconds

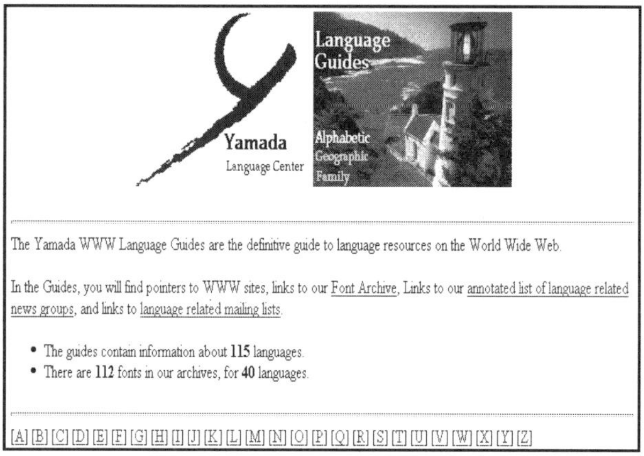

Language Guides

http://babel.uoregon.edu/yamada/guides.html

Created by the Yamada Language Center, this page provides access to language sites throughout the Web. Over 103 languages are included, with over 100 different font capabilities. Language-related new groups are listed. Languages can be accessed by alphabet, family, or geography. Check out What's New to see what fonts and languages have been added. There is a link to the Language Interactive Guide as well.

Site Details: Sound, Good Links
Load Time: 56 seconds

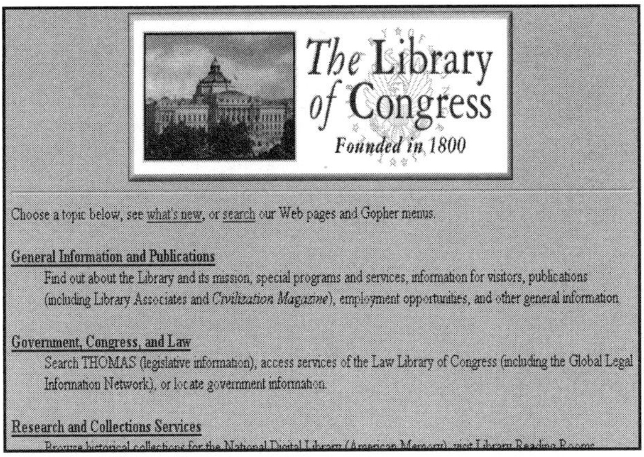

Library of Congress

http://lcweb.loc.gov

The Library of Congress site connects browsers to a vast maze of publications, searchable databases, and information about, well, everything—it's the Library of Congress, after all. Besides the wealth of information available through the Library's resources, it includes a wide-ranging selection of links. Search and view items from the Library's digitized historical collections, or browse its many electronic exhibits. The Newspaper and Current Periodical Room is worth special notice for its broad selection of newspapers and magazines.

Site Details:	Large Graphics, Good Links
Load Time:	23 seconds

Maps

http://www.cco.caltech.edu/~salmon/maps.html

Lost? Not for long. Visitors will find a map here for just about everything except Gulliver's travels. If you are looking for a hard-to-find map, such as the Galapagos Islands or the Beijing subway, or in need of something more domestic, like a map of Disneyland, earthquake maps of California, or the gargoyles of Duke University, turn your compass in the direction of this home page.

Site Details: Large Graphics, Good Links
Load Time: 5 seconds

National Archives Online Exhibit Hall

http://www.nara.gov/exhall/exhibits.html

Students will enjoy browsing the historic documents exhibited in the National Archives Online Exhibit Hall. The Declaration of Independence, The Constitution, and The Bill of Rights are displayed, along with high-resolution JPEG images of the original pages of the documents. Visitors can read transcriptions of the complete texts, and browse various articles by scholars discussing the history of and issues relevant to these historic documents. In addition, there are exhibits of modern artifacts, including the Japanese surrender document and posters from World War II.

Site Details: Video, Sound, Large Graphics, Good Links
Load Time: 15 seconds

On-Line Reference Works

http://www.cs.cmu.edu/Web/references.html

Here is a virtual reference shelf at your fingertips. Webster's Dictionaries, technical dictionaries, and foreign language dictionaries are available. Put your finger on that elusive word in a searchable Roget's Thesaurus, and the pithy quote in Bartlett's. The site lists a wealth of geographical resources including the U.S. Gazetteer, U.S. Census Data, and a currency converter.

Site Details:	Good Links
Load Time:	4 seconds

Planet Earth Home Page

http://www.nosc.mil/planet_earth/info.html

The Planet Earth Home Page (PEHP) is a virtual library, presently consisting of 13 rooms, each room containing 17 shelves of related information. Navigating the library can be done six different ways: by floorplan image map; by comprehensive image map; by text–only list; by search engine; alphabetically through HTML files and counters; and by popularity. This home page assembles thousands of Web resources for multimedia travels in science, history, government, education, and much more.

Site Details:	Large Graphics, Good Links
Load Time:	25 seconds

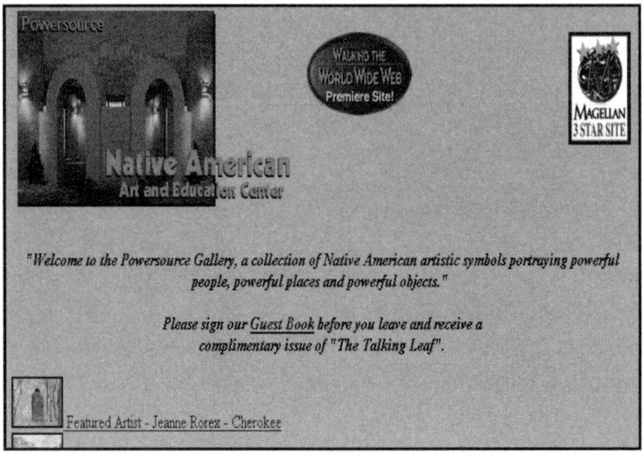

Powersource Native American Art & Education Center

http://www.powersource.com/powersource/gallery/default.html

Much more than an online gallery, the Powersource Native American Art & Education Center site features Native American Legends and Travel Guide, and Historical and Contemporary People of Power, such as Cochise, Chief Joseph, Sitting Bull, and Wilma Mankiller. This site includes reference guides to ceremonial dances and symbols of power. Users can follow interesting links to Native American-related subjects, such as The National Museum of the American Indian, A Guide to the Great Sioux Nation, the Indian Pueblo Cultural Center, and more.

Site Details:	Large Graphics, Good Links, Shopping
Load Time:	109 seconds

Project Bartleby—Columbia University

http://www.columbia.edu/~svl2

Offered by Columbia University, the Bartleby Project is currently one of the largest public collections of literature online, and is considered the finest example of public electronic publishing. Works by Walt Whitman, Robert Frost, and William Wordsworth are offered in their entirety. The project is named for the short story "Bartleby, The Scrivener" (1853), by Herman Melville, which is about a law copyist who was hired to transcribe full texts.

Site Details: Good Links
Load Time: 14 seconds

Publishing on the Web

http://www.cl.cam.ac.uk/users/gdr11/old-publish.html

This page contains useful information for anyone trying to publish on the Web. It includes information about using the Web, as well as how to add documents to the meta-libraries, searchable meta-indexes, and relevant subject indexes. There are links to a number of books about HTML and publishing on the Web.

Site Details: Good Links
Load Time: 15 seconds

United States of America

http://white.nosc.mil/states.html

Leave the car in the garage, cancel those plane reservations, and put away the encyclopedia. Users who want to know practically anything about the good ol' U.S.A. need only access this site. An overview of each of the 50 states, census and demographic data, maps, and a variety of related reference materials are included here. Details about travel, weather, geography, and more are provided—from the Atlantic to the Pacific, Canada to Mexico, and Alaska to Hawaii.

Site Details: Good Links
Load Time: 15 seconds

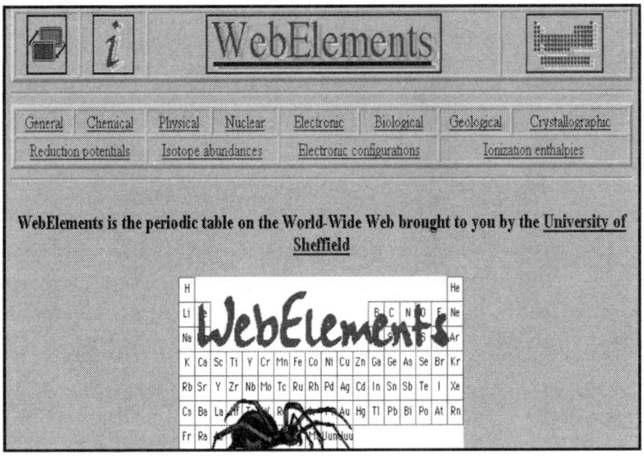

WebElements

http://www.shef.ac.uk/chemistry/web-elements/web-elements-home.html

This site contains a whopping 30-megabyte collection of 5,500 files about the periodic table. Different types of data on the elements are offered, from chemical to crystallographic, nuclear to biological. Also featured are reduction potentials, isotope abundances, electronic configurations, and ionization enthalpies for the elements. Clickable tables make it easy to find out the data for a particular element. Sponsored by the American Chemical Society, this site offers a huge number of links to other chemistry sites.

Site Details: Large Graphics, Good Links
Load Time: 71 seconds

Writing Resources

✯✯✯✯✯

http://www.missouri.edu/~wleric/writehelp.html

This page was created to assist writers who could use a little general guidance, advice, or inspiration. This master index provides pointers to resources such as online writing labs, writers' programs, clubs, book lists, playwriting and screenwriting resources, style guides, and reference material. It also links to the home pages of several renowned novelists and poets. A great general resource for writers, this page is one of the best sites to keep bookmarked.

Site Details: Good Links
Load Time: 14 seconds

WWW Virtual Library

✯✯✯✯✯

http://www.w3.org/hypertext/DataSources/bySubject/Overview.html

The WWW Virtual Library is a vast catalog of thousands of Web sites. A great research tool, its categories range from Aboriginal Studies and Aeronautics to Yeasts and Zoos. This Web database is staggering in scope and well worth examining, an excellent starting point for most online needs.

Site Details: Good Links
Load Time: 10 seconds

Religion

The Internet removes the constraints of time and distance to allow communities to form based on common interests. One major forum of common interest on the Web centers on religion and spirituality. Joining a community of like minds or learning about the world's religions has never been easier.

The Web offers numerous sites devoted to **Judaism**, **Christianity**, **Islam, Scientology** and others. Inspired writings from many religions can be found at the **World Scripture** site, while the **Christus Rex et Redemptor Mundi** page houses over 1,200 images from the Vatican Museum, the Sistine Chapel and architecture of ancient Rome. The **Electric Bodhidarma** covers Zen Buddhism, and **Tucker's Religious Resources,** while focusing on Roman Catholicism, has interesting links relating to all faiths. The **Christian Religion Resource Page** contains links to the many denominations of Christianity.

Those who want to learn more about the religions of the world will find many sites that offer comprehensive histories and practices. Those in search of fellowship with religious communities can find it on the Web.

A - Z of Jewish & Israel Related Resources

http://www.ort.org/anjy/a-z

A truly comprehensive resources of things Jewish, The A-Z of Jewish & Israel Related Resources provides links to sites such as a Chagall exhibit, Hebrew College's Academic Jewish Studies site, the American Jewish World Service, the Anne Frank Resource Package, the American Jewish Congress Online, and more.

Site Details:	Good Links
Load Time:	15 seconds

Christian Religion Resource Page

http://www.galstar.com/~rkjones/html/religion.html

To foster more informed discussions among Christians, this site provides information about numerous Christian denominations. Visitors may, for example, learn about the Jehovah's Witnesses, the United Pentecostal Church International, or the Seventh-Day Adventists. Also included are links to other religious resource lists, such as the World Council of Churches and the Christian Resource List. A hypertext Bible is also available. Anyone interested in doing scholarly Christian research will find this page useful.

Site Details:	Good Links
Load Time:	23 seconds

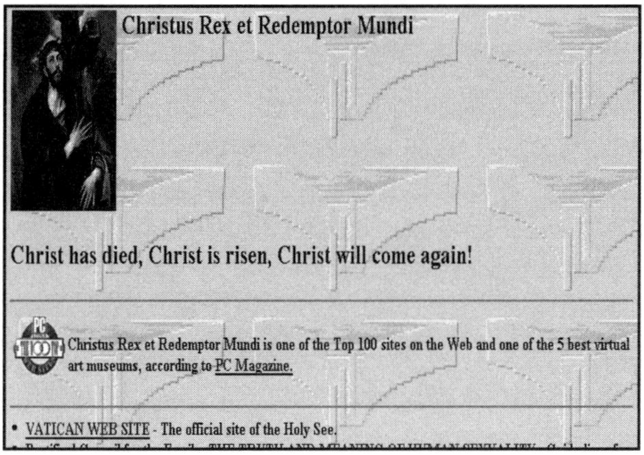

Christus Rex et Redemptor Mundi

★★★★★

http://www.christusrex.org

A major information resource for learning about the Vatican City, Pope John Paul II, or the art and architecture of the ancient city of Rome, this site contains over 1,200 images of the Vatican Museum, Sistine Chapel, and Vatican City. Visitors will find access to the Vatican Radio station, a worldwide tour of churches, and the complete text of speeches, homilies, quotes, and addresses delivered by His Supreme Holiness, Pope John Paul II.

Site Details: Large Graphics, Good Links
Load Time: 115 seconds

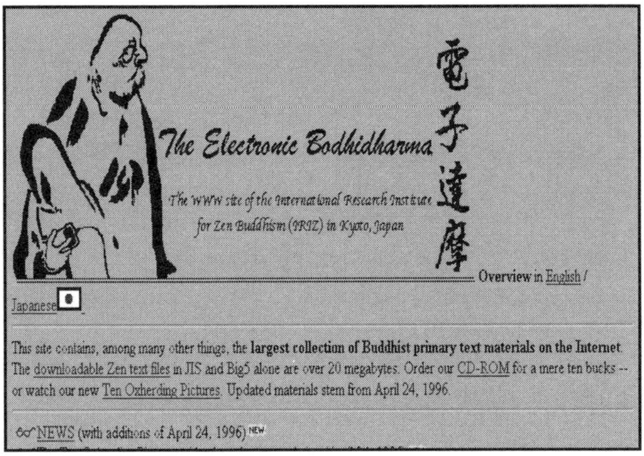

Electronic Bodhidarma

★★★★★

http://www.iijnet.or.jp/iriz/irizhtml/irizhome.htm

The International Research Institute of Zen Buddhism home page is a profound resource for the study of Zen, offering the largest collection of Buddhist primary texts on the Internet. Users of this site will find the Zen Knowledge Database, information on Chinese Zen masters, Zen stories, art, and specialized electronic tools—such as a 48,000 character Chinese database. This page will be of interest to people interested in religion, spirituality, meditation, or Asian Studies.

Site Details: Good Links, Shopping
Load Time: 5 seconds

Facets of Religion

http://www.biologie.uni-freiburg.de/~amueller/religion

Presented by the Web Virtual Library, the Facets of Religion home page is a repository of informational links to various world religions, including Christianity, Sikhism, Judaism, Buddhism, and Hinduism, among others. In addition there is general religious information and links to religious newsgroups.

Site Details: Good Links
Load Time: 76 seconds

Islam

http://www leland.stanford.edu/·-yusufali/islam/index.html

Here are revealed some splendid resources on the religion of Islam. This lucid exposition will take visitors on a journey through the history of the Islamic religion and culture. Pilgrims will find a thorough introduction, an Islamic glossary, dates of important events in Islamic history, access to the Shi'ite Encyclopedia, an overview of the Qur'an, and a list of Islamic laws, among many other resources. The page is a mix of insightful observations and factual presentations.

Site Details: Good Links
Load Time: 14 seconds

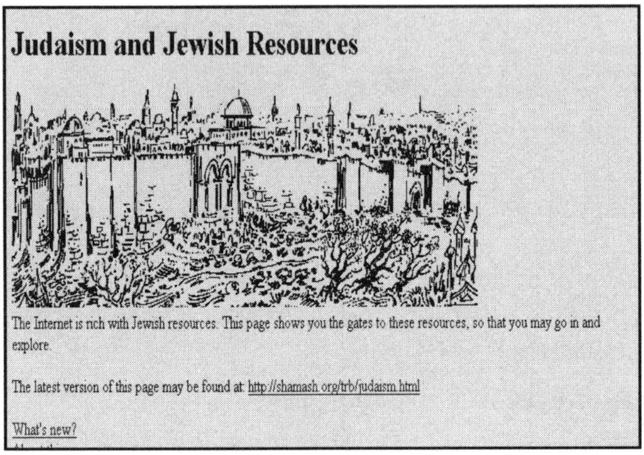

Judaism and Jewish Resources

http://shamash.nysernet.org:80/trb/judaism.html

This page has a wealth of Jewish resources. The site developer keeps us current with an extensive list of recent Web events. He also maintains a massive list of annotated Internet resources covering just about everything imaginable relating to the Jewish religion and culture. An interactive map of Israel allows connections to the selected servers there.

Site Details: Large Graphics, Good Links
Load Time: 11 seconds

New Advent Catholic Page

http://www.knight.org/advent

A virtual primer in the Roman Catholic denomination, the New Advent Catholic Page explains church doctrine in a clear and simple manner. The Pillar of Fire, Pillar of Truth section gives an introduction to the Church. Doctrine is presented in extensively hypertexed outline form. Under the heading God, readers will find St. Thomas Aquinas' five proofs of God's existence, information on the nature of God, and the Blessed Trinity. Many explanations are often offered in the form of Quick Questions. The Ten Commandments, Jesus Christ, saints, and much more, are covered.

Site Details: Large Graphics, Good Links
Load Time: 48 seconds

Religion and Philosophy Resources on the Internet

☆☆☆☆☆

http://web.bu.edu/LIBRARY/Religion/contents.html

Seekers of ultimate truth will find philosophy and religion resources to further their quest for enlightenment. A link to Boston University's library catalog is featured, as well as links to several other libraries nationwide. The religion archives are separated into various faiths, from Buddhism to Taoism.

Site Details: Good Links
Load Time: 9 seconds

Scientology

☆☆☆☆☆

http://www.scientology.org

Here's the official home page of the Church of Scientology, offering factual information on this growing religion and its founder, L. Ron Hubbard. The site offers virtual tours of prominent Scientology churches, and links to a virtual tour of the Hubbard Life Exhibition, to the award-winning Freedom magazine, and to an online bookstore featuring RealAudio excerpts of Mr. Hubbard's lectures, and a wide range of books, and other orientation materials. Also of note is a global locator that guides users to churches and missions worldwide. Check out this fascinating site.

Site Details: Real Audio, Video, Sound, Large Graphics, Good Links, Shopping
Load Time: 4 seconds

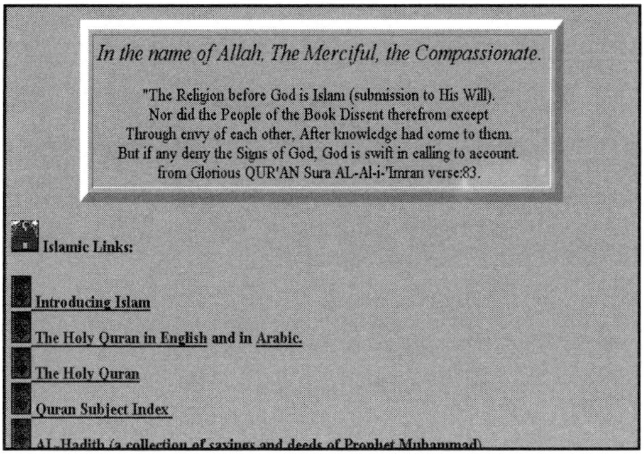

Thamer's Islamic Links

http://mars.superlink.net/user/tashour/islamlnk.html

Thamer's Islamic Links is a comprehensive resource of information relating to the world of Islam—the Holy Quran in both English and Arabic, a collection of the sayings and deeds of the prophet Muhammad, information about the Palestinians, the countries of Jordan, Saudi Arabia, Kuwait, and more. There are numerous links, lots of photos, and excellent graphics. The amount of information accessible here is astounding.

Site Details:	Large Graphics, Good Links, Shopping
Load Time:	12 seconds

The Holy See Vatican Web Site

http://www.vatican.va

Here the faithful can read the words of the Holy Father, Pope John Paul II; various papal addresses are printed in full. Recent communications posted here have included the Pope's Christmas message and a message celebrating the World Day of Peace. Still under construction at press time, the site will include news from the Holy See Press Office and the Vatican Information Service, as well as daily summaries of the Holy Father's activities. The devout everywhere can access the site; it is already available in Dutch, English, French, Italian, Portuguese, and German.

Site Details: Large Graphics, Good Links
Load Time: 64 seconds

Tucker's Religious Resources on the Net

http://convex.cc.uky.edu/~jatuck00/Religion/Religion.html

An immense database of resources relating to Roman Catholicism and Christianity, this information-packed site presents link after link of religious resources such as the Franciscan Homepage and the Way of the Cross. There are full text documents online such as the King James Bible and St. Jerome's Vulgate (Latin). The links enable visitors to explore other religions, such as Judaism, Zen Buddhism, and Hinduism.

Site Details: Good Links
Load Time: 34 seconds

Virtual Christianity

http://www.mit.edu:8001/people/aaronc/christianity.html

Here is an index of Christian-related sites that include the Christian Resource List, Kingdom Surf, World Christian Internet Resources, and the Christian Connection. In addition, visitors will find devotionals, links to Christian literature, Bible study topics, and Bible study newsgroups. Under the Miscellaneous section, there are links to the Secular Web, the Christian White Pages, and the Christian Bookstore.

Site Details: Good Links
Load Time: 4 seconds

World Scripture: A Comparative Anthology of Sacred Texts

http://rain.org/~origin/ws.html

This site contains passages from 268 sacred texts that represent the philosophies and ideologies of the many different religions of the world, including Hinduism, Buddhism, Islam, and Confucianism. The texts are organized around topics such as spirituality, salvation, atonement, sin, adultery, hypocrisy, liberation, and enlightenment, among many others.

Site Details: Good Links
Load Time: 4 seconds

WWW Bible Gateway

http://www.gospelcom.net/bible

The Bible Gateway's database contains five different versions of holy writ, each translated into seven different languages, which can be searched by keyword, chapter, and verse. In addition, passages can be pulled up by clicking on the name and chapter of the Bible book desired.

Site Details: Good Links
Load Time: 18 seconds

Shopping

With today's hectic lifestyles, it is hard to find the time and energy to enjoy shopping. Between working at a demanding job, paying the bills, running errands, and returning phone calls to friends, there just aren't enough hours in the day. What you do have time for is convenient and fun shopping on the Web.

The "cybermalls" of the Web are filled with everything from diamond jewelry to steel-belted tires, fresh flower bouquets to motorcycle accessories. The merchandise is unique, interesting, and, most importantly, right at your fingertips! Order a "Hot Box" Hot Sauce Assortment or a Copper Cookware selection from **Gourmet Gift Net** and have them delivered to your doorstep. Visit the **FTD Internet** site for a balloon bouquet for a special friend. Shopping that once consumed hours can now be handled on the Web in minutes.

In addition to saving you time, online shopping can be done at any hour of the day or night. Specialty stores and megamalls alike stay open 24 hours a day, seven days a week. Pick out the perfect salad bowl set from the William-Sonoma outlet at the **Dream Shop** or order a CD from **CDNOW** at 11 p.m. on Wednesday or 7 a.m on Monday. It's up to you!

Catalog Mart Home Page

★★★★★

http://catalog.savvy.com

This site offers a searchable database of more than 10,000 free catalogs in over 800 categories. Choose from allergy supplies to alarm systems, humidifiers to bird feed—simply click on the catalogs of interest, complete the address form, and the catalogs will be delivered to your doorstep. If you have a product catalog you'd like to list, the site offers a registration form for new vendors.

Site Details: Good Links, Shopping
Load Time: 75 seconds

Cyberspace Malls International

★★★★★

http://chili.rt66.com/cyspacemalls

One great convenience of the information superhighway is online shopping in the comfort of one's home. Cyberspace Malls International provides this luxury in its offering of numerous products—art, books, gifts, lamps, music, sports, and electronic goods. Select an item from a directory of stores, or browse each shop for that special set of dinnerware. The diehard shopper will delight in the variety of links to other great online malls found at this site.

Site Details: Good Links, Shopping
Load Time: 41 seconds

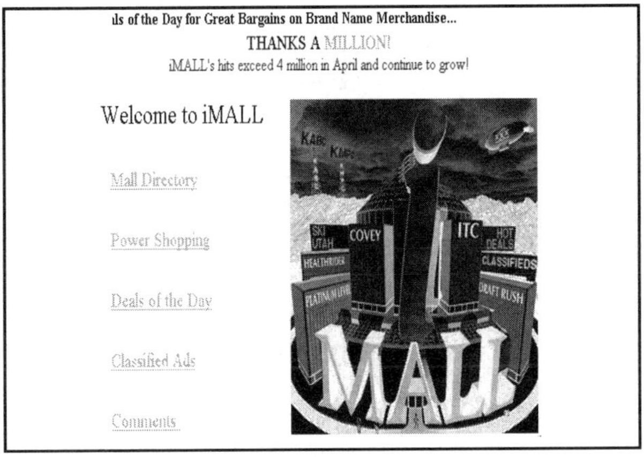

i-MALL

✯✯✯✯✯

http://www.imall.com

The concept of i-MALL is "power shopping" on the Web. The i-MALL offers a directory with links to products and services, free classified advertising to help you find something you need, and advertising to help you sell something you don't need. Check out the deal of the day or the monthly features. Most vendors on the mall offer online ordering.

Site Details:	Large Graphics, Good Links, Shopping
Load Time:	66 seconds

Internet Mall

http://www.internet-mall.com

Shopping enthusiasts will unearth a treasure chest of goods and services at the Internet Mall. Products for sale include everything from books, music, and clothes, to sporting equipment, computers, and furniture. Vendors range from the BTS International Meditation Institute to Dimple Records & Wild Things Online. This clean, well-organized site has a searchable database that helps you find the products you want.

Site Details: Good Links, Shopping
Load Time: 5 seconds

Internet Plaza

★★★★★

http://www.lupus.org

If the Internet were a city, this site would be downtown. A self-described "bustling crossroads for online commerce," XOR's Internet Plaza Web site features shopping at Card & Gift Drive, Fashion Boulevard, Career Way, Sports and Fitness Street, and Travel Avenue. Visitors can check out a new online magazine, the site of the month, and more. This site is well-designed, and the links are cool.

Site Details:	Large Graphics, Good Links Shopping
Load Time:	21 seconds

One World Plaza

★★★★★

http://www.wincorp.com/windata/OneWorldPlaza/OneWorldPlaza.html

One World Plaza affords shoppers a one-stop resource representing hundreds of merchants. The Gallery hosts vendors of boats, clothes, electronics, flowers, jewelry, and much more. Search for products by category where you'll find a listing of each business, displaying products, location, and ordering information.

Site Details:	Good Links, Shopping
Load Time:	26 seconds

Shopper

http://www.hummsoft.com/hummsoft/shopper.html

The Shopper Web directory is a bonanza for users who like to shop online or need information about a particular shop or mall. Access nearly 400 malls, indexed under the following categories: Large Cyber Malls, Regional Malls, Specialty Malls, International Malls, Small Malls, or Business. Users will also find links to other shopping directories. In addition to the many links available here, users can review a Top 10 list of tips for browsing online malls, a section with search hints, information on secure ordering, and additional shopping information.

Site Details: Good Links, Shopping
Load Time: 14 seconds

World Shopping Mall

http://worldshopping.com

The Internet is fast becoming a haven for convenience shopping. This site offers a huge collection of links to shopping pages, with jewelry, food, computers, children's clothing, and collectibles. A few of the links include Canadamalls, Acme Pet, Traveler's Checklist, and Sunnyland Farms. From sports to food, the Internet Shopping Page has the link.

Site Details: Good Links, Shopping
Load Time: 3 seconds

World Square

http://www.w2.com

The World Square has something for everyone. Users may travel from the home page to a selection of attractive pages with a wide variety of goods and services from purveyors of art, music, books, automobiles, and health products. The site also offers gateways to international museums, online magazines, and catalogs. In the arena of health-related links, World Square provides a list of nonprofit organizations involved in research for various diseases like Lyme disease, fibrositis, and scleroderma. Online entertainment in Kids' Korner offers RealAudio programs and a free opportunity to download the software.

Site Details: Large Graphics, Good Links, Shopping
Load Time: 94 seconds

World Wide Mall

http://www.olworld.com/olworld

The World Wide Mall Directory has over 18 categories from which shoppers can choose. Visit participating online vendors with products like arts & crafts, antiques, health & fitness products, nutritional supplies, wholesale items, and franchise information. In addition, Kids Club lets children meet other kids by e-mail, chat online, and play games. Teachers and parents are offered information about kid-safe sites on the Web.

Site Details: Large Graphics, Good Links, Shopping
Load Time: 61 seconds

1-800 MUSIC NOW

http://www.realaudio.com/CGI-bin/nph-redirect.cgi?100584

MCI offers this slick online music service where consumers can purchase their favorite tunes. Download a free copy of RealAudio, then choose from a large selection of audio files. Listening to the music is free, and the site is easy and fun to explore. Purchasing instructions are provided, along with a list of the most popular songs on DJ playlists around the country.

Site Details: Real Audio, Sound, Shopping
Load Time: 22 seconds

Amazon.com Books

★★★★★

http://www.amazon.com/exec/obidos/subst/index2.html/9165-5202824-522726

Amazon.com is an electronic bookstore offering over a million titles, usually at a discount. Browse the recommendations in any of 20 categories. Read reviews, bestseller list, award winners, and staff favorites. A searchable index is also available to locate specific titles. Would you like to know when your favorite author releases a new book? Amazon's notification service can do that for you. Place your orders online.

Site Details: Large Graphics, Shopping
Load Time: 29 seconds

Aphrodite's Love Palace

★★★★★

http://www.dircon.co.uk/purplet/love.html

Looking for the perfect gift for your beloved on St. Valentine's Day? Aphrodite's Love Palace offers many suggestions. Send a poem, say, Lord Byron's "She Walks in Beauty" via e-mail. How about flowers, wine, chocolate, lingerie, or a car? Attach a "cyberkiss," English or Italian style, to your gift. For those still looking for that special someone, links to several online dating services are also available.

Site Details: Sound, Good Links, Shopping
Load Time: 6 seconds

AutoMall Online

http://www.automall.net

Automall Online provides a quick, easy, and commission-free way to purchase your next new or used automobile. Shoppers use this free service by submitting the make, model, and desired optional equipment of the vehicle they wish to find. Automall will then send back a detailed proposal, including a price. Users can make arrangements to test drive the vehicle and finalize the purchase.

Site Details: Large Graphics, Shopping
Load Time: 25 seconds

British Books @ American Prices

http://British.Books@American.Prices.com/shop

British Books @ American Prices aims to provide books to the American consumer that would otherwise be hard to find. Cookery, biography, business, gardening, and, of course, fiction, can be ordered online. Check out new releases in categories like mystery, contemporary affairs, religion, music, and war.

Site Details:	Shopping
Load Time:	9 seconds

CDNOW

http://cdnow.com/cgi-bin/mserver/SID=843350263/RP/CDN/mainmenu.html

This site is the gateway to a huge Internet Music Store. Search for releases by artist, title, or genre. Visit the "artist of the week" segment for song lyrics, photos or a list of song titles. Get information on the top sellers, music discussion groups, reviews and reviewers. Access a wide variety of music magazines, world music titles, or hard-to-find releases.

Site Details:	Good Links, Shopping
Load Time:	73 seconds

Dream Shop

✯✯✯✯✯

http://www.dreamshop.com

This is cyber-shopping approaching near-perfection. Access great shops like Spiegel, Eddie Bauer, Horchow, The Sharper Image, and The Bombay Company. Browse their online catalogs, which are filled with discounts and specials for Internet shoppers. For affordable gift ideas, check out Gifts under $30. The site is tastefully designed and easy to navigate.

Site Details:	Large Graphics, Good Links, Shopping
Load Time:	62 seconds

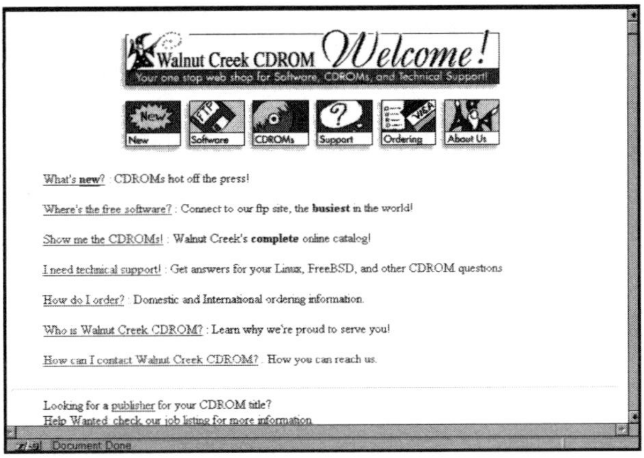

Electronic Catalog at Walnut Creek CDROM!

http://ftp.cdrom.com

From this online catalog, Walnut Creek CDROM provides access to an index of CD-ROMs, shareware CD-ROMs, and operating systems. You'll find graphics, fractals, programs, job listings, technical support, and much more. Give your feedback to the folks at Walnut Creek or order a product online.

Site Details: Large Graphics, Shopping
Load Time: 14 seconds

FAO Schwarz

★★★★★

http://www.faoschwarz.com/faohome.html

The treasures at this Web site will certainly delight the young and the young-at-heart. Choose from the beautiful Elizabethan Barbie, Christian Dior Barbie, Midnight Gala Barbie, or Peppermint Princess Barbie. Don't miss Ken as Rhett Butler from *Gone With the Wind* or Scarlett Barbie in all her finery. Visit the Ultimate Toy Catalog to view the Virtual Reality Headset Walkie/Talkies, a silver tea set, or a baby grand piano. In addition, there are specialty catalogs with such collectibles as a porcelain Betty Boop doll, a special edition G.I. Joe doll, and gold Matchbox Cars. Shoppers can order toll-free or print out an order form to fax or mail.

Site Details: Sound, Large Graphics, Shopping

Load Time: 24 seconds

FTD Internet

★★★★★

http://www.novator.com/FTD-Catalog/FTD-Internet.html

FTD makes it easy to have flowers delivered nationwide and even internationally (with three days notice). View images of arrangements, green plants, gourmet baskets, or dishgardens and place your order online. FTD provides a link to their customer service department which gives users information on delivery, products, and guarantees.

Site Details: Large Graphics, Good Links, Shopping

Load Time: 38 seconds

Global Furniture Network

★★★★★

http://www.gfurnet.com/gfn/index2.html

Visitors to the Global Furniture Network can access the online catalogs of a selection of furniture stores as well as a glossary of terms used in the industry. Furniture suppliers may read up on industry news including current market research and background information on the Network. The site also lists weekly sponsors and allows users to e-mail the chief executive officers of some of the industry's leading furniture dealers.

Site Details: Large Graphics, Good Links, Shopping

Load Time: 48 seconds

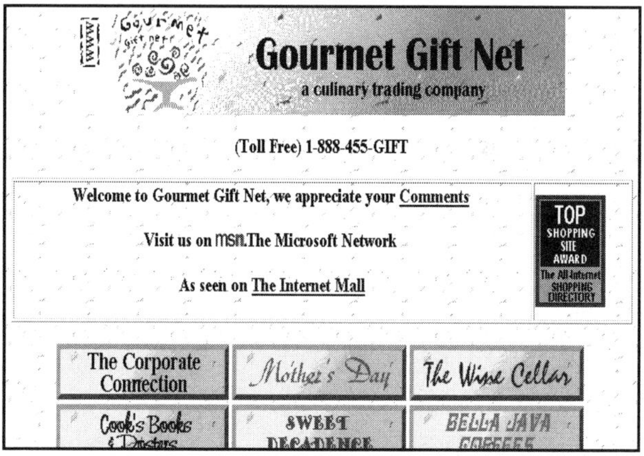

Gourmet Gift Net

http://www.gourmetgift.com/gift

Brew the perfect cup of coffee with the Gourmet Coffee Desk Set offered at the Gourmet Gift Net home page. This site presents a wide selection of gourmet gifts which include nuts, BBQ, baked goods, spices, cookware, candy, picnic baskets, and specialty seafood. Order by e-mail or by phone.

Site Details: Large Graphics, Good Links, Shopping

Load Time: 25 seconds

Motorcycle Shopper On-line

http://www.mshopper.eurografix.com

This online version of *Motorcycle Shopper* magazine offers a wealth of information for the motorcycle enthusiast. Visitors to this home page can find information on vendors, shops, articles, bulletin boards, swap meets, motorcycle clubs, news and classified ads. Helmets are optional for this ride.

Site Details:	Large Graphics, Good Links, Shopping
Load Time:	14 seconds

Naturally California Gourmet

http://www.magicwindows.com/~mwinfo/gourmet.html

Now Web users from all over the world may sample the gourmet foods of California. The Web site presents an excellent selection of shops with foods like olives, avocados, pretzels, and hot sauces. Specialty sausages prepared without preservatives and nitrates are available from San Luis Gourmet Sausage. Choose from a wide variety of flavors—Andouilie, Jamaican Jerk, Hot Italian, Pork Apple, and many more. Each vendor offers information on products, ordering, and pricing.

Site Details:	Shopping
Load Time:	8 seconds

Needlework Resources

http://www.islandnet.com/~arogers/needlework.html

Leave it to the Web to offer a site combining needlework and computer software. Needlework Resources features links to four unique companies that create custom needlework charts from supplied photos, offer cross stitch charts from PCX files for a variety of operating systems, and feature a host of related programs for weaving, sewing, quilting, and knitting. In addition to an online catalog, links to related software, books, magazines, accessories, supplies, gifts, patterns, and kits are provided.

Site Details:	Good Links, Shopping
Load Time:	39 seconds

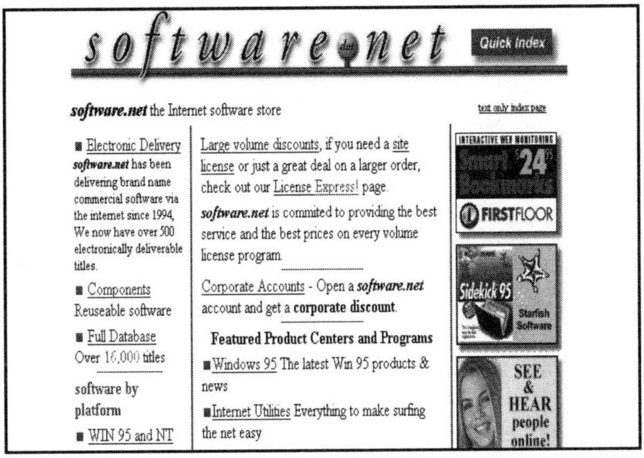

Software.net

http://www.software.net

Software.net is a software distributor for DOS, Windows, Macintosh, and UNIX products. Its search engine can be used to access information on thousands of computer programs. Check out the news and magazine sections for the latest events in the computer industry. Penny pinchers will love the Cool Deals and Free Stuff section for affordable software.

Site Details: Large Graphics, Good Links, Shopping

Load Time: 21 seconds

Sound Wire

http://soundwire.com

Sound Wire features eclectic music from a variety of independent labels. Listen to free sound clips in RealAudio from your favorite artist. If you need the appropriate audio player, you can download it from this site. Celtic music, R&B, soul, African, underground, and classical CDs can be purchased online.

Site Details:	Real Audio, Video , Sound, Good Links, Shopping
Load Time:	15 seconds

Sports & Recreation

The opening tip-off goes to the home team, the guard powers down the court for a picture-perfect layup, and the frenzied crowd jumps to its feet. Whether the excitement surrounds the first-half kickoff, the drop of the puck, or the snap of the starting gun, there's nothing quite like the thrill of competition. The loyal sports fan stays in touch with team stats, breaking news, and player trades.

Now the sports enthusiast with Internet access has the edge. Offering league standings, player stats, championship information, and scores, the Web provides up-to-the-minute reporting from slick sites like **ESPN Sportzone** and **CNN Sports**. Don't wait for the evening news or radio reports, QuickTime movies and RealAudio sound bytes bring you everything from last night games at Dodger Stadium to today's NBA highlights. Professional sports offer official sites of the **NFL,** the **NBA**, the **NHL**, the **PGA**, and **Major League Baseball.**

For those who dream of a climbing expedition to Nepal or a cross-country ski outing, **GORP- Great Outdoor Recreation Page** or **Ski Net** prepare you with photographs, itineraries, and conditions. Golf, tennis, running—the athlete can find club and tournament information, equipment recommendations, and tips for improving skills.

Big Wall Climbing

http://www.primenet.com/~midds

Information on the largest rock faces in the world is provided at this home page. Users can view the showcase of big walls from around the world or find out how a big wall rates in terms of difficulty. Also offered are details on big-wall climbs in Zion, Yosemite, Wyoming, Pakistan, and Mexico. Read the climbing stories or find out about the latest climbing equipment.

Site Details: Large Graphics, Good Links
Load Time: 46 seconds

Global Oceanic Surf Links

http://www.magna.com.au/~prfbrown/tubelink.html

Users who like to surf more than the Web should check out this home page for the most comprehensive index to actual—as opposed to virtual—surfing resources. Call it "real surfing." Resources are divided by geographic area, including Southern planetary regions, the Central Pacific Ocean (Hawaii), the Eastern Pacific Ocean and the U.S. West coast, the Northwestern Atlantic Ocean and the U.S. East coast, and three other areas. Additional commentary addresses the spirit of surfing.

Site Details:	Large Graphics, Good Links, Shopping
Load Time:	51 seconds

GORP—Great Outdoor Recreation Pages

★★★★★

http://www.gorp.com

Many of us look forward to outdoor adventures but lack specific inspiration. This home page offers a wealth of information about adventure destinations and activities. Experience Alaska by canoe or fish the rivers of Honduras. The links offered here are endless journeys through the National Parks system, sports-specific Web sites, and to maps that will help you plan the ultimate outdoor vacation.

Site Details:	Large Graphics, Good Links, Shopping
Load Time:	10 seconds

Mountain Biking

★★★★★

http://xenon.stanford.edu:80/~rsf/mtn-bike.html

This site has a complete list of places to bike in Europe, Canada, Latin America, New Zealand, Asia, and the United States. You'll find racing tips and information on the Olympic Games and the National Championships, along with scenic mountain biking photos.

Site Details:	Large Graphics, Good Links
Load Time:	41 seconds

Outdoor & MORE/Outdoor Network

✯✯✯✯✯

http://www.outdoornet.com

If you are happiest with the wind in your hair and your adrenaline pumping, take a break from the excitement long enough to visit the Outdoor Network Web page. The sports enthusiast will be well-outfitted here with product information on action sports, including snowboarding, windsurfing, mountain biking, and rock climbing. Order catalogs, or check out the links to adventure destinations.

Site Details:	Large Graphics, Good Links, Shopping
Load Time:	33 seconds

Road Runners Club of America

★★★★★

http://www.teleport.com/~rrca

The Road Runners Club of America is the national association of nonprofit clubs dedicated to promoting running as a healthy form of exercise and as a competitive sport. RRCA oversees more than 500 local clubs and 160,000 members in 48 states and Guam. This comprehensive, well-organized site includes everything from local club information to racing politics and funding, from club services to personal fitness and coaching. It's a can't-miss for anyone even remotely interested in lacing up the sneakers and hittin' the road.

Site Details: Good Links
Load Time: 18 seconds

Ski Net

★★★★★

http://www.microweb.com/brian/skinet

Those who love breathtaking beauty and invigorating alpine air will delight in Ski Net. Skiers no longer need to drive up the mountain to find out ski conditions. Visitors here will discover condition updates, sorted geographically. Other cool features include calendars of events, summer and winter activities, and lodging facilities for various ski resorts around the world.

Site Details: Large Graphics, Good Links
Load Time: 4 seconds

SnoWeb

http://www.snoweb.com

Skiers and snowboarders will find plenty of useful information on SnoWeb. A few of the features include a ski and snowboard events calendar, trail maps, an online magazine called *Cyberboarder*, and the beautiful and information-packed *Alpine World Magazine*. In addition, there are feature stories, classified ads, and entries on heli-skiing and ski-jumping. Skiers will find ski area information, sorted by geographic regions, including the United States, Canada, and, for Northern Hemisphere summer skiing, South Africa, South America, Australia, and New Zealand.

Site Details: Sound, Large Graphics, Good Links

Load Time: 29 seconds3

Virtual Flyshop

http://www.flyshop.com

Fly fishers visiting this site will find a resource of epic proportions. Just a few of the useful features include an online magazine, information on the fishing conditions of major rivers and water systems around the world, and a mall of virtual fly-fishing storefronts. A directory of fly-fishing resources on the Web, offering everything from weather conditions to related links, is also provided.

Site Details:	Large Graphics, Good Links, Shopping
Load Time:	25 seconds

World Golf

http://worldgolf.com

World Golf is one of the best golf resources on the Internet. Access nearly every golf course in the United States and around the globe. U.S. golf courses are listed by city and state. Find tips on how to construct golf clubs and improve play. Read guides to golf museums and libraries. Users can examine a digest of interesting golf-related tidbits. Visit the bookshelf of golf literature, the section on travel information, and golf classifieds.

Site Details:	Good Links, Shopping
Load Time:	57 seconds

American Racing Scene

http://www.racecar.com

American Racing Scene is an e-zine devoted to the sport of car racing in America. From the home page, select Indy Car or NASCAR for photo galleries of cars and drivers, racing schedules and results, online drivers fan club registration, and accumulated season points for drivers. Shop Talk is a live chat line for racing fans.

Site Details: Large Graphics, Good Links
Load Time: 47 seconds

Fastball

http://www.fastball.com/index.html

Fastball is your off-season source for baseball news and discussion. Dig in for Scores and Highlights, 1,000 Sports Stories, Stats and Schedules, Baseball Links, and Dugout Chatter (chat rooms for all major league teams, with feedback). Baseball fans will also want to check out the latest wire service stories, transactions, the off-season baseball calendar, a discussion about the new season, baseball quotations, and more. This page is a must-see for the diehard baseball fan.

Site Details: Sound, Large Graphics, Good Links
Load Time: 15 seconds

GolfWeb

http://www.golfweb.com

Presented by *Golf Digest*, GolfWeb is a comprehensive online golf information resource. Visitors to this site will find tournament reports, statistics about the PGA Tour, Senior PGA Tour, LPGA, European PGA, and Nike Tour, as well as all the results from tournaments. Find out about scoring rules, etiquette, and tournament play.

Site Details:	Large Graphics, Good Links, Shopping
Load Time:	23 seconds

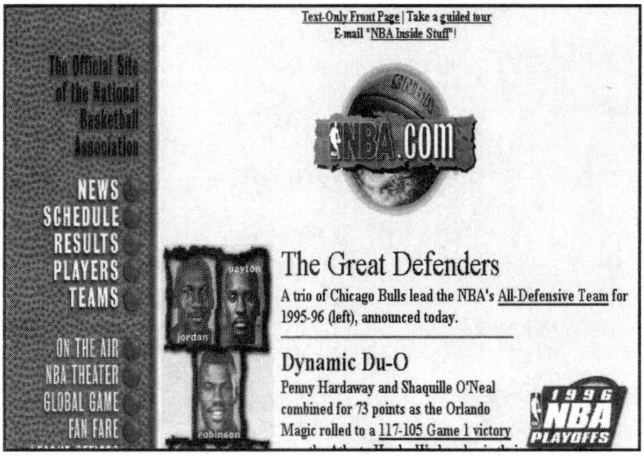

NBA.com

★★★★★

http://www.nba.com

The official home page of the NBA (National Basketball Association) is filled with interesting basketball facts and news clips. Basketball fans will find team schedules, game results, and feature articles about players. Television schedules, highlight clips, and sound files are available. Basketball lovers will learn in-depth information about their favorite players through interviews and statistics. The content and depth of this site are excellent.

Site Details:	Video , Sound, Large Graphics, Good Links
Load Time:	46 seconds

Web Site of the National Hockey League Players' Association

http://www.nhlpa.com

This is the official Web site of the National Hockey League Players' Association. Current statistics are available for the teams, players, and conferences. Among the features are a trivia challenge, player of the day award, and RealAudio interviews. Hockey fans will find this site fun and informative.

Site Details:	Real Audio, Large Graphics, Good Links
Load Time:	28 seconds

PGA

★★★★★

http://www.championship.pga.org

The Web site for the Professional Golfers Association (PGA) offers statistics on players, current news, and a review of the 77th PGA Championship. Users can get a hole-by-hole summary of the Championship at Riviera Country Club, including information about the course and past winners of the competition. An online catalog of PGA merchandise is available, which includes directions for ordering the officially licensed products.

Site Details: Good Links, Shopping
Load Time: 12 seconds

Pure WEB

★★★★★

http://caesar.atm.ch.cam.ac.uk:www/sports/webs.html

Soccer fans everywhere will find something to interest them at the Pure WEB site. It aims to collect all the football (soccer) Web sites in the world—and it looks to have made a good start. Just a few of the many general sites include the International Soccer Server from Finland, the Premier League from England, the WWW Soccer Information Service, and the WWW International Soccer Results Page. Pure WEB also provides detailed club, division, and league information for England, Scotland, Ireland, Germany, the Netherlands—most of the world! In addition, there are many more links, including Fantasy Football and competition information.

Site Details:	Large Graphics, Good Links
Load Time:	38 seconds

Skilton's Baseball Links

★★★★★

http://www.pc-professor.com/baseball/

Baseball fans, make this your first stop on the Web. With more than 500 unique links, Skilton's Baseball Links page makes it easy for fans of the game to find information quickly. In addition to a "Baseball Link of the Week," other categories include Major League Team Info, Minor League Team Info, College Baseball, and International Baseball. Access official team home pages, team and player statistics, game schedules and ticket information, as well as histories of some teams. There are nice photographs of players too.

Site Details:	Large Graphics, Good Links, Shopping
Load Time:	50 seconds

Team NFL

★★★★★

http://nflhome.com

This site invites everyone onto the NFL team—offering great news, chat, statistics, and articles about football. It highlights what's been happening in the National Football League. Football fans wanting to see headlines about the latest games can read This Week in the NFL. For statistics and matchups, look at the Team NFL section. Its NFL Library has sections about rules and records. Team NFL is definitely a winner.

Site Details:	Sound, Good Links, Shopping
Load Time:	53 seconds

Tennis Country

★★★★★

http://www.tenniscountry.com

Register free to join the club at the Tennis Country Web site. Polish up your tennis game with the playing and fitness tips available here. Users get information on major tournaments, the latest news about tournament players and winners, schedules, and rankings. Also available are sections about tennis travel and camps, tennis products and services, and tennis for kids, as well as chat forums where users can catch up on the latest tennis gossip.

Site Details:	Large Graphics, Good Links, Shopping
Load Time:	31 seconds

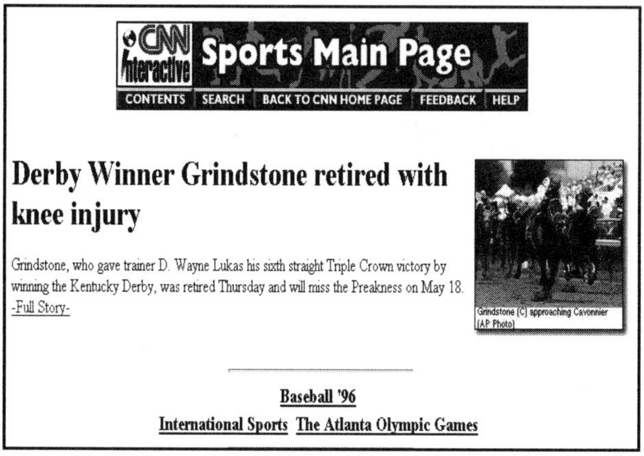

CNN Sports

http://www.cnn.com/SPORTS/index.html

For the latest news on major league baseball, check out this site at CNN Sports. It contains up-to-date information on standings, statistics, and schedules of all teams in professional baseball. For more in-depth information, the site offers recaps of last night's games and box scores. Whether the hot story involves an NFL player and drug charges, or baseball attendance on the rise, you'll find it at CNN Sports.

Site Details: Good Links
Load Time: 28 seconds

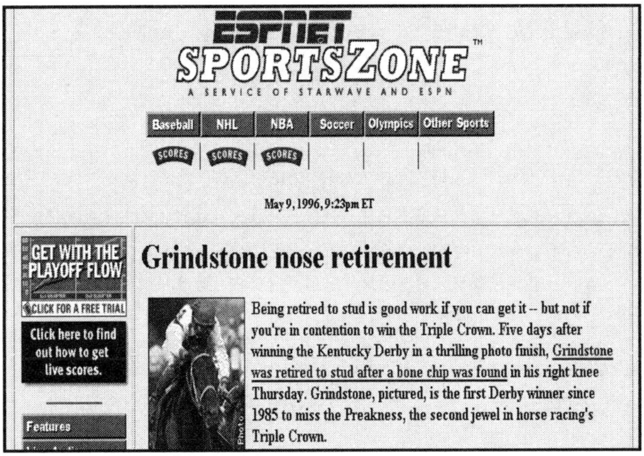

ESPNet SportsZone

http://espnet.sportszone.com

Working late at the office and wondering who's ahead in Monday night football? Click into the ESPNet SportsZone and get up-to-the-minute scores. Sports enthusiasts will love the variety of feature articles on such topics as the welterweight title replay or the Ricky Henderson trade to Cleveland. From amusing recounts of sports bloopers to sports trivia, this Web site is a must for the sports fan.

Site Details:	Video, Sound, Large Graphics, Good Links, Service Fee
Load Time:	60 seconds

Newbie's Guide to Sports

http://ug.cs.dal.ca:3400/sports.html

Here is all the sports information even the most fanatic fan could want. The Newbie's Guide to Sports is extensive, with a full assortment of schedules, stats, and commentary. You'll find the latest on baseball, basketball, football, hockey, soccer, tennis, fishing, surfing and rugby.

Site Details: Good Links
Load Time: 8 seconds

Official Guide to the 1996 Summer Olympic Games

http://www.atlanta.olympic.org

For the latest on the 1996 Centennial Olympic Games, sprint over to this Web site. Find out about planned events and venues or review the Official Program. If you want to make it to Atlanta in person, check out the information on travel and tickets. Users interested in the Olympic Arts Festival can request a brochure online or access details on the festival's schedule and programs. This Guide will be maintained by the Olympic Committee until December of 1996.

Site Details: Large Graphics, Good Links, Shopping
Load Time: 17 seconds

Sports Network

http://www.sportsnetwork.com

The Sports Network is a sports lover's dream with up-to-date news on professional baseball, football, basketball, hockey, golf, and collegiate sports. There are previews of upcoming games, team transactions, and player news. Get tee times for the 1996 Masters tournament or results from the NASCAR Winston Cup Series. The site offers great news briefs released on the hour covering everything from sports injuries to Mike Tyson's legal hassles.

Site Details:	Good Links, Shopping
Load Time:	56 seconds

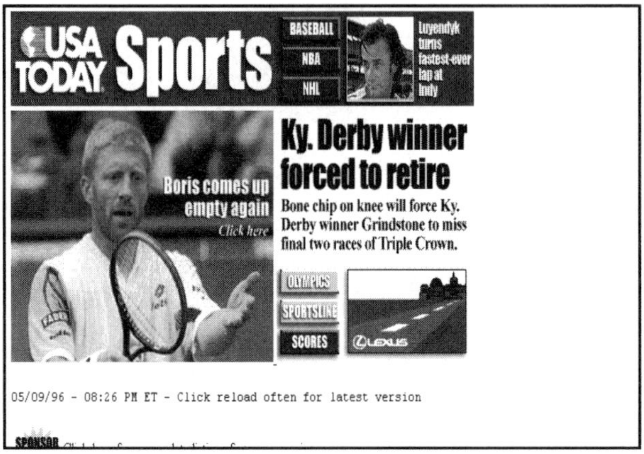

USA Today Sports

http://www.usatoday.com/sports/sfront.htm

The USA Today Sports Page is an electronic version of the national newspaper's sports section. The latest information about the NBA, NFL, NHL, NCAA, AAU, and golf, tennis, and boxing is presented in an easy-to-use and dynamic format. Scores, news, photos, and up-to-the-minute breaking cover stories are available.

Site Details: Large Graphics, Good Links
Load Time: 80 seconds

Travel Destinations

The human spirit longs to free itself through adventure and movement. Although time and money may sometimes limit our inclination to wander, the Web brings the world to us with images, sounds, and interactivity. The armchair tourist can experience the sounds of a South American rain forest or view the rugged seaside landscapes of Northern Ireland. If you're more the get-up-and-go type, the Web can prepare you for memorable journeys—a tropical island, an icy Himalayan peak, a romantic hideaway.

If you've always dreamed of an African safari, visit the **Africa-Virtual Tourist II** site for a photographic preview of the North Luangwa National Park. Plan an architectural tour of Paris with the help of the **Paris Pages**.

From New Zealand to England, Rome to Tokyo, many popular travel destinations are presented. If you don't see the particular place you are interested in, try one of the mega-travel sites like **What's On...In Europe** or **CityNet United States** for pointers to travel destinations throughout the world.

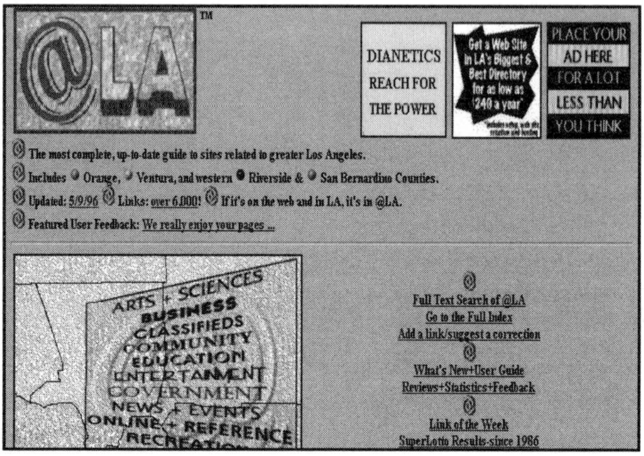

@LA

http://emporium.turnpike.net/A/atLA

@LA focuses on Internet resources in the greater Los Angeles area. Museums, coffeehouses, churches, synagogues, hotels—if it's in LA, and it's on the Web, you'll find it here. New links are added weekly. Find Catalina guides, including hotels, boat, and recreational ideas, as well as weekend entertainment: movies, theaters, and clubs.

Site Details: Good Links, Shopping
Load Time: 30 seconds

Amtrak's Station on the WWW

★★★★★

http://www.amtrak.com

All aboard! Web travelers who step on to Amtrak's Web site can access all the information necessary for planning a train trip. Read descriptions of the sights along train routes (maps included) or find out about accommodations on the Superliner or Single-Level fleets. Train travel tips are offered, in addition to FAQs about fares, reservations, and related details. Users can explore the sections on Amtrak's Great American vacations or other vacation packages. Take a chance at winning free tickets by filling out the questionnaire in the Contest and Promotions section.

Load Time: 12 seconds

Boston Online

★★★★★

http://www.std.com/NE/boston.html

Boston Online offers residents and visitors information about tourism, history, entertainment, recreation, sports, and weather with a witty and irreverent slant. Have some fun and access an electronic postcard or learn to talk like a native with the Wicked Good Guide to Boston English. Tourism information covers arts and entertainment events, food, lodging, and shopping. Points of interest are handily linked with public transportation routes.

Site Details: Good Links
Load Time: 15 seconds

Branson.Net

http://www.branson.net

Branson, Missouri, in the foothills of the Ozark Mountains, has fast become a popular destination for tourists because of its wealth of musical shows, theme parks, and other entertainment. The Branson home page is designed for tourists who want information about lodging, recreation, and upcoming events.

Site Details: Good Links, Shopping
Load Time: 32 seconds

CityNet United States

http://www.city.net/countries/united_states

The pages of CityNet make up in content what they lack in style and graphics. This expansive site will take visitors on a virtual tour of the United States—from Alabama to Wyoming. Information about U.S. territories is also available. This index of links connects users to cities, counties, local government, education, outdoor activities, media, and much more.

Site Details: Good Links
Load Time: 6 seconds

CNet—Canada

http://cnet.unb.ca/cnet

The CNet home page opens up with a large clickable map of Canada, whereby visitors can choose a place of interest and access information on the geography, religion, organizations, cultural composition, art, business, economy, tourism, government, and education in this vast and diverse nation. Armchair tourists will find everything they ever wanted to know and more about this gigantic and extraordinary land that shares a vast common border with the U.S. There is a search engine to facilitate the journey.

Site Details: Large Graphics, Good Links
Load Time: 54 seconds

Disneyland

★★★★★

http://www2.disney.com/Disneyland/index.html?GL=H

Original flagship of Disney parks and an American icon since its 1995 opening, "The Happiest Place on Earth" is one of the first stops people make when visiting California. Now it's a hot Web destination. The Disneyland site offers general park information: hours, prices, events, attractions, guest services, travel, and business information. A What's New section keeps visitors up-to-date on the ever changing Magic Kingdom. And there's plenty to try out in the Fun and Education section, which features QuickTime movies, trivia, and special Disney tips. Don't worry about missing anything: the Guided Tour ensures that you'll find everything at this magical site.

Site Details: Video
Load Time: 40 seconds

Go Native's Guide to Bed and Breakfast Inns

★★★★★

http://www.go-native.com

This site contains a complete guide to bed and breakfast inns and hotels, containing reviews, activities, points of interest, and accommodation features. Innkeepers present photos of their facilities. The resorts are listed by state, and maps often accompany the listings.

Site Details: Large Graphics, Good Links
Load Time: 49 seconds

Las Vegas Online

★★★★★

http://www.infi.net/vegas/online

Viva Las Vegas! This Web site is sponsored by a television station and contains a variety of resources related to the United States' gambling capital. Access news and current events surrounding the Vegas community. Las Vegas Online offers information about gaming, tourism, shopping, and other fun-filled activities. Users can also examine the business information center segment.

Site Details: Large Graphics, Good Links
Load Time: 47 seconds

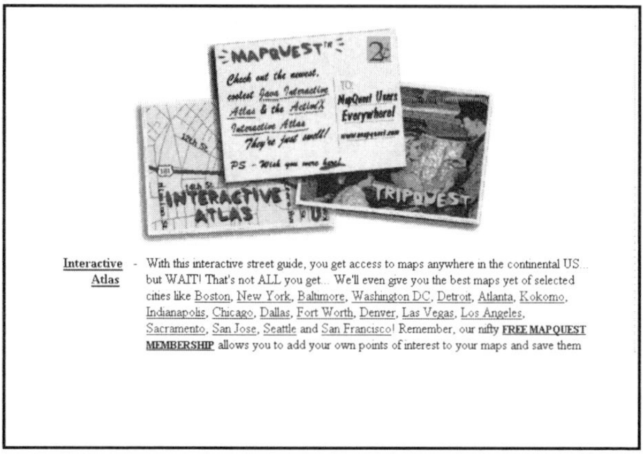

MapQuest

http://www.mapquest.com

Now there's an interactive street atlas of the United States on the Web! We put MapQuest through its paces by typing in our favorite obscure streets. MapQuest found them all—including a small street on Oahu—even though they only promise to cover the continental U.S. The level of detail is not as complete as CD-ROM mapping programs but it's more than adequate, especially considering that it's free. TripQuest, which can map out a driving route, and JavaQuest, are nifty features. See how MapQuest's clients are using customized interactive maps in their sites.

Load Time: 10 seconds

Metroscope

http://isotropic.com/metro/scope.html

Planning to see the U.S.A.? Spotlighting U.S. cities, Metroscope is a good place to start your travel research. Although not strictly tourist oriented, trip planners will find an ample supply of links to points of interest, event calendars, dining and lodging guides, and cultural resources. City residents will find government, educational, professional services, and business sites. The site isn't fancy, but it is cleanly designed and well-organized. A small number of international cities is covered.

Site Details: Good Links
Load Time: 96 seconds

Mexico: An Endless Journey

http://mexico-travel.com/

Whether journeying back in time to an ancient Mayan civilization or simply sitting on one of Mexico's gorgeous beaches, you'll love this Web site sponsored by the Mexican Ministry of Tourism. Its colorful, textured, 3-D home page leads to an index of topics that will help travelers get to know Mexico: Attractions and Activities, States, Regions, Cities, Beaches, Fiestas and Events, Travel Services and Tips, even Business Opportunities. There are also some great links to other sites about Mexican culture, history, education, government, and more. Everything is available in both Spanish and English.

Site Details: Good Links
Load Time: 40 seconds

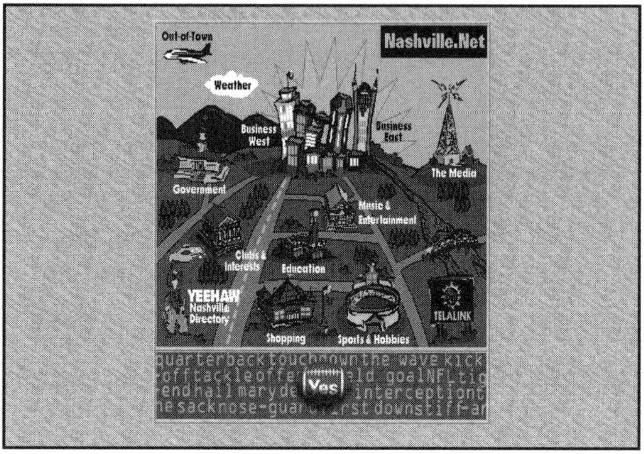

Nashville.Net

http://www.Nashville.Net/index.html

Discover the bright, tastefully designed pages of Nashville.Net, a service of public radio station WPLM FM90. The home page features a clickable cartoon map of the city of Nashville, Tennessee, where visitors can choose from music, entertainment, education, shopping, media, government, or nightlife resources. There is also a link to City.Net in the unlikely event that this site doesn't quench one's thirst for Nashville information.

Site Details:	Large Graphics, Good Links, Shopping
Load Time:	30 seconds

National Park Service

☆☆☆☆☆

http://www.nps.gov

The National Park Service Web site is a comprehensive source of information on the nation's parks. Search for parks by name, state, region, or theme. Find park phone numbers, as well as listings of National Park Service publications. Students and conservationists can peruse press releases and issue statements and papers. The Park of the Month features a great place to spend your next vacation.

Site Details: Good Links, Shopping
Load Time: 41 seconds

New England

☆☆☆☆☆

http://www.tiac.net/users/macgyver/ne.html

This large collection of resources is a good introduction to the states and cities of New England. The page is well-designed and organized and makes an excellent guide for travel, business, or entertainment. Listed resources are categorized by the following topics: Regional and State Indices, Metro Hot Spots, Cape Cod and Islands, Travel, Maps, and Commercial sites.

Site Details: Large Graphics, Good Links
Load Time: 10 seconds

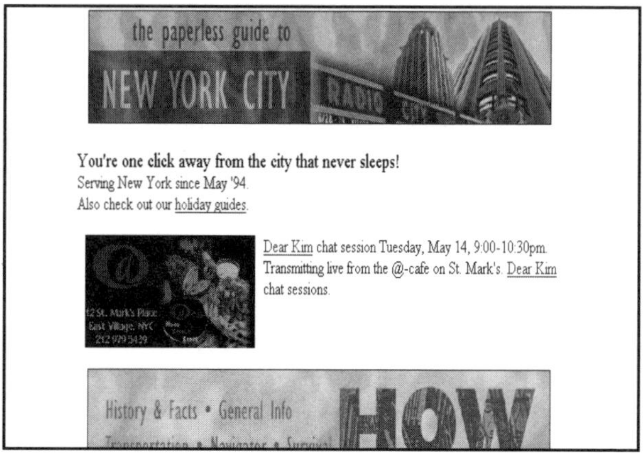

Paperless Guide to NYC

http://www.mediabridge.com/nyc

The Paperless Guide to NYC is one of the best guides to a major city we've seen. Divided into How and Wow sections, everything a visitor needs to know is easily accessible. Users can learn about the history of the city, view a map of the subway system, even type in a Manhattan street address to find its location on a map. In addition to all the transportation tips, tourist information, and big-city survival advice, the Wow section lists restaurants, shopping, museums, and sights. Users can click on a map of New York to get in-depth information on such attractions as Central Park and Greenwich Village. The hotels are listed by name or by location.

Site Details: Large Graphics, Good Links, Shopping

Load Time: 78 seconds

Seattle, the Emerald City

✯✯✯✯✯

http://www.seanet.com/Seattle/SeattleHome.html

Residents and visitors in Seattle will find a wealth of useful information here. Under Basic Information, find transportation information, weather reports, earthquake and volcanic data, and public transit information, as well as population, land area, and crime statistics. The Entertainment section has scores of things to do, while the Government section carries a host of local, county, state, and federal links. There are Shopping and Business sections, as well as a great Neighborhood section with community information. The Outdoors section details the multiple recreational opportunities available in and around Seattle.

Site Details: Good Links, Shopping
Load Time: 20 seconds

Six Flags Theme Parks

★★★★★

http://www.sixflags.com

The Six Flags site, under construction at press time, promises to be as fun and action-packed as the theme parks themselves. The number-two theme park company in the United States, Six Flags currently has eight parks nationwide. Bugs Bunny and the gang greet you on the home page, and there is a preview of the new Superman ride. You can view construction photos, and an artist's rendering of the completed ride. Be sure to return to check on its progress.

Load Time: 5 seconds

South Beach–The American Riviera

★★★★★

http://sobe.com

Who knows why a town suddenly becomes hip? It's easier though, to determine when it becomes hip—Sean Penn buys real estate, Madonna is seen out on the town schmoozing with Cher, and movie shoots no longer turn residents' heads. The current mecca for the beautiful people is South Beach, Florida, a charming art deco enclave with tropical heat. This site gathers together visitor's guides, virtual magazines featuring local columnists, and pointers to hot spots. Those who yearn to join the fun can view listings for real estate, rentals, and hotels.

Site Details: Good Links, Shopping
Load Time: 1 second

Universal Studios Hollywood and Florida

http://www.mca.com/unitemp/index.html

Like their real-world counterparts in Orlando and Hollywood, the home pages for Universal Studios are exciting, entertaining, and packed with multimedia—and both pages are accessible from here. At the Hollywood site, there's an interactive, illustrated adventure (Waterworld's Quest for the Mariner). The QuickTime VR clips in the Entertainment Center offer a taste of the theme park's attractions. At the Florida site, visitors will find QuickTime videos, photos, and facts about favorite rides, shows, and tours.

Site Details: Video, Good Links,
Load Time: 1 second

Virtual Chicago

http://www.nexchi.com/chi/virtual.chicago.html

Welcome to the windy city home page, a database spotlighting all the hot spots and services located in Chicago, Illinois. Divisions of the site include Internet providers, universities, art, businesses, entertainment, food, and government. Links to Chicago's libraries and museums are presented, as well as connections to the city's music scene, theater performances, publications, and much more.

Site Details: Good Links
Load Time: 58 seconds

Walt Disney World

✯✯✯✯✯

http://www2.disney.com/DisneyWorld/index.html?GL=H

Disney World, the younger, bigger brother of Disneyland, is home to more than one theme park: the Magic Kingdom Park, Epcot, the Disney-MGM Studios, and three water parks. The colorful and well-designed home page provides reservations and lodging information, downloadable maps, pictures and descriptions, QuickTime movies and live camera shots. A special events calendar allows visitors to plan ahead for one-of-a-kind or annual attractions. Another feature will list all the new park features since your last visit. A Dream Maker tour guide selects tours of Disney World for families with or without children.

Site Details:	Video, Shopping
Load Time:	10 seconds

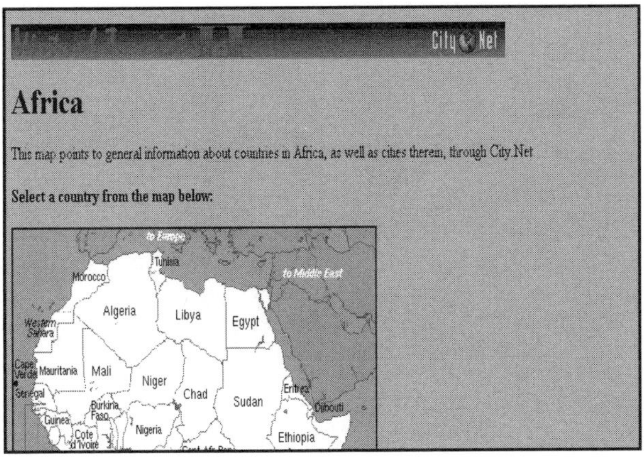

Africa–Virtual Tourist II

http://wings.buffalo.edu/world/vt2/africa.html

The virtual tourist can explore the continent of Africa and its cities through this Web site. The page includes maps, language databases, travel advisories and links to additional detailed regional information. Also included is information about each country, its culture, entertainment, government and community services.

Site Details: Good Links
Load Time: 28 seconds

Australia Travel Directory

http://www.anzac.com/aust/aust.htm

This site is a comprehensive travel resource on Australia. Access information countrywide or state-by-state. National travel products and miscellaneous Australian link sources are also listed. Everything from hotel accommodations to packaged tour companies to rail travel information can be located. Information is available either directly from the provider or through links to other Web sites.

Site Details: Large Graphics, Good Links
Load Time: 10 seconds

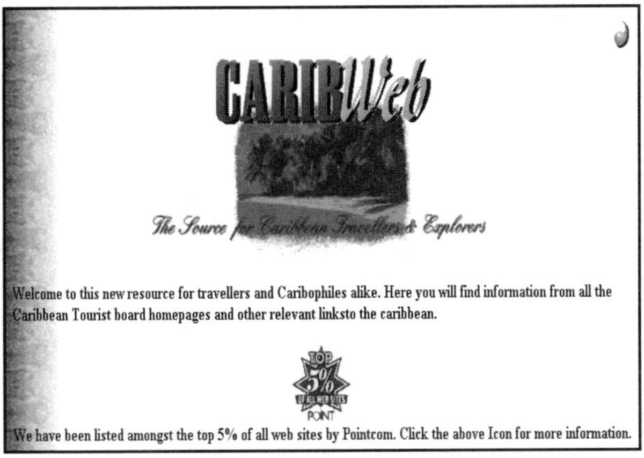

CaribWeb

http://www.caribweb.com/caribweb

Barbados, Montserrat, Martinique, St. Barts—the names evoke trade winds, silken seas, and tropical flowers. Whether you are planning a trip to the Caribbean or just feeling nostalgic for the islands, a visit to CaribWeb will be satisfying. Trip planners can access CaribSearch, a database of hotels, restaurants, and yacht charters; and Island Guides, which contains links to various islands' home pages. Beachcombers can exchange stories in CaribTalk, which is sorted by island and topic.

Site Details:	Large Graphics, Good Links, Shopping
Load Time:	23 seconds

Hong Kong Online Guide

http://www.hk.super.net/~webzone/hongkong.html

The Hong Kong Online Guide is a spectacular presentation of what to do and where to go while in Hong Kong. This wonderful Web page will take you on an exotic journey to the best restaurants, airlines, hotels, shopping areas, and tourist attractions. Glance through the virtual menu, and make a stop to learn the history and government of Hong Kong. Find out how to do business in Hong Kong and learn tips for bargaining during shopping hours. Check out the top 10 restaurants in Hong Kong or cook one of the recipes provided here yourself.

Site Details: Large Graphics, Good Links, Shopping

Load Time: 70 seconds

Ireland: Virtual Tourist Guide

http://www.bess.tcd.ie/ireland.html

Various gateways to Ireland are available at this server. Among other things, you can access information about Irish universities, literature, language, economics, politics, current affairs, genealogy, and tourist guides. There are a number of fine maps of the country, as well as current weather reports. Link to the C.I.A. World Factbook for further information.

Site Details: Large Graphics, Good Links

Load Time: 19 seconds

London Guide

✯✯✯✯✯

http://www.cs.ucl.ac.uk/misc/uk/london.html

This is one of the best sites about England on the Web. Visitors will find photos of the city of London and listings of its restaurants and pubs, as well as all the major hotels (with brief descriptions and rates). Find museums, bands, dancing, theatre, tourist information, and clickable maps at this site.

Site Details: Large Graphics, Good Links
Load Time: 18 seconds

New Zealand Guidebook

✯✯✯✯✯

http://www.akiko.lm.com/nz

Through this site, browsers can take a virtual tour of New Zealand. Access travel and tourist information, geography and natural history data, government, university, and business organizations. Find out about other Web sites linking New Zealanders with lovers of this land. There is also a section providing the most current New Zealand news events. Link back to the Akiko home page for even more New Zealand information and online data.

Site Details: Large Graphics, Good Links
Load Time: 29 seconds

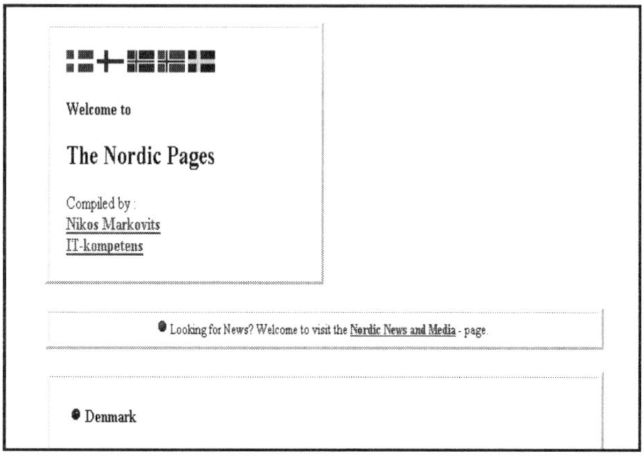

Nordic Pages

http://www.algonet.se/~nikos/nordic.html

Check here for Internet sources relating to Denmark, Finland, Iceland, Norway, and Sweden. The section for each country features government links, clickable maps, tourism information, and university resources. Additional features include news, art links, and museums. Users can find Viking history links as well, such as the Viking Home Page, The Viking Navy, and the Viking Network Web, to name a few.

Site Details:	Large Graphics, Good Links
Load Time:	41 seconds

Paris Pages

★★★★★

http://www.paris.org

Those planning a visit to the City of Light will find The Paris Pages *tres formidable*. The pages contain a Calendar of Events, tourist information on hotels, hostels, airports, restaurants, and the Metro, and Embassy, Consular, and Tourism addresses worldwide. The Paris Weather and Currency Exchange Rate pages ensure that the traveler will arrive well-equipped. Cafes are an integral part of Paris life; Cafe Pages list them by *arrondissement*. There are, of course, museum and monument debriefings, as well as shop listings. Bon voyage!

Site Details: Animation, Large Graphics, Good Links

Load Time: 47 seconds

ROMA 2000

http://www.roma2000.it

Don't be surprised to find yourself humming arias after a visit to the ROMA 2000 site. The opening screen—a heavenly blue sky dotted with white clouds and frolicking cherubs—prepares you for the baroque wonders of Roma. You'll find the addresses of restaurants and hotels that have a five-, four-, or three-star rating. Find out what time the Sistine Chapel opens to visitors, and view images of monuments and piazzas, statues, and paintings. Viva Italia!

Site Details: Good Links
Load Time: 140 seconds

Si, Spain

★★★★★

http://www.civeng.carleton.ca/SiSpain

Provided by the Embassy of Spain in Canada, this page posts information about the social, political, economic, and cultural climate of Spain. This thorough exposition displays the history, geography, politics, social services, education, tourism, science, and environment of Spain, in an organized and easy-to-use format. The site is in both English and Spanish, and it contains a rudimentary Spanish language course for beginners.

Site Details: Good Links
Load Time: 28 seconds

Tokyo Q

★★★★★

http://pobox.com/~ian

Find your way to the Jump and Jive night at Colors nightclub with the help of this online guide to the city of Tokyo. Everything from bar-hopping sprees to a plunge in a hot sauna is described for the Web traveler. Links are provided to information about popular Tokyo restaurants, upcoming concert events, and tips for excursions in and around the city.

Site Details: Large Graphics, Good Links
Load Time: 39 seconds

TravelASIA

http://www.asia-online.com/travel

Traveling to Asia? You'll want to take a look at this Web site before you plan your trip. The TravelASIA hotel chain sponsors an attractive and easy-to-navigate site that contains very valuable information concerning several Asian destinations. Users will find essential data about climate, entry regulations, customs regulations, tipping policies, local transportation options, health issues, local electricity, water, and banking. A list of TravelASIA hotels is provided, along with links to other Asian travel resources.

Site Details: Large Graphics, Good Links, Shopping

Load Time: 61 seconds

UK Directory

http://www.ukdirectory.com

The UK Directory is a content-rich, comprehensive guide to the United Kingdom. Just a few of the features here include community services, jobs, local and national politics, magazines and publications, sporting facilities, entertainment resources, medical services, and education links. Guests may also choose to view the listings alphabetically.

Site Details: Good Links

Load Time: 105 seconds

United Kingdom Pages

http://www.neosoft.com/~dlgates/uk/ukindex.html

This site is chock-full of useful tourist, cultural, academic, government, and regional information. Access in-depth data on cities across the UK, some of which include virtual tours. A WWII Evacuee's Registry allows UK citizens who were evacuated to the countryside during the war to share their experiences with others. A photo album contains photographs of the Royal Family, thatched cottages, and Constable paintings. There are links to political parties, Westminster Online, the Central Government, and more.

Site Details: Large Graphics, Good Links
Load Time: 50 seconds

Virtual Irish Pub

http://www.misty.com/ulysses/vip/index.html

Pick up a pint from the friendly bartender, then select a "table" and get comfortable. Depending on your mood, settle down for a chat with the amiable patrons, explore Ireland by clicking on a map, or find lodging information or ideas for things to see and do. Rather talk about Yeats? Just have a seat at the Literature table. More in the mood for rugby and soccer? Mosey over to the rowdy Sports Table. Whether your interest is Irish history, hobbies, or theatre, you'll find like-minded patrons in the Pub.

Site Details: Large Graphics, Good Links, Shopping
Load Time: 42 seconds

What's On In Europe

✯✯✯✯✯

http://www.telepac.pt/whatson

This is the definitive page for any and all information about Europe. The multiple window layout and information content make this a sure hit. Travelers can choose from a list of European countries such as Belgium, France, Luxembourg, Holland, and Great Britain to find resources that include entertainment, accommodations, music, magazines, sports, travel, real estate, and much more.

Site Details: Good Links
Load Time: 189 seconds

Travel Guides

We've all known one—the Charmed Traveler who roams the globe from Bali to Panag, Paris to Madrid. The Charmed Traveler never suffers from tropical fevers or arrives in a capital city just as the military stages a *coup*. Armed with humor, flexibility, and a sense of adventure, the Charmed Traveler also knows the secret—travel planning on the Web.

Checking the **Air Traveler's Handbook**, the CT plots a course through the endless corridors of Heathrow to make a flight to Paris. Inoculation recommendations and travel advisories from the **Travel Health Information** and the **State Department's Travel Advisories** home page keep the CT safe and healthy.

Unruffled by the channel trip, the Charmed Traveler emerges from the Métro at Pont Marie, pausing to gaze at the bâteaux mouche on the Seine. Before leaving home, the CT planned a tour of Paris Gothic cathedrals with the help of **Webfoot's Travel Guide** and the **Subway Navigator**. The bells of Notre Dame sound as the CT arrives at the small, elegant hotel on the Ile St. Louis, which was also found on the Web.

Like the Charmed Traveler, you can use the travel resources of the Web to make your next vacation a rewarding one. Whether you're planning a journey to the jungles of Mexico's Copper Canyon or a trek to the sacred temples of Indonesia, the Web can guide you there.

Air Traveler's Handbook

http://www.cs.cmu.edu/afs/cs.cmu.edu/user/mkant/Public/Travel/airfare.html

Whether you travel for business or pleasure, by air, rail, boat, or dog sled, bookmark this site. Much more than an air travel guide, the Air Traveler's Handbook is an essential resource. Users will find links to international, national, regional, and commuter airlines. There are links to Frequent Flyer programs, airline ticket consolidators, courier services, and charters. Interested in a cruise? Link to the major cruise line companies, tour operators, and travel agents. Link to hotel home pages, Bed-and-Breakfast directories, hostel guides, and home exchange archives.

Site Details:	Good Links
Load Time:	9 seconds

Airlines of the Web

http://haas.berkeley.edu/~seidel/airline.html

Created by a UC Berkeley graduate student, the Airlines of the Web page seems to feature every airline on the planet. Passenger carriers are listed by geographical region. Frequent-Flyer Programs, Airline Stock Quotes, Medical Airline Transports, Cargo Airlines, Manufacturers and Suppliers, Commercial Aviation Organizations, Related Internet Sites, and Former Related Sites are all offered at this comprehensive page. A short history of the site is given at the end.

Site Details:	Real Audio, Sound, Large Graphics, Good Links
Load Time:	41 seconds

Connected Traveler

http://www.well.com/user/wldtrvlr

Beautifully presented, this travel journal features articles by some of the best practitioners of travel writing today. A recent edition included pieces by Jan Morris, Arthur C. Clark, and Peter Mayle. Read about A Bad Day In Borneo by the site's author, Russell Johnson, and join Georgia Hesse on an Inuit sled.

Site Details: Large Graphics, Good Links
Load Time: 33 seconds

Foreign Languages for Travelers

★★★★★

http://www.travlang.com/languages

The subtitle of this site could be "How to Survive in a Foreign Country When You Can't Speak the Language." Containing useful phrases from 24 languages, including Finnish and Serbian, users can hear the sentences and words pronounced. You won't become fluent, but it can make traveling a little smoother. Links lead to online translation dictionaries and other travel resources.

Site Details: Sound, Good Links
Load Time: 26 seconds

Internet Guide to Hostelling

★★★★★

http://www.hostels.com/hostels

This all-purpose, practical guide is a compendium of addresses for budget accommodations to low-cost housing options for travelers across the world. Tips and directions for penny-pinching travel can be found at its Tips and Tales section. Planned ski trips will be less expensive after a virtual trip to Ski Country Hostels. Sell or purchase travel equipment using the Classified Section. An excellent resource for travel and touring needs, this guide should be bookmarked by adventure seekers.

Site Details: Large Graphics, Good Links
Load Time: 68 seconds

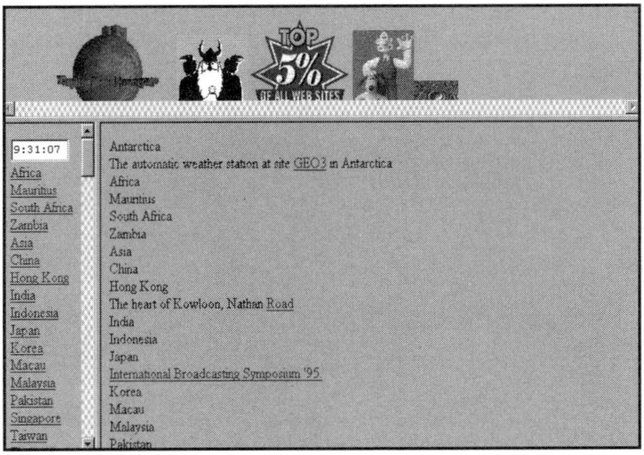

Live Camera

http://www.ts.umu.se/~spaceman/camera.html

This photographic tour will take you for a spin through city streets, mountain ranges, college campuses, office buildings, and aquariums. The seemingly endless collection of photos and movies is easy to navigate and invites interaction from the viewer on several occasions. It's a great way to see the world without leaving the comforts of home!

Site Details:	Animation, Video, Sound, Large Graphics, Good Links
Load Time:	58 seconds

rec.travel Library

http://www.solutions.mb.ca/rec-travel

A *New York Times* writer calls this site "one of the most extensive databases of travel information," and rightly so. From the home page, users can access TravelWise, the discount mail order travel bookstore, or click to a specific continent to find an alphabetized list of countries with travel information, currency rates, news articles, accommodation listings, and a wealth of general information. Other features found here include travel agents and tour operators, airlines and cruise reviews, health guidelines, and FAQs.

Site Details: Good Links, Shopping
Load Time: 63 seconds

The Rough Guide

http://www.hotwired.com/rough

The Rough Guide is a traveler's paradise. This easy-to-use directory is organized by region, state, and city. Virtual tourists may explore the United States, Canada, or Mexico. Phone numbers and addresses of accommodations, restaurants, dance clubs, shopping centers, bars, and coffeehouses are listed. This is an excellent traveler's resource.

Site Details: Large Graphics, Good Links
Load Time: 22 seconds

Subway Navigator

★★★★★

http://metro.jussieu.fr:10001

The Subway Navigator is your underground travel guide, enabling you to search for subway system routes for many cities around the world, from Caracas to Calcutta to Calgary. Many subway system home pages contain clickable maps and street search capabilities. This invaluable tourist resource is offered in French and English.

Site Details: Large Graphics, Good Links
Load Time: 6 seconds

Tourism Offices Worldwide Directory

★★★★★

http://www.mbnet.mb.ca/lucas/travel/tourism-offices.html

The Tourism Offices Worldwide Directory consists of a database filled with international tourism offices. Although plain in its design, the page offers a valuable resource for the traveler. Type in the name of any country for listings of addresses and phone numbers.

Load Time: 3 seconds

Travel Advisories

http://www.stolaf.edu/network/travel-advisories.html

The U.S. State Department provides advisories to warn travelers of potential safety hazards when visiting foreign countries. From this site you can subscribe to an Internet mailing list to regularly receive travel advisories. In addition, it has links to the Stanford Travel Medical Service, the Perry-Castaneda Library Map Collection, and the World Tourist site.

Site Details: Good Links
Load Time: 21 seconds

Travel Health Information

http://www.intmed.mcw.edu/ITC/Health.html

Before you start to pack, even before you update your passport, check in at the International Travelers Clinic Travel Health Information Web site. The site includes features on medical essentials for traveling abroad and precautions for pregnant women, along with disease and immunization information.

Site Details: Good Links
Load Time: 27 seconds

Web Travel Review

★★★★★

http://www-swiss.ai.mit.edu/webtravel

With over 2,000 vivid photos coupled with provocative stories, the Web Travel Review takes users on a trip around the world and introduces the on-the-road writing of Philip Greenspun. View the pristine hills of New Zealand, the delicate plants of the Great Barrier Reef, and the scenic wonders of the Grand Cayman Islands. This site is quite an exploration.

Site Details: Large Graphics, Good Links
Load Time: 42 seconds

Webfoot's Travel Guides

★★★★★

http://www.webfoot.com/travel/guides/guides.top.html

This Web page is an excellent source of travel and tourism information for areas around the globe. Find an extensive set of resources about Austria, the Virgin Islands, France, Germany, Italy, Spain, Vatican City, and Hawaii. Users will find general, historical, and cultural backgrounds of these exotic locales. City sections for each Web link provide details on each country's cities. Users will also find helpful hints on transportation, lodging recommendations, and how to pack for trips.

Site Details: Good Links
Load Time: 2 seconds

Appendix A - Internet Terms

Archie: A method used to search databases on the Internet. Archie finds **FTP** sites related to the title, keyword, or subject you indicate.

ASCII: American Standard Code for Information Interchange. The most common character code used on PCs and for communications, it consists of 128 upper- and lowercase letters. Since the ASCII code makes no provision for non-English letter accents and forms, currently most computers use an **extended character set** that accommodate technical, graphic, and non-Western characters.

au. files: A filename extension that denotes audio data.

Audio files: See au., midi, and wav. files.

bandwidth: A measurement of network capacity and the amount of data that can flow through a communications circuit per second. The broader the bandwidth, the more data can flow.

baud: A measurement of the speed data travels. Related to, but not identical to, **bps.**

BMP files : A data file or structure which corresponds bit for bit with an image displayed on a screen. A bitmap is a map of bits when taken altogether and viewed through bitmap programs, the patterns of bits form a picture.

bps: Bits per second. A measurement of data transmission speed. A 14.4 modem transmits data at 14,400 bps.

Browser: An online application that provides a window to the Web. Permits the user to read hypertext documents and to navigate from one document to another. Most browsers are user-friendly, with button bars and pull-down menus. Many support images, forms, and sound files.

Appendix A - Internet Terms

CERN: The European Laboratory for Particle Physics. Located in Switzerland and France, CERN is the place where Tim Berners-Lee first originated the World Wide Web in 1989.

CGI: Common Gateway Interface: A standard for running external programs, or gateways, under a World Wide Web server.

DNS: Domain Name System. A distributed data query system used to translate hostnames (205.94.220.10) into Internet addresses (squeegee.com).

E-cash: A way to make purchases over the Internet through an electronic transfer of funds. Eliminates the need to transmit a credit card number over the Internet. Security is maintained using a public key digital signature. E-cash software holds electronic money on the user's computer.

Email: Electronic mail; also, e-mail. Responsible for reviving the lost art of written communication. You can send correspondence down the hall or across the planet in seconds.

Emoticons: A way to convey tone in written conversations in lieu of spoken and physical cues. Emotions such as happiness, sadness, and tongue-in-cheek signals are displayed with the use of colons, dashes, periods, etc. Tilt your head fully to the left, horizontal to the page, and read: **: = (**

FAQ: Frequently Asked Questions. Originally referring to a list of questions and answers aimed at new users of a Usenet newsgroup, FAQs are also employed on the Web as well, as a way to convey information concisely and quickly.

Frames: A Web page layout tool which creates numerous windows on one Web screen and offer improved navigation.

Freeware: Software available without charge through the Internet, bulletin boards, and user groups. Not synonymous with **shareware**.

Appendix A - Internet Terms

FTP: File Transfer Protocol; also, Anonymous File Transfer Protocol. A way to download software files from other computers. Anonymous means you don't need an account to get the files.

GIF: Graphics Interchange Format. A color graphics file format useful for higher-resolution images because of its file compression feature.

gopher: Menu-based program allowing access to information on the Internet. You can gopher to a **Telnet** or an **FTP** site.

Graphics files: see BMP, GIF, and JPEG.

Home Page: The top-level **HTML** document for a Web site. Other pages can be accessed by following **hyperlinks** from the top-level page.

Hotlist: Also, hot links. A **hypertext** list of links to, in someone's opinion, interesting or valuable sites on the Web.

HTML: HyperText Markup Language. The formatting language of the Web, it determines the appearance of and defines the links in a Web document.

Http: HyperText Transport Protocol. The basis of the Web, this protocol allows for the exchange of HTML documents. In a URL, it is the first part of the address that indicates that the rest of the address is a Web site.

Hypertext links: Called **hyperlinks**, or more commonly, **links**. How information on the Web is connected. Clicking on the highlighted text in a Web document takes you to another page of that document or to another Web site. This seamless connection is changing the way we get and use information. Instead of processing information in a linear way, hyperlinks let us get the information in the order that makes the most sense to us.

Appendix A - Internet Terms

Internet: Originally used by the military, scientific and academic communities. Can be thought of as a worldwide network of networks, utilizing a common addressing format. The resources available on the Internet cover everything imaginable—Hubble space telescope photographs of Jupiter, a virtual tour of the Louvre Museum, audio and video clips from the latest rock bands, the complete text of Homer's Odyssey—the range is mind-boggling. Not originating from any one source and owned by no one, the Internet has taken on a life of its own--much like an alien lifeform. The Internet is constantly changing and growing—by connecting to it, you become part of it.

IRC: Internet Relay Chat. Networks where users can conduct real-time conversations with other users, within virtual chatrooms.

ISDN: Integrated Services Digital Network. A digital communications network that can carry voice, data, and video transmissions. To give an idea of ISDN's speed, a two-channel ISDN line transmits at 112 kilobits per second, and a 28.8K modem, at 28 kilobits per second.

JAVA: Java, created by Sun Microsystems, is simple, object-oriented, dynamic general-purpose programming language. Supporting programming for the Internet, Java applets create animation, speed, and interactivity within Web documents.

JPEG: Joint Photographic Experts Group. A digital image compression standard, JPEG is designed for compressing either full-color or gray-scale digital images of "natural," real-world scenes.

LISTSERV: An application which uses distribution lists, or mailing lists, to send one email message to many servers at once.

MIDI: Musical Instrument Digital Interface. A hardware protocol for exchanging musical information between computers, synthesizers, and instruments.

Mirror site: A server where another site's files are duplicated, or "mirrored." Users can choose to connect to their closest site. For example, a popular U.K. site may be mirrored at several sites in the U.S. to speed users' access time and reduce the load on the originating site.

MPEG: Moving Pictures Experts Group. A standard for compressing moving images for transmission .

Netiquette: What constitutes good manners on the Internet. As in any community, good manners makes life more pleasant for everyone. ***The Netiquette Home Page*** is a good place to bone up on good Internet deportment, especially before joining a **newsgroup** discussion.

Newsgroups: Discussion groups on **Usenet**, a network that is not the same as the Internet, but can be accessed from the Internet, among other channels. Newsgroups consist of millions of people posting and reading thousands of messages about innumerable topics. See **Usenet.**

PGP: Pretty Good Privacy. An encryption application created by Phillip R. Zimmerman. PGP allows the private and authenticated transmission of data over communications networks. Using Public-Key Cryptography technology as a base, PGP does not require the use of secure channels.

POP: Post Office Protocol. An application that allows users to obtain their email from a server.

Protocol: An agreed set of procedures that ensures compatibility between the receivers and the transmitters of data.

QuickTime: A digital video standard developed for Apple Macintosh computers. Special viewing applications are needed to run QuickTime movies.

Real-time video: Video transfer in which, by the use of streaming rather than downloading, users can view the video file almost instantly

Search Engines: Tools for finding information on the Internet. Search engines compare electronically strings of text entered by the user and locate matches on the Internet. Just a few of the many search engines you can find on the Web are ***Yahoo, Lycos, and InfoSeek.*** Evolving from **search engines, Spiders** serve up only sites that are evaluated for content, rather than the indiscriminate collections of the search engines.

Shareware: Software, distributed for trial use without charge. The author requests payment if the user continues to use the software after a trial period.

Shockwave: Shockwave is a software application which transforms Web pages into dynamic, interactive multimedia productions that load as quickly as static images. It provides media-specific compression, network linking through Universal Resource Locators (URLs), and helpful authoring techniques.

SGML: Standard Generalized Markup Language. Providing conventions for other markup languages, SGML defines the formatting of a text document, including hypertext, by describing a document's information rather than its visual components.

SLIP/PPP: Serial Line Internet Protocol/Point-to-Point Protocol. Protocols that allow a computer to use a modem and phone line to function as an Internet site.

Super Mosaic: Luckman Interactive's Web Browser.

T1: A super-fast, super-expensive, data transmission line, transmitting at 1.544 megabits per second. For comparison, a single ISDN channel transmits at 56 kilobits per second, and a 28.8K modem, at 28 kilobits per second. A kilobit is a thousand bits per second, and a megabit refers to a *million* bits per second.

Appendix A - Internet Terms

TCP/IP: Transmission Control Protocol/Internet Protocol. Two protocols by which all information is sent over the Internet.

Telnet: An Internet tool you can use to log in remotely to a distant computer, as if you were part of its network.

UNIX: Designed by AT&T, and written in the C programming language, UNIX is a multi-platform, multi-user, multitasking operating system.

URL: Universal Resource Locator. Each Web page's unique address. Made up of distinct parts, it can tell you what kind of host is the source of the site. For example, in the URL address http://harvard.edu, the ".edu" appellation designates an educational institution. Commercial and nonprofit organizations are, respectively, ".com," and ".org." Other appellations include ".gov, for government, .".mil" for military, and ".net" for network.

Usenet groups: Use r Net work. A decentralized, networked system of news and discussions topics, called **newsgroups**.

Veronica: A tool, similar to Archie, used to search Internet **gopher** sites.

Video files: See MPEG, real-time video.

VRML: Virtual Reality Modeling Language. A language that allows for more than one user's participation in interactive 3-D simulations on the Web. The simulations describe "virtual worlds" that include interactivity and hyperlinks with other virtual worlds, or other HTML Web pages. Now in an early stage of its development, VRML promises to become more sophisticated and interactive in the future.

WAIS: Wide Area Information Server. A commercial indexing tool for keyword searches of text documents on the Internet.

.wav files: A filename extension that denotes Windows audio files.

Web Browser: A browser—such as Luckman Interactive's Super Mosaic or Netscape—provides a window to the Web, allowing you to effortlessly follow hyperlinks, which may take you from networks in New Zealand to Zurich, and from Zurich to Africa, with only a few clicks of the mouse.

Web Page: A **Web site** is made up of a series of Web pages, connected to each other with hyperlinks. Government organizations, companies, charities, universities, and individuals are putting pages on the Web.

WinSock: Windows Sockets Specification. Provides an Applications Program Interface standard for Windows TCP/IP software development.

World-Wide Web: Also known as the **Web**. The most user-friendly part of the Internet, offering graphics, sound, video, and hypertext links to Web sites.

Worm: A robotic indexing program creating a searchable database which can be accessed or keyword searched.

America Online

800-827-6364

703-448-8700

http://www.aol.com

CompuServe

800-848-8990

614-457-8600

http://www.compuserve.com/

Prodigy

800-776-3449

http://www.prodigy.com/

Microsoft Network

http://www.microsoft.com/

Genie

800-362-1296

800-847-5260

http://www.genie.com/

Appendix B - Online Services

National Internet Service Providers

Arrownet

517-371-7100

571-371-2188

http://www.arrownet.com/

AT&T WorldNet

1-800-WORLDNET

http://www.att.com/worldnet/wis/index.html

BBN Planet Corporation

800-472-4565

617-873-3599

Dephi

800-695-4005

617-491-3393

http://www.dash.com/

Free.org

715-743-1700

http://www.ferryboard.com/

InternetMCI

800-360-2304

http://www.mci.com/fornet/home.shtml

InterRamp

800-827-7482

703-709-0300

http://www.psi.net/indivservices/interamp/is.html

Netcom

800-353-6600

http://www.netcom.com/

Pipeline USA

800-453-7473

http://www.usa.pipeline.com/software/software.html

PSINet's Pipeline USA

800-827-7483

http://www.usa.pipeline.com/info.html

SPRYNET

206-957-8997

http://www/sprynet.com/sos/member/tellme.html

Index of Keywords

Index of Keywords

Index of Keywords

D

Index of Keywords

Index of Keywords

Index of Keywords

Index of Keywords

Index of Keywords

Index of Keywords

Index of Keywords

Index of Keywords

Index of Keywords

Index of Web Sites

Index of Web Sites

Index of Web Sites

Index of Web Sites

Index of Web Sites

Index of Web Sites